Afloat

Afloat

Small Boats, Swell and Seaspray

DAVID GANGE

WILLIAM
COLLINS

William Collins
An imprint of HarperCollins*Publishers*
1 London Bridge Street
London SE1 9GF

WilliamCollinsBooks.com

HarperCollins*Publishers*
Macken House, 39/40 Mayor Street Upper,
Dublin 1, D01 C9W8, Ireland

First published in Great Britain in 2026 by William Collins

1

Copyright © David Gange 2026

David Gange asserts the moral right to be identified as the author of this work in accordance with the Copyright, Designs and Patents Act 1988

A catalogue record for this book is available from the British Library

ISBN 978-0-00-841358-3

All rights reserved. No part of this publication may be reproduced, stored in a retrieval system, or transmitted, in any form or by any means, electronic, mechanical, photocopying, recording or otherwise, without the prior permission of the publishers.

Without limiting the exclusive rights of any author, contributor or the publisher of this publication, any unauthorised use of this publication to train generative artificial intelligence (AI) technologies is expressly prohibited. HarperCollins also exercise their rights under Article 4(3) of the Digital Single Market Directive 2019/790 and expressly reserve this publication from the text and data mining exception.

Typeset in Granjon LT Std by Palimpsest Book Production Limited, Falkirk, Stirlingshire

Printed and bound in the UK using 100% renewable electricity at CPI Group (UK) Ltd

This book contains FSC™ certified paper and other controlled sources
to ensure responsible forest management.

For more information visit: www.harpercollins.co.uk/green

To Morgan, for getting me back *in* the sea
(and taking the jellyfish stings).

And to Tim Robinson, Mairéad Robinson, Fionnlagh MacLeòid, Norma MacLeòid, Sandra MacLeòid, Peter Bailey and John Gillis: each a great interpreter of coastal life who helped shape this project but is sadly no longer with us.

Contents

Maps	xi
Preface: The World in the Wave	1
Introduction: The Lives and Love of Little Boats	7
1. *Conamara/Connemara*: In Search of the Donkey Boat	25
2. *Leòdhas/Lewis*: The Shores Boats are Built From	38
Interlude: Of Clinker, Carvel, Birchbark, and Sealskin	62
3. *Sápmi*: A Pine Tree at Sea	70
4. *Føroyar/The Faroes*: Down Comes the Puffin from the Cliff	92
Interlude: Crossings and Connections	118
5. *Kalaallit Nunaat/Greenland*: Home Is Where the Umiaq Is	130
6. *Ktaqmkuk/Newfoundland*: London Is a Ladder up the Cliffs	163
7. *Maine and Massachusetts*: Forest Seas	195

8. *Barbados*: Sea Flower, Sea Moss, Moses Boats   228

Epilogue: To Understand What's Beautiful   249

Select Bibliography   253

Index   265

De saat dat coorses trowe	The salt that courses through
dy veins is de lifeblöd	your veins is the lifeblood
o an aulder converseeshun,	of an older conversation,
wan dat ebbs and flodds	one that ebbs and floods
joost as de tide.	just as the tide.

  Roseanne Watt, 'Saat i de Blöd', *Moder Dy* (2019)

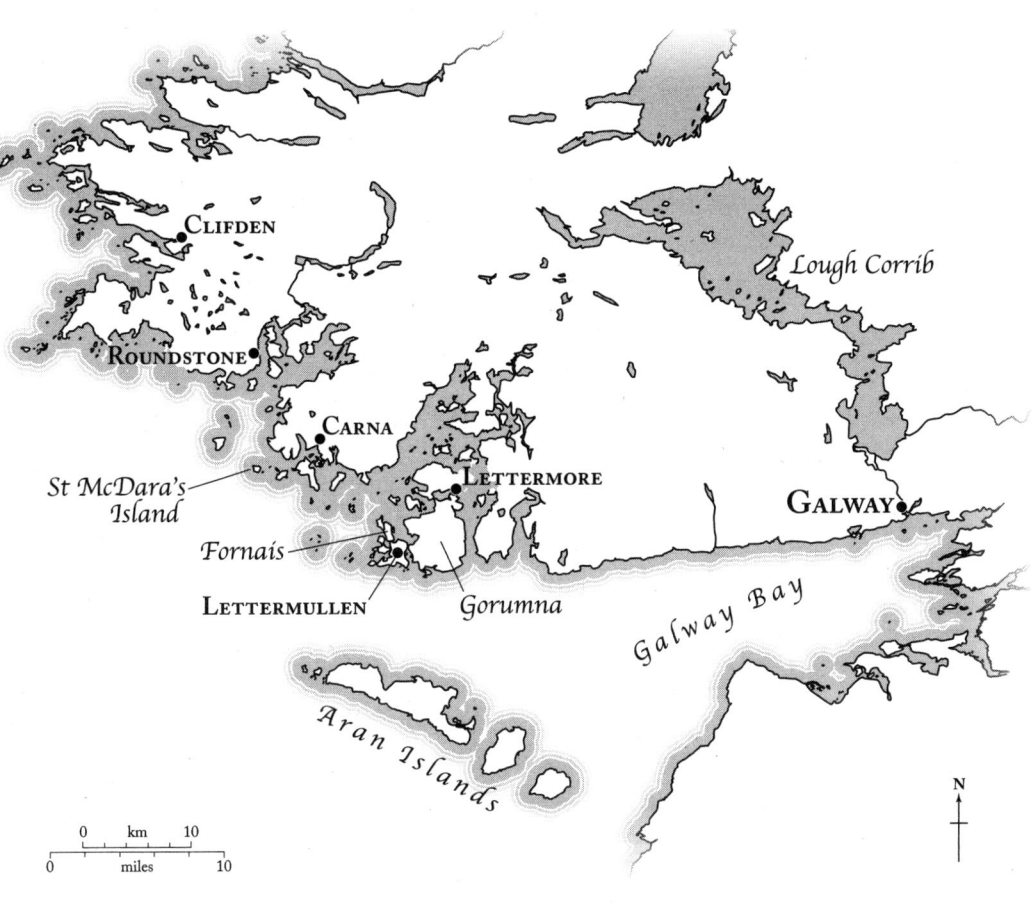

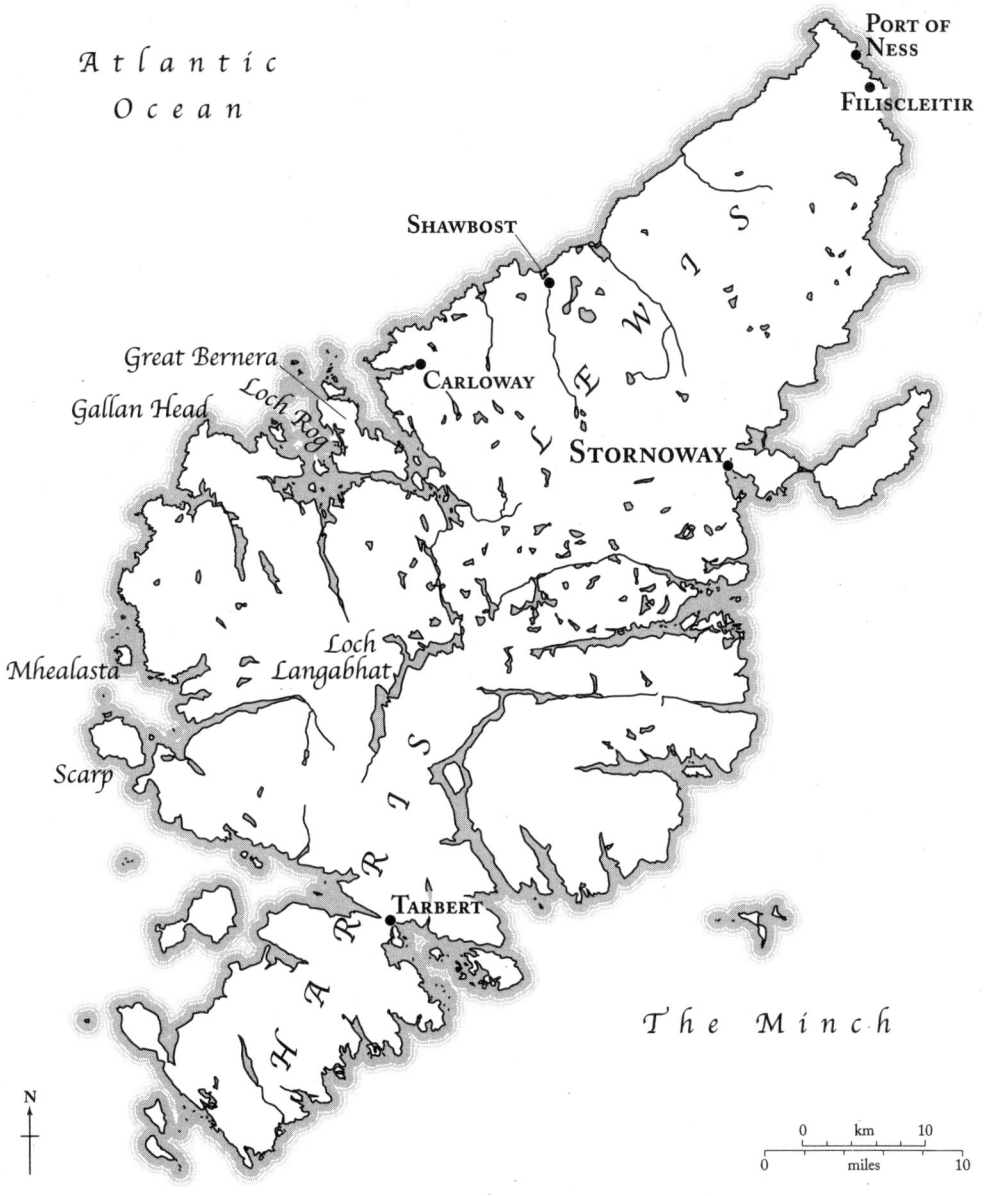

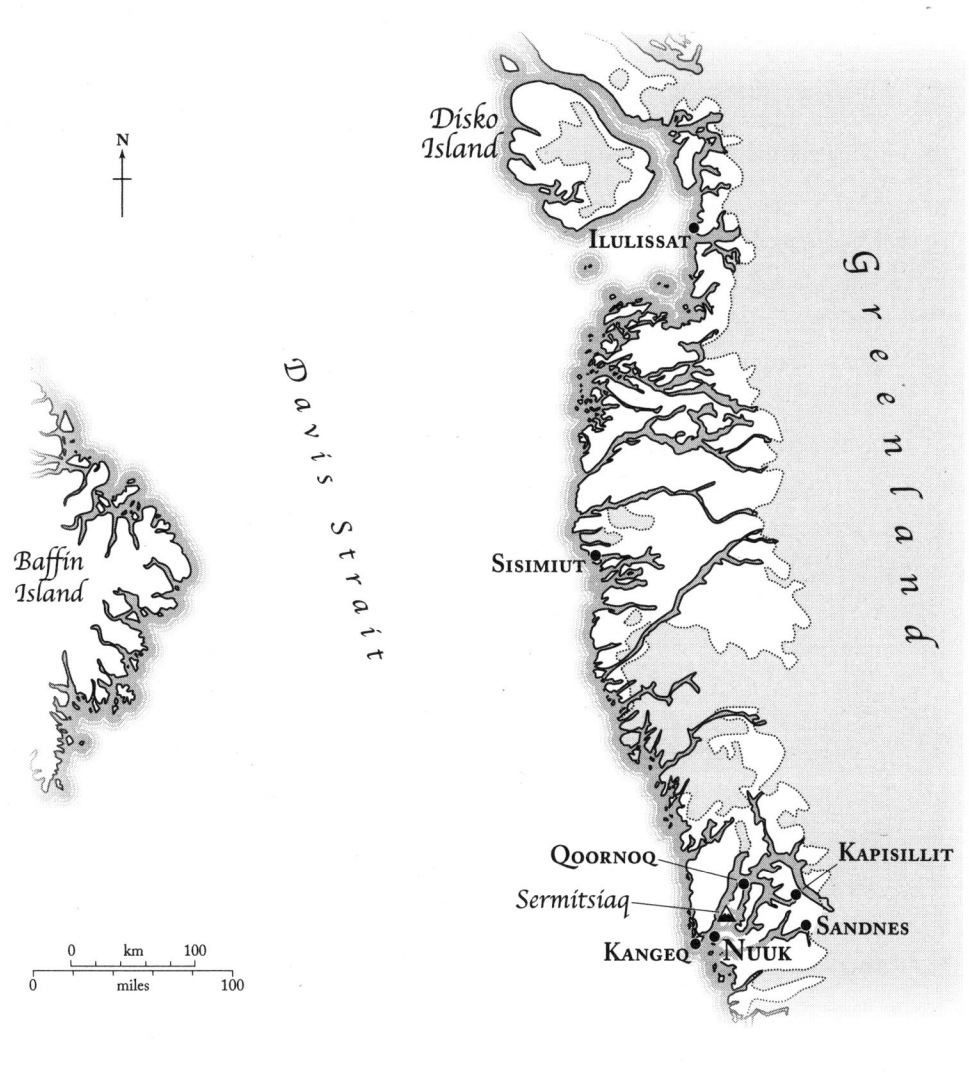

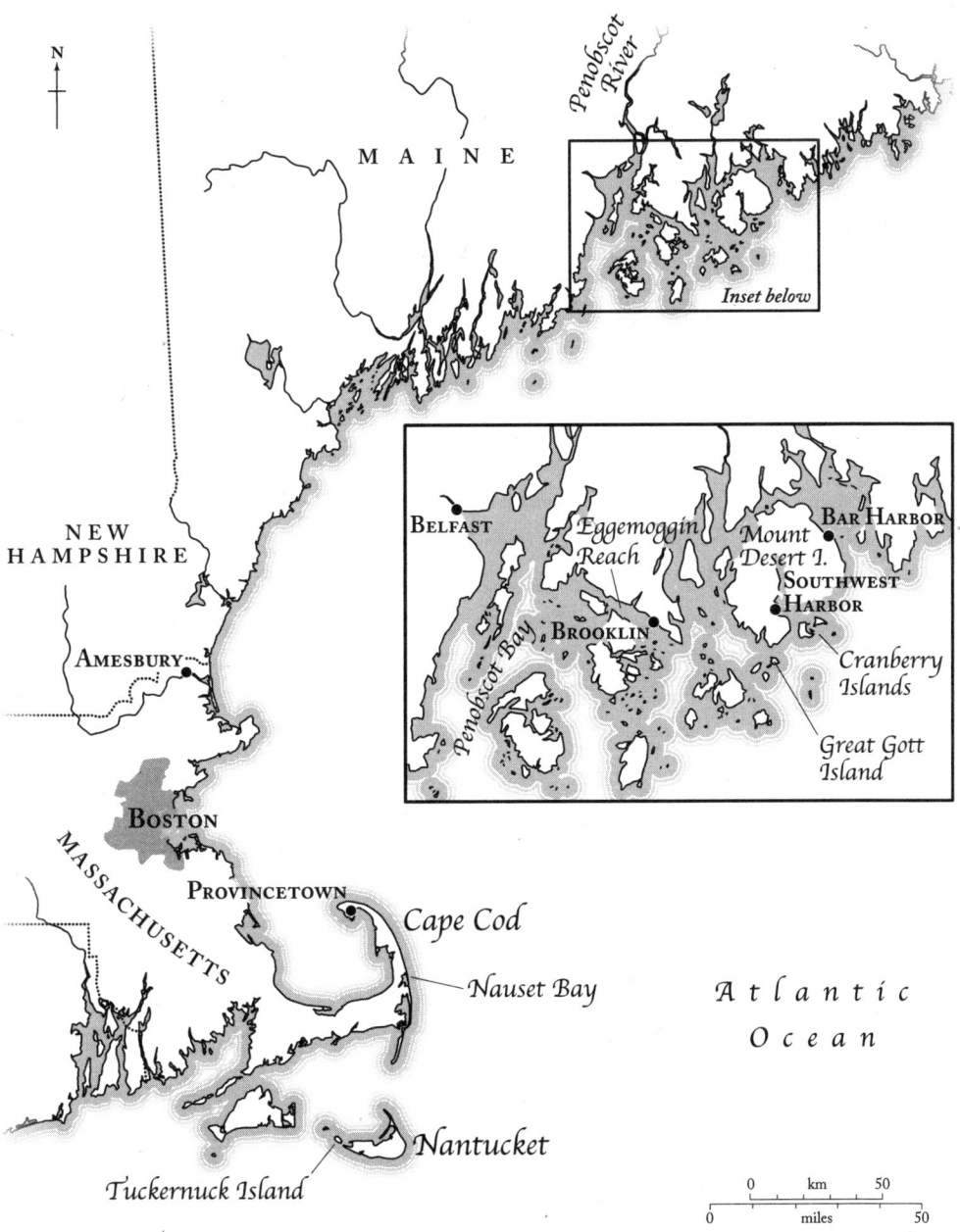

Preface

The World in the Wave

THERE'S A MOMENT when, in a heavy swell, you make the choice to turn the bow of your little boat to shore and let the breakers tower above you as you ride their raging crests towards a beach. If this has been a long journey, and this is a shoreline you don't know, there's fear in the possibility of a black rock reef or other unseen danger amid the swirling foam. But once the breakers grip you, there's no hope of stopping and little chance to turn.

It's the point just before committing to the chaos that's most memorable. One moment the swell lifts and drops you dramatically but gently. It carries you up and down twenty feet in the space of seconds while you guide your boat along a low-risk line. Suddenly, though, you're staring at the backs of rows of water that are angry and angular. They appear wilful and alive in the strange shapes they seem to choose to take. What was slow, inky swell now runs white and turquoise and is violently, frantically, loud in all directions.

There's a moment, looking at the back of the towering breakers, but before the white water hammers down on you, when you imagine what it will feel like to be in their midst. You experience a stunningly vivid empathy with a version of yourself who is just two short seconds in the future but who feels an infinity away. That moment of visceral imagining is both accelerated and slowed. Full of joy and fear. You are committing yourself completely to a drastic risk, taken in faith that perfect safety lies just beyond the bruising clatter into sand.

This moment always lodges itself in memory in ways unlike anything else. It returns in dreams. It flashes suddenly into focus when waiting in a queue or immersed in office admin. What I love most about the way this sublime split-second echoes through memory is that it means that once you've had the ocean roar around you, it'll never truly let go. It feels, paradoxically, like you're scarred by joy. You return to everyday life a little wilder: you're emotionally slightly unmoored, and psychologically salt-rimed.

These moments that twist time and skew perspectives do so in many ways: they can seem to carry you beyond the present completely, evoking fellow feeling with those countless others whose daily lives involved confrontation with the ocean. The voices you hear on the wind might be men in sealskins or tweeds shouldering oars or paddles, or women in thick woollens, wading waist deep in sea to drag their boats ashore. They're voices joined in the chanted rhythms, often wordless, that happen wherever a community comes together to haul its boats. That this moment in the wave could be situated at a specific time between deep past and present seems as improbable as dry feet in a sea storm: nothing could make me feel more like a fragment out of time, or more like I was renewing a timeless dance of people, boats, and sea.

To be a historian is to seek out the meanings of experiences like these. It involves observing their fabric and pulling at its threads to unravel any knowledge they might reveal. This book's journeys among small traditional boats on North Atlantic seas, like its conversations with boatbuilders and seafarers, and its nights spent in a waterproof sleeping bag on elemental shorelines, are attempts to attune empathy with past people of the coasts. They are also the starting points for conversation ashore. Coastal memory is strong, in part because oral cultures survived on rural coasts longer than elsewhere, and so traditions of hospitality for seafarers persist. Every part of this book is shaped by that distinctively coastal generosity. I can't count the number of times I crashed into coastal rocks, tired and damp, without land transport of my own, and was approached by a stranger who invited me for tea, coffee, or a beer, told me coastal stories, and sometimes even drove me to a boatbuilder they knew, from whom I learned about the place I was travelling. There are many people (in Newfoundland in particular, where dropping my phone in the sea meant losing the details of several wonderful families) whom I wish I could thank more fully than I've managed to.

I consider such hospitality so important in part because it shapes the arguments this book makes. One of these is that the cultures of coasts have been unique in their perspectives on past, present, and future: the small languages and dialects of the coastline aren't just grammars and vocabularies, but philosophical outlooks, rich with unique visions of what land, coast, and sea are and mean. Another is that we urgently need those visions if our societies are to flourish: awareness of and support for cultures from Scottish Gaels to Kalaallit Inuit or Bajan fishers can make the difference between tourism draining or sustaining communities, and between seas recovering from a century of industrialised overexploitation or sinking further into degradation.

I believe these things are true even when, as in the case of Faroese or Inuit seafaring, those values clash with modern urban norms; after all, it isn't the whale or seal hunts of small communities but industrialised and globalised ways of life that have made seas inhospitable to every species from phytoplankton to whales and humans. The vision of societies such as the Faroes' that appear in this book are therefore of cultures with deep knowledge of the ocean environment and strong commitment to its custodianship: even though encounters with cetaceans are the highlights of my life, the depiction of the

Faroe Islands in this book is far from the cartoonish myth of conscienceless whale-slaying that runs through much global media.

But this book is less an attempt to convince anyone of anything than a deep dive into how shorelines can be experienced and perceived. It shows how viewing our societies from little boats at their salt-rimed edges makes them profoundly unfamiliar. The deep small-boat histories of tiny settlements such as Mikladalur (the Faroes) and Conne River (Newfoundland) make them as important to North Atlantic seafaring as Southampton or New York; the artists of Dorset-culture Greenland become as significant to the arts of the ancient world as the sculptors of Greece or Rome.

This book is formed around long rowed and paddled journeys. These were originally intended to be continuous over a year, in 2020, and planned to involve twelve unbroken months of travel. But when the Covid-19 pandemic made those journeys impossible, the planned year's voyage had to be spread across a longer spell from January 2022 to October 2024. Boat travel plays different roles in each chapter. The first chapter, for instance, involved short journeys in search of a boat that no longer exists, while the second entailed a lengthy winter in the Isle of Lewis exploring boats' contexts through strings of short voyages to the most important sites of Outer Hebridean small-boat life. Neither of the first two chapters featured sustained expeditions. But later chapters involved the most dramatic sea voyages I've ever undertaken, round swell-battered headlands, beneath icebergs as tall as mountains, and in the fierce, hot seas of a circumnavigation of a Caribbean nation. In each of these chapters there's sea rock and spindrift as far as the eye can see. The skies are full of seabirds and the waves full of fins and faces, and these are perceived through the craftwork, stories, and writings of myriad peoples, past and present, whose lives have been built on water.

This book features a small proportion of the photos I took at sea and a select bibliography. There is a further resource at www.david gange.com/afloat, which hosts hundreds of further images, and links to the work of the boatbuilders, artists, and authors who appear in these pages, as well as notes on sources for researching boats and coastal cultures.

Introduction

The Lives and Love of Little Boats

I

The Mind of a Boat

FIFTEEN YEARS OF kayaking has brought me more joy than I'd ever imagined possible. My kayak has taken me under towering cliffs packed with tens of thousands of seabirds. It has carried me through hollow islands where networks of sea caves are haunted by seal song. It has given me freedom to wander places otherwise entirely inaccessible. Little feels so serene as paddling a stilled and silent ocean, or so thrilling as running surges of swell that bear down on you like moving mountains. And so I think of kayaking as a wild intensification of experience and I long, when ashore, for the roar of the ocean in my ears.

But it was only a few years ago, in the sound between the Coigach Peninsula and the Summer Isles, that I was first given the chance to sit in a traditional wooden boat and pull oars through sea. There was something completely new in the texture of the oar's grain, the creak of the ash planks, and the camaraderie of other rowers. The mountains of Wester Ross towered over the sunlit sea of this first row. Eider cooed and great northern divers cackled. There was a breeze to push sea and boat along, and to let them sing with the elements, but not enough to make the waves a battle: circumstances could hardly have aligned more perfectly to leave me wanting more. That night, I went to a screening, in a hall designed to look like an upturned boat, of a film about the building of the style of little boat I'd been rowing. The room was packed with local people, gathered to celebrate the revived rowing tradition that plays significant roles in many coastal places.

The language in the film, among its viewers, and in the boatish conversations I pursued in the following months was unlike anything I'd heard before. Boats weren't talked of as mere objects or tools, nor in terms that made them sound like wild creatures, pets, or human strangers, but as though they were beloved members of the family. Phrases were full of intimacy and care. Boatbuilders seemed to consider it obvious that 'a boat is the nearest thing you can build to something that is living'. They talked of boats having 'their own brains, their own way of moving, their own music'. When I met families in Ireland who owned good boats, they had such pride in them that they became entwined in all their stories, and there seemed to be a consensus that you'd repaint your boat before you repainted your home. This relationship was the richest, deepest, love, and I was beguiled by it.

That this was love didn't mean it was free from the complexities and challenges that come with all relationships: boats, after all, made decisions of their own. People described them as proud and wilful, responding to slights or rough treatment by sulking or taking revenge. Rowers or paddlers came to ruin who failed to 'listen to their boat'. A boat might hold a grudge for decades if someone made the error of trying to take it out to sea while drunk. But they were also depicted as unfailingly generous, willing to repay every kindness or mark of respect a hundred times over: the most frequent stories of all were of boats 'making choices' that evaded dangers and saved lives.

That first stretch of sea I rowed was the very place the poet Norman MacCaig had in mind when he wrote that a wooden boat need have no more than 'a crew of one alone' for it to carry 'a meaning, a cargo of centuries'. I was becoming increasingly aware that the histories of whole islands were built upon their boats. I read of small Shetland islands whose people had to leave their homes forever because new, more distant, fisheries left the community without young men to do the daily rowing of boats. I heard of islanders in the Outer Hebrides for whom the loss of rowing boats, even without the loss of human life, had led to the abandonment of cherished settlements. Today's love for these living boats contains the memory of times when life itself was built on their planks and thwarts. I knew that if I was to understand these coasts I loved, I had to immerse myself in this wet, wooden world that felt like the past revivified.

I quickly learned that there were far more small-boat traditions around the North Atlantic than I'd ever imagined, and that their diversity expressed the stories of land, sea, people, and all the species of the coastal zone. Adaptation by tiny adaptation, boat forms came to speak of centuries of human negotiation with specific bays or headlands, tidal streams, or prevailing winds. Responses to rock and water are built into their curves. They were often made entirely from local resources, whether oak wood, spruce root, or birchbark, pine tar, sealskin, reindeer antler, or bear fat. This meant that to learn of them was to learn how the communities who built them interacted with their worlds.

But these diverse localities were also interlinked, and the North Atlantic was a shared space of exchange and encounter. One reason for the range of small-boat cultures in these regions is the vast forests that flank the ocean. Huge boreal zones give timber to people who live in them, but also generate driftwood for every treeless island in between. Even a century-old treefall can be strong enough to form a boat or house around, and driftwood is one of the great forgotten resources of the world. Tides and ocean currents were highways that linked specific treeless bays in Greenland or Shetland with continental shores of northern Canada or Norway. By shaping where wood accumulated, they determined where boatbuilding centres, and whole coastal societies, came to be. Every wooden or skin boat expresses deep knowledge of a place, the trees that grew or washed ashore there, the movements of wind, tide, shoaling fish and flocking seabird, and the dynamic interactions of wood, water, and animal and human ingenuity. Every small adaptation made to a boat style is thus a sophisticated, poetic, response to history's changing tides. The highways of history are not just roads between cities but also tides between disparate coasts.

If the shore shapes a boat's form, the boat, in turn, informs the culture that grows from it. It is a bond uniting place and people, nature and culture. This deeply communal meaning is easily missed today, because a builder of traditional boats is often seen as a lonely figure who stubbornly preserves a few fading skills against wider flows of change. But this is to misinterpret what it is these builders are preserving. When small boats were the lifeblood of communities, it was rarely a single person's task to craft a vessel. A huge range of social activities went into the provision and preparation of materials, as well as the tasks of construction. As one craftsman in a Newfoundland outport put it, 'everybody could take a shift and build a boat'. I was constantly surprised by how much today's workshops bustle with activity, as visitors and volunteers drop in. Boatbuilders aren't isolated individuals cut off from changing communities: what they preserve is the idea of community itself.

These are just a few of the reasons coastal communities have defined themselves by their boats. In every region this book treats, distinctive little boats reveal a whole local world at work. Many of

THE LIVES AND LOVE OF LITTLE BOATS

these communities have outlooks shaped by small languages with unique marine lexicons, or by dialects rich with ecological vocabulary. Most imagine humans as part of their ecology: with less difference between a human and a whale, or even a human and a wave, than inland cultures have maintained. When I paddle or row long stretches of coast, and try to learn their terminologies, my greatest desire is to find myself slipping towards the outlooks of past coastal peoples, because exploring the many ways in which a shore can be experienced and perceived seems to me to be a life-enriching thing.

In giving voice to these visions, this book focuses on those open boats that are closest to the water: light and low in the waves, all are crewed by just one to four people. Many travelled large distances in weeks away from their home quays or beaches, but they were never part of the placeless worlds of the permanently ship-confined mariner. All were rowed or paddled more often than driven by the wind. I chose these boats partly because I'm a paddler and a rower, not a sailor, and partly because rowed and paddled boats show us people and places whose significance has often been ignored amid the multitude of sailing stories.

Where decked, sailed vessels were often commercially owned, these tiny undecked boats were possessed by individual families. This is part of the reason they evade historical attention. History books tell the tales of sail or steam. They tend to centre on ships that moved between the big port towns. This makes it a surprise to some that, wherever we have statistics, small rowed and paddled boats vastly outnumber sailboats. Irish rural coasts were far closer to centres of commercial shipping than most coasts in this book, but even there the statistics are striking. The first date we have Irish figures for is 1836. Then, 73 per cent of vessels were small, open rowing boats. Only 2 per cent were decked sailing ships. Yet the 2 per cent accounts for almost all the documentation left behind, because big ships were involved in formal markets. The places they went, and the things that left and entered their holds (the legal ones, at least), were scrupulously recorded in the name of commerce. Small family boats, in contrast, rarely left a single written word. For centuries, their forms went unrecorded in handbooks or manuals. Their stories were rarely shared in books, but were told instead on sea journeys, round open fires, at community gatherings, or during the communal process of building and repair.

This book tells the stories of these boats and their worlds as I learned them through rowing and paddling their coasts. It celebrates the sophistication of these vessels and the people who used them. I don't for a moment believe in the assessments that inland writers, from the eighteenth century to the present, have made of these regions. Visitors from cities depicted them as backward, naturally prone to poverty and famine, and in need of outside intervention to 'catch up' and modernise. All the research I do strengthens my conviction that, rather than failing to conform to the values of commercial society, these communities were passionately committed to different values altogether. Far from 'outmoded', these communities were – and are – vanguards of viable alternatives to the destructive world views that dominate our present.

All around rural Atlantic shores, famine, abject poverty, and environmental degradation were most often the result of outside intervention. They were rarely caused by harsh environments or communities' failings in confronting hostile seas. A great deal of violence went into dismantling the cultures that relied on small boats. Inuit children were forced into western-style schooling to strip them of their values. Gaelic-speakers were banished across the ocean to clear their coasts for sheep. The Beothuk people of Newfoundland were slaughtered and marginalised till the only Beothuk left were those who'd intermarried with Mi'kmaw or Innu communities. Sámi people saw their boats burned and were forced to turn their migratory reindeer into industrial beasts of burden at inland silver mines. Even though the cities of the eighteenth and nineteenth centuries claimed to be spreading enlightenment and tolerance, they brooked no competition from the small communities at the ocean edges who were, and sometimes still are, viewed with condescension and suspicion.

Some of this dismantling of coastal cultures might be considered well-meaning blunder. When governments set themselves the goal of providing education and healthcare to all, they were forced by necessity to limit the cost of their task. This meant consolidating populations into areas easily supplied by road. In doing this, they claimed, they gave new life choices to communities whose options had been limited by geography. But one important option was stolen from these communities: the chance to continue their existing ways of life. In the late twentieth century, the construction of welfare states was driven by visions of equality that refused to acknowledge difference and defined the nation by assimilation. This was, as the Sámi artist Hans Ragnar Mathisen puts it, 'welfare politics' as 'land grab'. In Sámi lands, 'progress' was also deeply regressive: a society with a remarkable degree of gender equality was transformed rapidly into one where women and children lived in permanent roadside homes to comply with national education policies, while only men pursued traditional Sámi life at sea or with the reindeer.

In every place these changes happened, later visitors met people who wished to have their own small voices heard amid the sweeping self-congratulation of states. When many Newfoundland outports were emptied in the 1960s, one resident told the writer Farley Mowat,

> It's been fine you came to visit us ... But still and all, I'm wondering, could you, maybe, do one thing for we? Could you, do you think, say how it was with us? ... We'd like for everyone to know we never would have left the places we was reared, but ... we ... was ... drove!

Politicians and administrators believed they were doing the right thing. They didn't resort to violence but offered coastal families money to relocate. When a few young people and skilled workers chose to take such funds and move to cities, each departure sapped the strength of communities. Coastal people experienced these processes as far more forceful and compulsive than those who enacted them intended or understood. Even many who actively made the choice to leave devoted their later lives to writing songs, plays, and novels recounting their sense of betrayal: the glistening promises of urban 'progress', they insisted, had failed to exceed the quality of communal life in coastal settlements. Hundreds of songs symbolise this loss by evoking wooden boats with mouldering, mossy planks and weeds growing through them. Boats came to symbolise whole lost or threatened worlds.

Part of the reason for this devaluing of coastal life was that administrators were often driven by singular measures of 'poverty' that incorporated only formal income and understood only a binary of employment and unemployment. They failed to comprehend the informal economies of exchange, mutual care, foraging, and craftwork they destroyed. And they rarely understood how much was at stake in the changes they wrought. They didn't see that knowledge of how to live well with marine environments, far from cities, could die with coastal communities. As the chronicler of Irish shores, Tim Robinson, put it: 'Without the occasional renewal of memory and regular rehearsal of meaning, place itself founders into shapelessness, and time, the great amnesiac, forgets all.'

In these examples, it wasn't necessarily even that administrators chose the wrong option from those available to them. But those choices, in so consistently working against the diverse local ways of life of the little boats and in favour of the singular and integrated outlook of the big ships, have cost all our societies a great deal. They limited both our practical resilience in the face of a changing world, and the equally significant richness of cultural existence.

By the dark days of the 1960s, many coastal communities lay empty. Boats rotted on shores until varieties of vessel that had thrived just a generation before became extinct. Specific skills fell out of daily use, as did the vocabularies of seafaring, and with them whole philosophies and world views. Even most people in communities this book features had begun to buy into the belief that small-boat life and communal values had to be rejected in order, urgently, to become modern and market-oriented. To emulate the cities was the only way to escape urban condescension.

Yet every place featured in this book experienced a revival of interest in its traditions in the 1970s. That decade's global reinvigoration of diverse local ways of life, after the bleak cultural annihilations of previous decades, is still only partly appreciated and understood. Gradually, since then, the dynamics of loss and fragmentation have come to face new forms of resistance. Building a wooden boat became as powerful a statement of values and intent as petitioning a parliament. Boatbuilding is now a feature of indigenous activism around the world, at a time when the resurgence of indigenous knowledge and practice is the most important intellectual movement of our era.

At Nuuk, in Greenland, where hardly a qajaq (traditional Greenland kayak) would have been present in 1960, huge crowds now gather once a year to watch the most accomplished kayakers in the world compete in races and qajaq-rolling competitions while celebrating the people who used these boats in the past. At Six Men's, in Barbados, the lives of old working boats are celebrated in a summer festival of seafaring that unites the whole village like no other occasion. In the Faroe Islands, St Olaf's Day combines the reopening of parliament with boat races and, every year, the launch of a newly built wooden vessel. Several times each summer, Galway Bay is filled with the elegant deep-red sails of Galway hookers, and the oars of currachs, as they gather to race the stunning seas between the Aran Islands and the Irish mainland.

These developments are sometime referred to with terms such as 'leisure revivals' and 'leisure craft'. But these descriptors are far from adequate, because they imply that the boats aren't fulfilling practical purposes of great significance. They suggest that the racing is what matters when, in fact, it's just a hook on which to hang a cultural renaissance. These occasions are celebrations of local histories and customs, which reflect a vibrant upsurge of belief in the power of community. Because of this, these boats express whole ways of life that, though they came close to sinking, still defiantly ply the seas.

These ways of life are the heart of my interest: the boats made them possible and are therefore the keys to unlock them. There's a strange phenomenon in the history of writing about these boats that leaves many links between the boats and their people unmade. Several writers on specific boat styles have published a volume on the technical aspects of a boat and its construction, while promising a second book that would elaborate the boat's place in the life of its communities. The great historian of Inuit seafaring, H. C. Petersen, put it like this in his introduction to *Skinboats of Greenland* (1986):

> It is an immense task to try to preserve the Inuit knowledge of and experiences with the kayak and umiak for posterity. I have divided the work up into two parts, the first being this book, a description of the kayak and umiak and their gear, along with the use of the umiak. The description of Man and the Kayak, the cultural area which the kayak has created in the lives of the Inuits, I hope to have the necessary time to prepare at a later date.

Every time this sequence has been promised, volume one has been a masterpiece, written by a scholar with deep knowledge of the societies they studied. But volume two has always gone unwritten. Since I first became interested in these coasts, I've longed to read these imaginary books. What knowledge was lost when H. C.

Petersen passed away with his planned project unwritten? The present book can't replace what those volumes would have been, but it exists in the space they left open, exploring what ways of life were built upon such vessels and asking how we might know them by the boats they left behind.

II

North Atlantic Drift

It's widely recognised today that anyone wanting to understand the past holistically will quickly find themselves stepping outside the archives and libraries that have traditionally been the haunts of historians. The profession and its archives developed in tandem, in eras when few imagined that historians might one day wish to hear voices from beyond corridors and courts of power. Increasing numbers of historians now turn to the work of their hands, feet, and senses as points of access to the past. They walk, ride, sail, or sled old routes on land or sea, grow old varietals of grain or fruit and veg, and cook historical recipes with old ingredients and utensils. They make traditional craftwork in textiles, wood, metal, or stone, dance traditional dances, and sing or play old songs. They recognise that past communities *made* their worlds and *built* their knowledge through practices such as gathering berries and weaving baskets: they never had static world views made up of book-bound thoughts. We stand at a moment of unprecedented creativity among historians, when the discipline overlaps more with the arts and with craftwork than ever before. But this is also a time when many historians have moved so far from the archival core of their own craft that they aren't certain they're even historians any more.

I feel all the excitement and neurosis of this moment. To comprehend the worlds I feel urgently compelled to learn about, I know I need to immerse myself in swirling air and ocean, surround myself with past people's workplaces on cliff edge and skerry, and travel the sea routes past families traversed. I need to seek what is sometimes called 'silent knowledge': the kinds of understanding that have to be intuited with the body rather than learned from documents. I know that telling the stories of this experience is as important as recounting facts of the past. Yet the phrase 'silent knowledge' evokes its evanescent nature. Every journey in search of past ways of doing things is an impossible experiment: a quest to use relationships with waves as the foundation for imagining new connections to old things.

Just as lots of writing about the regions in this book assumes that communities of the coasts lived hardscrabble lives defined by harsh environments and limited resources, books formed round travel or adventure tend to emphasise the challenges, hardships, and obstacles posed by their arenas of action. But emphasising these things would contradict my experience. All the research I do, especially in boats, leads me to believe that life on these coasts was capable of greater sophistication and happiness than history books allow. There will be storms in this book (with whole weeks spent wet), as well as confrontations with immense seas that left arms and mind sapped beyond the point of any ordinary exhaustion. But there were only a handful of moments that entailed real risk or hardship in this whole year's travel.

It's no coincidence that many of these shores produced not just boatbuilders and seafarers of great repute, but artists, storytellers, poets, and musicians whose names ring down through generations. Indeed, as Tim Robinson put it, coastal tradition on Irish-language shores 'is still so voluble in story, song, and placename that one wonders if . . . days and nights were longer formerly, to hear all that was said and sung in them'. Whether on the sea ice of the Davis Strait or the rugged, gale-bitten cliffs of the Outer Hebrides, traditional pursuits that demanded leisure, resources, and community cohesion existed in extravagant surfeit. I've wondered whether the high value placed on darkness in many of these cultures – the dark and inspiration going hand in hand, and the day beginning not at dawn but earlier – relates to the long hours of leisure that winter brought after the intensive labour of autumn harvests. In northern Greenland, the arrival of sea ice strong enough to be crossed by dog sled, alongside the rapidly shortening days, led to November being seen as the time for sharing stories and being given a name that translates as 'month of news'.

For all these reasons, hardships are less significant in this book than pleasures and revelations. A day paddling forty kilometres through a shifting maze of sea ice, and sleeping by the boat on a cold, rocky shore, might feel difficult; but a day commuting to a city-centre office and working eight hours under the scrutiny of a line manager is far more heroic. Lack of choice in occupation or material goods might mean that modern measures of quality of life don't judge the times and places covered in this book kindly. But the incredible epidemics of mental health conditions in precisely those times and places where quality of life is considered highest show they're not the final word on what makes for good living. Judging past lives by the standards of the present can lead us to see spectres of discomfort in things that were, to those who lived them, pure joy. The greatest challenge of projects like this is always returning to an indoor urban life.

The journeys around North Atlantic shores that frame each chapter in this book were calculated to link sites of small-boat building with the seas of their daily use. I looked, when choosing my routes, for places with rich cultural heritage which are distant from today's port towns. Some of these places – long uninhabited – are remembered only by the most committed custodians of memory in a few local settlements. Many of them are places where change over the last two centuries is a matter of absence: there are no new buildings, paths, or roads for miles around, while old ones are reduced to ridges and scratches in the earth. They are not remote. Nowhere beside the connecting sea can ever be truly isolated. To me, as to those who live nearby, these places are at the heart of what matters. But modern politics and technologies have made them seem remote to urban viewpoints.

The goal was always to travel slowly, with time to stop at every possible point of interest. Only at a slow glide would it be possible to tie the fragmentary textual sources on past communities to the observation of the worlds that existed round them. Everywhere, there were elements that undercut accepted truths, such as regions widely assumed to have suffered from bad soils and lack of grain, which were nonetheless scattered with millstones. Conversations with locals told, too, of ill-regarded resources, like dogfish, driftwood, limpets, or bladderwrack, that were rarely recorded in statistical accounts but turned out to be rich with past uses: the stuff of wealth not poverty. Just as whale oil lit wealthy city streets, the skins of dogfish caught from little Atlantic boats sanded smooth the curves of the most prestigious musical instruments on the planet: every multi-million-pound Stradivarius violin was rubbed with dogfish before resting under the chins of the most refined virtuosi. Salt dogfish toasted in the fire on a Sunday morning was a delicacy, in many coastal places, to rival caviar. But these regions are far more than the sum of their resources; and, everywhere, the stories and songs that have been handed down contain joy, wonder, and fierce protectiveness in relation to spectacular coastal places. Many such accounts long predate romanticism, which conventional wisdom suggests first spurred these responses to 'wild' places.

I'd never journeyed before in many of the climates this project took me to, whether the freezing seas of Arctic Greenland or the turtle-filled tropics of Barbados. In each Atlantic region, I found people committed to the values associated with wooden or skin boats, who were willing to take me out onto the water and share stories of people, places, and vessels. We left technologies such as sonar and GPS behind, looked to sea and sky, and rowed or paddled. Doing this, we could experience coasts in ways mediated by stories and histories more than by modern tech.

What was only occasionally possible, however, was to undertake long-distance, multi-day journeys in these historic craft. In the northernmost reaches of Norway, and the exposed coasts of Cape Cod, I borrowed full-size kayaks to venture further afield. For paddling Lewis, I could use my own sea kayak. But to indulge my desire to travel to every little site on other coasts I required another means of water-travel. I secured my freedom of the seas by carrying a tiny inflatable boat in my pack, with paddles strapped to the rucksack's sides. Mixing paddling with hiking, and carrying a waterproof sleeping bag, everywhere was accessible. The dimensions of this boat are such that I think of it more like an item of clothing than a vessel: a kind of wearable technology. Weighing just 1.2 kilograms, and little over two metres long (only thirty centimetres by twelve when packed), this seatless, deckless craft demanded that I know and work with the elements. I couldn't force my way against the flow of sea ice, or battle with a speeding tide, so I had to learn their movements. I didn't have the luxury of ignoring a viciously unfriendly wind as I might in my full-size sea kayak. Instead, every journey in my boat-suit involved the kind of cooperation with nature that past shoreline communities were famed for (in many, the highest compliments were phrases that indicated successful, caring negotiation with environments). By carefully coordinating a lift from a tidal stream, or waiting out an offshore wind among coastal ruins, I was forced into a kind of elemental immersion that generated ever greater distance and detachment from those indoor urban worlds that are insulated from weather and reality.

The journeys move, chapter by chapter, from northeast Atlantic to southwest, taking in a long arc of the northern ocean, from rocky shores beyond the rich fertility of Ireland, via the Outer Hebrides of Scotland to the edges of the Atlantic and Arctic oceans in Sámi Norway, then west to the sea rocks of the Faroes, the ice floes of Greenland, the ocean crossroads at Newfoundland, and the grand forests of the eastern seaboard of the United States. The voyaging ended on Caribbean coasts that are connected to the starting point by both the Gulf Stream and the tides of history. This is a profoundly interconnected geography, but obviously far from exhaustive: with another year, I would have rowed and paddled Senegal, the Basque Country, Iceland, Nova Scotia, the Carolinas, Carriacou, Bahia, and many other boat-filled coasts.

I hope to show, in writing of these places, that small is beautiful, and that the persistence and restoration of coastal communities on their own terms is a social and environmental good that's worth rallying round. If, in the twentieth century, our legal structures had worked to protect small-scale local fishing, and discourage vast factory ships and dredgers, our seas would be healthier and our supplies of food from the ocean assured. If the skills of wooden boatbuilding had been preserved instead of scorned, then the current pivot from oil-guzzling cargo ships to sailed ecoclippers would be far more easily and cheaply achieved. If our politics had worked to recognise local needs, in education, healthcare, housing, transport, energy, and agriculture, rather than seeking to encourage integration and assimilation as apparent social goods, then we'd have a far wider range of options from which to find responses to social and economic catastrophe. If small coastal languages, with their vast ecological vocabularies, had been protected, we'd be far better equipped to guard against ecological impoverishment. It's not just that knowledge has been lost whenever peoples of small boats were forced from their coastlines. It's that loss rendered shorelines blank for exploitation: forests aren't destroyed, or waters despoiled, when people in power know and value their stock of stories. Such stories are powerful things, and they follow, like leaping dolphins, in the wake of little boats.

All of this is given new inflections by the world of the 2020s. The phrase 'small boats', along with slogans like 'stop the boats', have become symbolic of social crisis and political division. From Britain to Belize, the idea of powerless people crossing borders in tiny vessels has been conceptualised as threat by people who wield unprecedented wealth and power. This marks a new stage in millennia-long histories of small boats operating at the edges, testing the boundaries of state authority and control, and becoming a last recourse for those suffering injustice. It's my hope that perspectives from small boats can allow us to see our world anew and imagine ways to make it better.

I

Conamara/Connemara
In Search of the Donkey Boat

I

Lost Boats

SOUTH CONNEMARA IS as famous for its writers and singers as for its dangerously rocky shores. In writing about the fractals of the shore, Tim Robinson showed how this storied richness emanated from the infinite length and vast diversity of the coastline. But these same fractals make this a place of many perils. Along hundreds of complex miles of peninsula and island shore, most regions have rocks so razor sharp they'd shred a traditional cowhide currach in moments.

The land, too, has long been labelled 'difficult'. When the English philanthropist James Tuke travelled here in 1880, he described

> a very wild, stony, desolate region, covered for many miles with boulders and large granite slabs and stones along the shores of little bays, near which were scattered many villages and houses scarcely discernible at times from the huge rocks against which they are sheltered. It seems incredible that any sustenance can

be gained at all amidst this wilderness of rock, rivalling Petra in its barrenness.

It is perhaps unsurprising that this rocky edge developed some of the most sophisticated boat technologies ever to have existed. Even a casual glance quaywards will show that highly specialised local craft, built from wood or canvas, have never been replaced by mass-produced and crudely multi-purpose vessels. From 1976 onwards, an extensive revival of seagoing traditions has made Connemara waters the envy of the wooden boat world. In regattas and on saints' days, dozens of boats are brought together for celebrations of the seaways. Crowds descend on tiny piers with little infrastructure. Cars block lanes. Boats are moored three deep along the jetties. Mass might be said in a lifeboat station, where a miraculously unscratched chip van is squeezed between dry-stone walls.

In February 2020, I wandered the South Connemara islands with Peter Bailey, skipper of the Galway hooker *An Capal*. We drove through the Lettermullen rain to visit the region's most celebrated boats, as well as a few shoreline shells of once-famous craft, lost for lack of crew to love them or funds to renew sails or hulls. Peter knew, in detail, the ancestry of every living vessel or broken pile of planks for miles around. We bumped into owners of these craft, who embodied, perhaps more than anywhere else I went, the habit of speaking of vessels as members of the family, with feelings and minds of their own. I spent my afternoons indoors, helping out on restorations of Galway hookers in two of the workshops on the Claddagh. I loved the way that when old, mouldering boats were renewed, their pieces were replaced one by one with new wood. In a method guaranteed to catch a historian's attention, old forms become the template for renewal and the past guides the construction of the future.

I'd prepared for this trip by talking boats in London with the great chroniclers of Connemara life, Tim and Mairéad Robinson.

With their input, and that of families such as the Baileys, I'd felt a welcome sense that my quest for the small boats of Connemara would feel like collaboration with many lovers of Atlantic life. But by the time I made my next Connemara journeys, three years later, much had changed. The Covid-19 pandemic had caused the seemingly vigorous revivals to falter. Festivals struggled to draw their customary crowds, while many vessels that sparkled with fresh paint in 2020 had gone unused so long that they'll need huge investment ever to sail again: local people could reel off, with frowns, the list of celebrated boats laid up ashore. More sadly still, most of those I'd talked with on the previous trip, including Peter, Tim, and Mairéad, had passed away. My ocean pilgrimage and writing felt, now, like a tribute to, rather than a collaboration with, the extraordinary generation of seafarers, storytellers, and singers who'd led Connemara's great revival in appreciation of the sea.

I returned to Leítir Mealláin (Lettermullen), this time to visit Pádraig Ó Sabhain, whose recent doctoral dissertation captures and preserves the memory and knowledge of past *bádóirí* (boat men and women). We wandered the islands, just as I had three years before, and dropped in on owners and builders of local boats, seeking stories. We drank tea and blackberry wine while annotating maps with spots on small islands where renowned rowers once lived and worked. My interest had been piqued by a unique style of rowed boat that's almost completely lost from memory: Pádraig's thesis is one of only two or three texts ever to have done more than simply list its name.

The boat that had caught my interest was a rowed class of Galway hooker that's tied, intimately, to the extremely localised geography of south Connemara's islands. Nothing has been more iconic of the Connemara cultural revival than the sailing hooker. In the 1970s, these boats re-emerged, labelled 'leisure craft' rather than 'working boat', and large regattas became the centrepiece for celebrations of far more than just sea travel. Reading accounts of the first events is an emotive affair, as old Connemara people, teary-eyed, describe the bristling thickets of masts of the gathered Galway hookers. These, they stressed, were sights from their youth that they'd never imagined could occur again. The largest hookers have a huge carrying capacity (up to twenty tonnes) and are distinctive because of the way they combine this practicality with jaw-dropping flamboyance on the water. To see them lean as they turn a narrow bend is like watching a breakdancer; or perhaps it's as if Transit vans had been designed as the most elegant vehicles on the road.

Since the revival began, lists of the classes of hooker include four sailing vessels. The full-size *bád mór* (meaning simply 'big boat'), like Peter Bailey's *An Capal*, transported peat and limestone between the Aran Islands and shores to north and south. The vast tourist industry on Inis Mór began when a *bád mór* skipper with creaking joints started letting visitors aboard on condition they pay their passage by unloading his peat on the island. His descendants run the thriving ferry business now.

The next class of boat was the *leath bháid* ('half boat'). More agile in tight bays or channels, this was the seaweed boat, hauling large volumes of the lucrative algae from where it settled on skerries to coastal towns and villages. Many Connemara women walked large distances, heavy burdens on their backs, to exchange this seaweed for wool from the slopes of the Twelve Bens, which they'd then turn into the finest flannel clothing.

The other two classes of hooker are sized similarly to each other. The *gleoiteog* – a name derived from the Irish for 'pretty' – is like a miniature *bád mór*, rigged with a large mainsail and two small foresails (known as 'gaff rigging'). The *púcán*, however, has a single sail (a 'dipping lug'): unlike the others, it is rigged so that it needs no more than one sailor.

This list of boats usually accounts for the entire family tree of the Galway hooker. Yet in the era of working boats, the tree had a fifth branch. There were very few, then, of the two smallest sailboats, and in their place was the vessel that was the object of my interest. This was a mastless ship known simply as a *bád iomartha* ('rowed boat'). *Báid iomartha* were unique to this region of south Connemara, where they did the work of canvas-hulled craft elsewhere. Their form was as elegant as the sailing hookers, though often even sturdier. They had the larger boats' beautiful sweeping lines (there's supposedly never a straight line in a Galway hooker). And, at the top of the hull, they had the same extravagant curve inwards called a 'tumble-home'.

This craft was far, far heavier than most rowed boats. Where rowers in other local vessels sat one in front of the other, each with two oars of around twelve feet, each rower in a *bád iomartha* held one great eighteen-foot beast of an oar. They sat with the starboard rower in front, port behind. In the worst weather, a third rower would hold a steering oar astern so the storm couldn't drive the bow askew. With the potential to carry three tonnes of cargo, this was among the most demanding rowing boats ever made. But it ran straight and true in weather fierce enough to discombobulate a currach, and in the right hands it could navigate the most windswept rocky channels. On the rare occasions when *báid iomartha* are mentioned, it's the exceptionally long sweeping strokes made by their skilled rowers that receive remark.

On the islands of Leitir Móir and Fornais, I visited two people who recalled, as children, watching *báid iomartha* race, and so Pádraig and I began a search for written records of such occasions. Before the 1970s revival, two small regattas stuttered on in little sea-edge townships, and the people we visited remembered *báid iomartha* taking part in both. But we could find just one written record, which dated to a race day in 1938. The weather had been rough and there was much disruption of clashing oars and splintering wood. But a *bád iomartha* mustered 'all the speed she had' to defeat every local currach.

When widespread interest in traditional boats was revived after 1976, all rowed races were conducted in small, light currachs in which anyone could get involved. The *bád iomartha* was seen as ill-suited to leisure boating, since only long-term use could build the specific strengths to row it far. Perhaps more significantly still, the rough and rocky seas in which it thrived were ones no rower today would be asked to brave.

For two hundred years before the decline of the peat trade, *báid iomartha* had been crucial to the Galway hooker's world. They navigated shallow coastal waters to load up bigger boats, and rowed peat and seaweed out to islands when the weather wasn't right to raise sail. They were most significant as ferries: social boats taking island children to school and adults to visit friends across the sounds. One island I'd paddled out to on a cold and breezy afternoon, Inis Bearachain, was famous for its *bád iomartha* rowers. There's a tale of an island woman, her waters breaking, who somehow took her boat across the sound to Leitir Móir alone, in order to seek a lift to Galway and give birth in hospital. Local priests took *báid iomartha* from island to island to deliver Mass. Small shops beside the water (some without road access) might have a dozen pulled up at their frontages, and many shopkeepers had their own *báid iomartha* as their chief delivery vessels.

Today, there's not a single *bád iomartha* still in use. Nor are there any in museums or in dry dock. Some were left rotting on the shoreline, but others were sawn in half, then rebuilt with extra planks and a mast: many of today's racing *gleoiteoga* and *púcáin* were made from working *báid iomartha* in this way. With the help of local boatbuilders, I collected the names of converted boats, and information on where a few could be found. Yet it always took time for people to see *why* this was the focus of my interest. Peter Bailey, as the last skipper of a sailing hooker to carry oars aboard, had seemed like someone who might be sympathetic to rowed boats. But when

I'd told him I wished to write not about the elegant sailboats like his own *An Capal* (which means 'the Horse') but the bulky little *báid iomartha*, he couldn't hide confusion: 'Why would you write about those? No one's interested in those. That's the donkey boat!'

Soon I was drawing comfort from the refrain 'no one ever asks about those', and coming to love the idea of *báid iomartha* as salt-strewn donkeys. This made them far more interesting, I thought, than the waterborne equivalents of a thoroughbred racehorse might be. It was once a mistake of much historical research to assume that the sophistication of a society, or the complexity of an economy, was revealed only in luxury goods and long-range trade. There's at least as much magic in goods moved locally in bulk (like peat or seaweed), in ordinary, everyday transport (such as donkeys or rowed boats), and in the songs and stories people make from these 'small' things. To hear the splash of oars in water is still as eloquent of the storied coastal past as is the sound of braying echoing across a bay. And life on the little islands once relied on *báid iomartha*, just as fully as a family's well-being demanded a donkey. No boat could be more beguiling or profound.

I scoured boat surveys for mentions of *báid iomartha*. The only things I found were expressions of surprise at the number of their rotting hulls along the shore. The most recent survey, in 2015, voiced sentiments that were perfectly predictable (because they appeared in each earlier survey too): 'The number of *Báid Iomartha*, 44 encountered [9 per cent of the total boats surveyed], came as a surprise to the survey team, even those with an intimate knowledge of the area and its boats.' That these failures of memory can be repeated every decade shows the power of this boat to reveal dynamics of memory and forgetting, tradition and innovation, survival and revival. They raise the question of how we value those parts of the working past that sit uneasily with both the practical needs of cultural revivals and the requirements for documentation or preservation of surviving objects without which historians and heritage professionals can't do their usual work.

II

The Sea Saint

After conversations in kitchens and days in workshops, the only way to enter further into the *bád iomartha*'s world was to head to sea. I made my way to Mace Pier, some two miles southwest of Carna. From this small structure at the end of a single-track road I'd join one of the great Atlantic pilgrimages: the Irish equivalent of festivals such as those for Nossa Senhora dos Navegantes (Portugal) and Bom Jesus dos Navegantes (Brazil). Just over a mile from the mainland, across a suitably stormy sound, is a gem of an island, where orange-tinged granite is swathed in green. This tiny rock on the edge of a vast ocean is the spiritual home of all Connemara boats. It would once, on its saint's day, have been the destination for hundreds of *báid iomartha*.

Oileán Mhic Dara (St MacDara's Island) is now uninhabited. The first edition Ordnance Survey map (1839) shows two houses. But the small and charismatic stone church, with steeply raked roof and decorative finials, is today the only building. It was built in the twelfth century, reputedly by sailors who'd stolen a bull and ram from the island and wished to do penance; when the revival of the hooker tradition began in 1976, restoring the chapel to its former pristine state was one of the first tasks on the revivalists' agenda.

The local folklorist Seán Mac Giollarnáth told of Páidín Rua, who lived on the island in the late nineteenth century. Few were the families, then, who owned more than two cows, but Páidín Rua's household had seventeen because wealth could be made from kelp and carragheen. There wasn't a day of the seaweed season when

Páidín Rua didn't choose to work both ebb tides so that he could, during every other month, live in leisure. A small scrape of an islet, Oileán Muiríleach, just metres south of St MacDara's Island, was the spot where swell carried kelp from miles around. The very tides seemed, under the guidance of the saint, to bless Páidín Rua and his rowing boat with extravagant luck.

MacDara himself is barely recorded in history but expansively exceeds its bounds. His first name, Síonach, seems to be built on the Irish word for sea squalls, *síon*, evoking elemental borrowings from pre-Christian ritual and belief. Urbane authorities have questioned his legitimacy. Indeed, when a missionary attempted to visit the island on the saint's day in 1851, to implore the locals to forgo their 'ancient rite' and worship in more modern ways, he was 'surrounded by a mob of both sexes, shouting and throwing stones'. 'Thanks to the Lord,' he added, 'I was only struck by three.'

Past festivities on St MacDara's Day took place in the expansive style of local seafarers, fuelled by gratitude for a year's safety at sea. There were so many hours of song, dance, and drinking, that pious visitors claimed pilgrims returned even 'greater sinners than they were before'. But these tributes to the sea saint seem to work. It's said no boat has gone down near Oileán Mhic Dara. The promise God is reported to have given the saint, that on one side or another of his island a rower would always find shelter, holds true to this day.

Mac Giollarnáth recounted in detail the feast day as it happened in the early twentieth century. He described the gathering of pilgrims:

> People come from all directions ... from Iorras Mór to the west, Leitir Mealláin to the east, and from Árainn, and in olden times they came from County Clare and from Joyce Country beyond Mám Éan.

He told of the reasons for their coming. When families feared for a stormbound traveller or fisherman, they prayed to MacDara and promised to make his pilgrimage. If a person fell ill, loved ones would step outside and turn their faces to the island to pray, vowing to pay their respects through pilgrimage in thanks for a speedy cure. Any child born in the months leading up to the saint's day in July (often any born after Christmas) would wait for their christening till the pilgrimage day, and many boys christened then would take one of the sea saint's names.

Mac Giollarnáth described the sequence and sites of pilgrims' actions but also insisted that in times past the pilgrimage was only one aspect of the island's festive pull:

> In the past many people came to the island who didn't make the pilgrimage at all but were there to be part of the gathering. In years gone by there was food and drink and confectionary available. There were boat races and foot races for the young men. It's a long time now since that came to an end. Mass is celebrated there now. Not many go, apart from those who attend the Mass and take Holy Communion and then make the pilgrimage.

In the late twentieth century, all those traditions were revived in dramatic fashion. People now travel, once again, from far and wide to visit the island and watch rowed races in the sound. But I arrived, in 2023, on a saint's day so stormy that the island Mass was cancelled, and locals shook their heads at the sorry number of boats willing to cross the wind-whipped sound. This was a day far too vicious for my tiny inflatable, and I'd still not managed to secure a crossing when other thwarted would-be pilgrims began to peel away to watch the All-Ireland Gaelic football. But I hung around, reluctant to take off the borrowed buoyancy aid that signalled my desire to make the crossing.

I was on the verge of giving up, when I saw a family clambering down into a little boat and found, to my surprise, that they were cheerily willing to make space for one more. Most of the few boats crossing were wooden currachs, of a style invented in the twentieth century, with outboard motor instead of oars (not entirely dissimilar to *báid iomartha*, though far lighter and easier to use). We launched through an exceptionally bumpy swell, and I happily took my first soak from an Irish ocean since February three years before. The children aboard complained of the drenchings, till their mother convinced them this was 'just like *Moana*', and they attuned themselves to the thrill of a wild crossing.

By now, there were four beautiful Galway hookers in the sound: the famous *bád mór An Tonaí*, a *leath bháid*, *Norah*, and two *gleoiteoga*. They ran fluid lines close to shore, instead of the circuits round the island that happen on more placid saint's days. Gradually, the skies over the island cleared, in ever greater contrast to the dark cloud burdening the land, and we turned into the cove where, even on this day of attenuated activity, there were more small traditional boats than I'd ever seen in a single bay before.

This year, perhaps even more than others, the defining feature of this event was its informality. The feast day has been described as 'like a second Christmas, halfway through the year', and those on the island were treating the festivities with the full range of attitudes inspired by Christmas revelry. For some, this meant immersion in the ascetic ethos of the early saints; having left phones at home, they slowly and seriously did the full round of island holy sites. Others enjoyed a celebratory day on the beach. One family set up a tent on the slope, and some of the picnics I passed were feasts in the truest sense.

While I walked a circuit of the pilgrimage sites I didn't hear a single word spoken that wasn't in Irish. There was an old couple dressed in full sea gear of waterproof trousers, macs, lifejackets, and thick wool-lined hats, but with only saintly sandals on feet that glistened with seawater. They seemed so happily but reverentially absorbed in their shared experience of the rites that I wished I had some access to the feelings it evoked for them. I wandered past a family who, passing a pair of binoculars between them, were absorbed in deep and technical discussion of the manoeuvres each hooker was making half a mile away.

The most recent academic study of this festival paints a picture of an event shorn of historical meaning and religious purpose. Even the organisers, its authors write, 'do not seem to be burdened with much factual knowledge' about the meanings of the pilgrimage or the history of the island. My experience was wildly different. I saw a community gathered to honour its boats and celebrate ties to these shores in a wide range of styles. Even on this stormbound day, over a hundred people had risked the windswept waters in small boats to renew their links to Connemara, and to each other, with piety, picnics, or both. Everyone I spoke to was invested in local traditions in one way or another, so that I have never felt more connected to communities bonded by seafaring.

Though the donkey boat is gone, its world does remain. It's not for lack of local love that the whole hooker tradition is in danger of following in the *bád iomartha*'s wake. Rocketing costs of timber, sails, and even nails, mean that local love can't be enough. Only outside investment in this jewel of global heritage can save these beautiful, practical, and sustainable vessels. Tragically, it's the family and community structure of ownership – one of this tradition's most important features – that makes it so precarious. Institutions baulk at funding families rather than corporations; but if they leave living boats to sink, they take the risk that in the future they'll save only their wrecks. There's no reason why, in times to come that might take sustainability and beauty seriously, all five Galway hooker classes might not have revived practical purposes. Ecoclippers, after all, are showing historic technologies to be more advanced than steam or diesel. The tragedy would be if the hookers' usefulness was rediscovered after the dissolution of both their structural integrity and the skills required to sail and row them.

In this way, the *bád iomartha* is a symbol and a cautionary tale. Donkeys will continue to bray all across Connemara, but *bád iomartha* oars may never slice inter-island seas again. What their absence conjures shouldn't be a sense of how much has been lost, but of how little. Every other class of Galway hooker, and almost every kind of currach, persists. The task of knowing, and showing, why they all matter – whether they're marine mule or sea stallion – is ours.

2

Leòdhas/Lewis
The Shores Boats are Built From

I

The Shieling of the Pools

IT HAS BEEN nearly a century since the last *báid iomartha* rowed peats between the south Connemara islands. But on many Atlantic shores, the living worlds of small boats are closer to us in time. In the 1960s, Dan Morrison produced a rich photographic account of Ness, the northernmost district of the Isle of Lewis. Ness is a beautiful wedge of rough land in the North Atlantic. It is, as Morrison's photos show, oriented towards the ocean. That's partly because it's the centre of constellations of islands. North Rona and Sula Sgeir, forty miles to the north, are bucket-list paddles for any ocean kayaker. Their wild, tidal grandeur contrasts starkly with the hundreds of gentle islets in sea lochs further south. It's characteristic of this region that even the most distant offshore islands were as much part of the Ness community as was the local moorland.

Morrison depicted a world in which every family had their horse, cart, plough, and harrow. Each grew oats, barley, and potatoes, kept sheep to make tweed and cows to churn butter, and owned nets and rods for fishing from the rocks. His pictures of the townships of Ness show tools such as frames worn over the body for carrying milk in buckets, and creels for loading peat onto the back. They show the turf-covered roofs of shielings on the moorland where summers were still spent with cattle. And his images of Port of Ness show beautiful wide boats, with two rowers seated side by side, heading far out to sea to their fishing grounds.

Perhaps because the past feels so close and vibrant here, there's an exceptional local commitment to preserving the memory of that boat-borne way of life. There's still a group of shieling huts at Cuishader, frequented for leisure in the summer months, which is a rarity in modern Europe. And there are still two seagoing examples of the local wooden boat, the sturdy but nimble *sgoth Niseach*, which have travelled as far as Orkney in recent decades. These boats are thought of today as sailboats. It's widely forgotten, even in the islands, that only the development of commercial deep-sea fishing, late in the nineteenth century, led boatbuilders to adapt for sail forms that had long been launched from surf-strewn beaches under oar.

At the start of 2022, just after the final pandemic quarantines were lifted and with travel still limited but movement finally feeling ethical again, I relocated my life to Ness to learn about these boats. I sold my house in Birmingham and, from January till May, rented a former tweed mill in Adabroc, beside Port of Ness, from which I could watch northerly winter storms strafe the sea by day and northern lights dance across Atlantic skies by night.

These months were guaranteed to include weeks of fierce seas, and I saw them as my opportunity to learn more of how these boats belonged in the complex worlds of moorland, shore, and sea that made the communities of Ness so vibrant and distinctive. These were the months when storms thrust tonnes of wood ashore, so the building of next summer's boats began by combing winter beaches. I chose zones to walk and paddle, from the cliffs in the east of Ness, round the Butt of Lewis in the north, and down the bleak west coast, through an array of small isles of the most staggering richness, to Scarp, forty miles to the south. And I travelled this region, on foot, and by boat, dozens of times.

Standing in storms on west Lewis beaches made it seem not just unlikely but impossible that past people launched their little boats from here. Rank after rank of ten-foot-high breakers beat endlessly on the golden sands. Ness seas, warmed by the Gulf Stream, face winters far scarcer in resources than those at similar longitudes elsewhere, where sea ice opens endless possibilities to fish and to hunt. In contrast, the wet and stormy winters here close off the sea's resources. Past islanders' response was to develop rich practices of fermenting, pickling, salting, and smoking their plentiful summer foods: winter was pungent and flavourful to say the least.

My first boat journeys of the winter did not take me out to sea, but along inland rivers and into past Lewis summers, seeking the moorland pastures of the shielings. Without these, I felt, I couldn't comprehend the life in which seagoing boats played crucial roles. Almost all shieling sites are watery. Those at Borve, in west Lewis, are typical. Here the shielings cluster round a stream of delicious fresh water. Summer months on the moor meant freedom from the clergy's gaze. Here locals have mapped the links between current households by the shore and the specific shieling ruin that their ancestors spent summers in.

But at Filiscleitir, in northeast Lewis, an even more evocative arrangement existed. Here the shielings were built on the cliff edge. This is where John Nicholson, known locally as An Fiosaiche ('the Seer'), chose to build his spectacular clifftop chapel. He was a Lewis man who found evangelical religion in the United States, and returned with an American wife who introduced the Gaels of Ness to such luxuries as harmonium music and oranges. The chapel this couple founded in 1905 expressed great flair for drama, requiring that worshippers walk a narrow, vertiginous clifftop path, on which they could ponder the sublimity of their God and their own mortality, as they approached the tiny ocean-facing door.

Even in the English language, the evangelical hymnal is full of sea storms and their influence. I imagined lines such as 'Our life is like a stormy sea' ringing from these walls, and realised just how often the songs Nicholson and his wife taught their parishioners would have made Christ a boat's pilot or anchor, and used the symbol of a boat for the church itself. Did this alter Ness folks' perception of their family vessels? Surely some, at least, thought of An Fiosaiche as they launched into seas that were like a judgement on their souls. Today, this building, and the shielings round it, stand as some of the most atmospheric ruins in all Scotland, leaving visitors to imagine parting conversations between preacher and parishioners, shouted in the doorway over roaring storms.

But the shielings that interested me most were south from here and further from the sea. Scattered round the fresh water of huge Loch Langabhat are hundreds of ruins, which I'd started to see as the rowing boat shielings at the heart of Lewis. During February, I took every opportunity I could to visit these extraordinary places. I dragged my sea kayak into the Grimersta River and paddled up routes that large shoals of salmon once leapt. Fierce westerly winds assisted me against the white water's northeasterly flow, and smart little dippers sounded shrill alarms as I came round each bend. Even low in this ascent, small islets in every thickening of the stream housed squat stone ruins from eras when the salmon were plentiful. But the great revelations arrived when the high loch opened out at the site of Àirigh nan Linntean (the 'Shieling of the Pools'). From these places, and only these places, I felt I could begin to envisage the rich boat-bound life of the summer dwellings.

Loch Langabhat is both long and complex: its shores, when combined with those of its adjoining lesser lochs, are well over a hundred miles in length, yet it rarely reaches a quarter of a mile across. It is bounded to the south and east by the small, rough mountains of southern Lewis and Harris. To my mind, it's emblematic of the ways the most important places are often the most easily forgotten. In winter the loch today feels wild and remote, with the nearest roads or formal paths miles of boggy trudge away. Yet every part of the loch's shores bustle with past activity. Because of the distance from modern crofts, the stones of these buildings have never been taken for reuse, and so their intricate walls, sometimes square but often the rounded corbel domes of beehive houses, stand as they stood when they were built.

In some stone structures a fireplace can still be seen, while in others I could store my lunch in the rocky alcoves where cheese and milk were once cooled. There's no way of knowing how many of the shielings round this loch were ever occupied simultaneously, but the impression their presence gives is of a historic summer city on the moors. The sites of these shielings, not next to the running water of small streams but beside easy points of access to the loch itself, suggest that they were interconnected by rowing boat rather than path: their locations make little sense unless lochs linked, rather than separated, them.

The second time I made this journey, I took books in which visitors in the eighteenth and nineteenth centuries recounted their wonderment at stepping into this extraordinary world. They tended to bring preconceptions that underestimated the sophistication of life here. They assumed the people they encountered would be illiterate, until they saw them reading. They assumed conditions of 'bare subsistence', until they saw how rich subsistence could be. And they imagined a parochial peasantry, until they learned of regular exchanges with passing ships in which local herring was swapped for Bordeaux wines. The same astounded wonderment fills them all.

I ate my bread and cheese in beehives much like those a physician and antiquarian, Arthur Mitchell, described after travelling here in 1866:

> By the side of a burn which flowed through a little grassy glen – a sort of oasis in the midst of a great waste of bog and rock – we saw two small round hive-like hillocks, not much higher than a man, joined together, and covered with grass and weeds . . . Out of the top of one of them a column of smoke slowly rose, and at its base there was a hole about three feet high and two feet wide, which seemed to lead into the interior of the hillock.

Mitchell soon encountered the community who lived there, and, though a well-travelled man who lived to write up his antiquarian journeys, found himself almost lost for words:

> we found one of these beehive-houses actually tenanted, and the family happened to be at home. It consisted of three young women . . . None of them could speak English; but they were not illiterate, for one of them was reading a Gaelic Bible. They showed no alarm at our coming, but invited us in . . . and hospitably treated us to milk. They were courteously dignified, neither feeling nor affecting to feel embarrassment. There was no evidence of any understanding on their part that we should experience surprise at their surroundings. I confess, however, to having shown, as well as felt, the effects of the wine of astonishment. I do not think I ever came upon a scene which more surprised me.

Mitchell's favourite theme when writing of shielings was the connection they made between present and past. The niches in the walls of these beehive houses, he observed, contained 'little milk tubs' with thin 'slaty stone' discs for lids like those excavated at sites of his antiquarian activities. He told of some structures, already long disused, in which bones of seal, sheep, deer, and dog had been found, many of them shaped as tools centuries ago. But he stressed that there were people alive in the second half of his own century who had built some of these structures, and many people living who had been born in them.

By the early twentieth century, when other visitors to Lewis photographed and wrote about these spots, they found no one dwelling within. Another visiting antiquarian, W. M. Mackenzie, described, in 1904, 'a scene of pastoral richness, quiet, and beauty, over which the shy deer boldly move among what were once the habitations of men'. Some of the shielings Mitchell decribed had already been destroyed, because landowners had feared that poachers were using them as cover. But the fact that many stand intact today, on such gale-swept moors, is testimony to the skill of their construction. The views from those on higher slopes are so extraordinary that it seems their sites were chosen for the scope and grandeur of their vistas. They are tiny observatories for the vast dramas of weather and water that sweep across the glittering tapestry below.

I paddled between these beehive buildings (cleits) on the slopes of a hill named after them (Ascleit) and the many square, stone shielings beneath the charismatic little mountains that fringe the loch. Bedraggled sea eagles often sat like trig points on any high ground. By boat, this was a small, contained world in which the garden-like green of one shieling was just minutes from the beautiful, loch-side verdure of another. On foot, the same short trips would be tortuous journeys: the best part of a day's walk, with rivers to wade. Fittingly, the names of shielings, from the Shieling of the Pools to Àirigh nan Loch nan Learg (the 'Shieling of the Loch of the Red-Throated Diver'), suggest communities oriented towards the water.

The task of bringing driftwood, by horse or mule, to build a boat would have been arduous. But boat materials were carried far further elsewhere, and it seems entirely implausible that these were terrestrial rather than amphibious settlements. We have no evidence, however, that a boat was ever used here in the long eras of the shielings. No visitor described one. No remains have ever been looked for. This is how completely the memory of small boats like those that must have been the medium of life here can be lost.

II

The Riches of the Sea

As spring arrived, the string of successive storms finally spluttered out, and the sea turned from milky froth to rippling dark swell. This was the moment to launch onto the ocean. While seas remained wild, I spent day after day paddling the deep fractals of Loch Ròg, the great indentation in west Lewis, with its multitude of tiny islands. This single sea loch would repay a lifetime's wandering, because each small island's history and geography are different and full of stories. On the north side are Carloway, with its dramatic dun and windswept harbour, and Callanish, with its stone circles and gentle bay. On the south are the great cliffs of Gallan Head, the rounding of which has inspired multitudes of songs and stories. In the centre is the largest island – Great Bernera – whose rowers and sailors were once so renowned throughout the islands that they were said to be rivalled only by those of Scarp. Sweeping out from the depths of the loch towards the open sea are a succession of sheltered bays and flat islands that gradually give way to fierce exposure and the high towers of rocky islets.

It isn't just the land, but the stories, that change as the exposure to the ocean grows. Within the loch, the tales are domestic and the place names indicate the everyday uses each area was put to. My time at the moorland beehive buildings made me seek out their coastal twins. I spent a night on tiny Eilean Fir Chrothair (the 'Island of the Men of Croir'), where a little beehive hut sits limpet-like within reach of seaspray. Its name records the use of this rock by the family who lived at Croir on Great Bernera, for whom it provided shellfish and a little grazing.

In the outermost islands of the loch, by contrast, the great heroic figures of Lewis seafaring, such as Dòmhnull Cam Macaulay and Neil MacLeod, played out the grand politics of island life. In the poetic 'oar songs' that fill Gaelic verse, the heroes are distinguished by their boats. They rowed no 'ramshackle old crates', or 'bulging, rusted tubs', but deft and daring little vessels. My most dramatic landing in this region was on the cliffs of Bearasay, the stunning sea rock on which a band of Lewis men held out in 1598 against James VI's attempts to 'civilise the most barbarous Isle of Lewis' in the name of commerce and the Scottish nation. There's no landing here but for one stretch of rock that's slightly less vertical than the others. These kinds of islands are among the most significant sites in Europe never to have been excavated or the subject of serious scholarship.

Figures like Dòmhnull Cam are recorded in history as pirates and nuisances: stubborn men who delayed the proper development of the islands and rarely turned up for their lawful trials and executions. Dòmhnull was young, it seems, when James VI's mercenaries (known as the Fife Adventurers) swept through Lewis, and his father was one of the farmer-fishermen who lost their land and living to the adventurers' demands. Fortunately, a learned nineteenth-century Lewis man, Donald Morrison, known as An Sgoilear Bàn, 'the Fair-Haired Scholar', went to great pains to collect from oral tradition every tale he could of the outlaw life Dòmhnull lived thereafter.

A huge and formidable man, Dòmhnull came to be considered almost invincible, despite the injured eye that gave him his epithet '*Cam*' (which literally means 'crooked'). Many tales take him to distant coasts, and some have him row little boats long distances in terrible conditions. Indeed, his records read like a testament to the place of the small rowed boat in island culture. Once, for instance, Dòmhnull and Neil MacLeod escaped royal forces who held them captive at Ullapool but couldn't leave the mainland before the alarm was raised. The order was given that every township for a hundred miles secure their boats and remove their oars to prevent Dòmhnull's flight to Lewis. But eventually, many miles to the south, opposite the north of Skye, the fugitives found a rotting rowing boat full of holes, which they repaired with only clods of earth. They tore down the doors of a cowshed to use for oars and, still wearing heavy chains round neck and feet, rowed their leaky boat to Dunvegan Castle on Skye. It's said that Dòmhnull Cam's heavy chains, removed by the castle's blacksmith, were displayed in Dunvegan for many years, so that older generations could show youngsters how strong were the rowers of the past.

There are many Lewis sites associated with Dòmhnull, including a dramatic, almost inaccessible promontory, Stac Dhòmhnuill Chaim ('Dòmhnull Cam's Fort'), whose steep and precarious sides his daughter was said to scale with a bucket of milk or water on her head so that her hands were free for climbing. Far away, in the island's east, is *Àirigh* Dhòmhnaill Chaim ('Dòmhnull Cam's Shieling'); and further north is a sea cave called Priosan Dhòmhnuill Chaim ('Dòmhnull Cam's Prison').

But closer to home, in a tiny, pretty loch in the hills above Loch Ròg, there's another 'fort'. This one is smaller in footprint than a terraced house. It is reached from land by a series of underwater stepping stones that, in Dòmhnull Cam's time, were set in zigzags to confound would-be attackers. This spot is associated with yet more tales that give a fuller picture of Dòmhnull Cam's life in his rowing boats. During his time at this miniature fort, Dòmhnull adopted a young boy, John Du Craig, who had survived the Lewis men's capture of an English ship. Dòmhnull and John lived on the island in the loch, hunting venison and fishing far out to sea. Once, it's said, John's cheeky quips so enraged Dòmhnull while they fished the rough water at Gallan Head, that John, in fear of his life, threw Dòmhnull's oars overboard and swam for shore. The raging ocean, the lesson seems to be, was less formidable than Dòmhnull Cam's wrath. It's said that Dòmhnull returned home weeping, believing his young apprentice had surely drowned. He was overjoyed, as he approached the fort, to find the lad home, with the floor swept and a fire laid. But, in true island style, while feeling deep relief in every bone of his body, he mustered all his reserve to walk impassively in and say, 'Make the supper, John.'

In many of the tales of Dòmhnull Cam, the drama begins when he's engaged in everyday coastal life from a small boat. Dramas begin at home while he's off fowling on the Flannan Isles or fishing for ling. Like all the renowned Lewis seafarers who were considered pirates by the state, he was an ordinary small-scale farmer and fisher, made famous by the disrupted times he lived in. That Dòmhnull Cam's particular repute came in part from his extraordinary propensity for violent rage means he's in no way an attractive figure, but this grisly reputation perpetuates his fame today as a cautionary tale for unruly Lewis children: 'Dòmhnull Cam will get you.'

The tales of Dòmhnull's time are of figures whose chaotic lives were the result of centralised efforts to stamp out, not their violence, but their everyday peaceable interactions with the world around them. And it's telling of both the good times and the bad on these coasts that even the most renowned of leaders rowed their little boats through every story rather than commanding others to fix a sail. The questions closest to my heart were what that life had been and how, from this distance, to get behind the heroic tales to ordinary realities.

These would be found, I thought, far from the exposed islets in the gentle innermost bays of Loch Ròg. Sure enough, the sheer amount of life around my boat showed the plentiful resources of the sea loch. Otters and great northern divers busied at the water's surface, while bivalves, urchins, and algae bustled beneath. I returned repeatedly to one spot that seemed to sit at the confluence of land- and sea-life. Here two past settlements, called Ganstotl and Loch an t-Sròm (Strome), sit either side of a tiny peninsula at the point where two sea lochs converge.

This is a spot that can feel extremely remote today. But it was once central to sea routes. There are ruins of large and complex habitations in the deep shelter of the bays, and there are tidal coves beside them brimming with shellfish. I found scallops and picked one up before returning it to the water, where it spurted cartoonishly away. I found beds, barely beneath low tide, of old, gnarled, healthy oysters. Martin Martin, a Gael from Skye, was the first great travel writer on the Outer Hebrides. In his 1703 *Description of the Western Islands of Scotland* he told how an unusually low tide could leave fifteen to twenty horse-loads of these oysters on a single island beach. There were limpets and black periwinkles, which Martin explained were the key ingredients for a wholesome broth that was favoured by nursing mothers. And pretty, subaqueous gardens of red, green, and brown seaweeds ran throughout the bays. Martin recorded their uses too, describing the seaweed known in Scots as 'slake' (and by the Welsh as lavabread) as a kind of superfood: an adequate diet in itself, if cooked in a little butter, for the most robust and energetic people. Had I passed through at high tide, rather than spending days in this bay, I would have seen little of this largesse.

This was a striking place to imagine past worlds from. The calm, enclosed launch from Loch an t-Sròm, perfect for the rowing boats that would have been dragged up these beaches, gave direct access both to the best white-fishing zones imaginable and a sea loch famed for herring and salmon. It would have been possible, too, to row miles at sea without risking open ocean, visiting the many larger settlements along the coast. The land was once well enough grazed for it still to glow green two centuries later, and there are yet more shieling structures where the rich, deep peat begins. At Ganstotl, a half-completed millstone lies in the earth, revealing this verdant world to have been a site for quarrying the tools of arable life. The extraordinary number of nearby mill ruins undermines the often-repeated idea that grain played limited roles in the diets of the Highlands and Islands. In the work of local writers such as Finlay Macleod, the little mills, which were actively smashed up by landlords who sought to commercialise this landscape, have come to symbolise the way of life that centralised, monetary society destroyed.

Stories abound of exchange and intermarriage between Loch an t-Sròm and an area south of Gallan Head, a half-day's row away. One day in March, I followed in their oarstrokes through the bleak Atlantic bluster at west Lewis's great headland, and spent a gorgeous night on Eilean Mhealasta. This is an island with staggering westerly exposure. Its treacherous tidal sound is a very simple crossing on the right day, but utterly unnavigable when strong winds turn north-westerly. With calm weather promised for days, I paddled over to a gentle world of juniper, primrose, marram grass, and seaducks. The eider were so busy with their hoots and murmurs that it seemed they thought the spring already here.

The township opposite the island, Mhealasta, no longer exists, though it was once among the largest and most significant in south-west Lewis, sustained by the resources on its many islands and skerries. On one small sea rock, I found a beehive dwelling that isn't listed even in the most complete compendium of such buildings ever made. And Eilean Mhealasta itself is riddled with evidence of largely undocumented pasts. There are five buildings in the fertile north of the island. Each was already a ruin on the first edition Ordnance Survey sheet (1854) and none are marked on any later map. There's place-name evidence for mills in the south of the island, though no discernible structures. There were almost certainly inhabitants here in the seventeenth and eighteenth centuries which history doesn't record. The high ground is surprisingly rich in fresh water, and the seas are full of fish and shellfish even today. Luxury bedding would come from the seabird fowling cliffs of the Flannans, which look spectacular from Eilean Mhealasta's western edge. A skerry to the southwest, Gaisgeir, was once famed as the site of the fattest seals, whose skins made for cosy boots and jackets and whose oil lit winter nights. Irish merchants, local memory holds, once passed through here regularly and exchanged luxury goods for fish, feathers, and seal oil.

My experience of the richness of these places, and their potential for supporting fulfilling human lives, is contrasted dramatically and abruptly by the archival record. Beyond names, the ordinary lives lived at Loch an t-Sròm or Eilean Mhealasta are almost entirely absent from textual sources. Instead, one name dominates the documents. In 1830, an Inverness speculator, Alexander Macrae, was granted land in the west of Lewis by the Seaforth estate so that he might raise sheep and eke some profit from the land.

Macrae seems to have been a man of the land, who didn't much like the sea, the islands, or their people. Within three years, he'd become so irked by sharing the shore of Little Loch Ròg with the local community that his letters to the Seaforth estate took on a tone of deep frustration. Concerning Loch an t-Sròm, he wrote:

> I am sadly annoyed by the Tenants of Strome, whose cattle destroy my Grass, as well as my Corn . . . and in order to get rid of so troublesome and disagreeable neighbours, as well as with the view of doing more justice to my stock, I will feel much obliged by your letting me have the Farm of Strome . . . for which I shall pay you the Rent these tenants pay, besides it will be putting me in possession of a Vote for the County Member.
>
> If the Honourable Mrs S Mackenzie knew how I am situated, I have no doubt she would order me every encouragement, and

this faith I have likewise in you Sir, particularly to a Tenant who pays his rent when asked.

In a way entirely typical of the 1830s, it took no more than Macrae's requests for a place that might have been continuously occupied since prehistory to be emptied forever. Its sophisticated forms of mixed subsistence were replaced overnight with an ovine monocrop. Small wooden boats would never again leave the little bay on fishing trips or make social visits to nearby islands. The archival presence of the loch was a monocrop too, built on documents produced only by people whose world views were irreconcilably different from those of the communities they removed.

On the other side of Gallan Head, Macrae's influence was equally malign, although it was manifest differently. In the documents of the later 1830s, Macrae comes to seem less like a hard-hearted but canny financial operator, and more like a feckless bandit. In 1838, despite Seaforth's acquiescence to his every whim, Macrae stopped 'paying his rent when asked' and was threatened with prosecution. As a consequence of the arrears he built up, sixteen families from Mhealasta were cleared to Ness, many miles to the north. There are records of families cleared in this way living for months or even years on Ness beaches, with only their upturned boats for shelter. This was the same moment of change used to smash the mills, so that communities now had to pay for use of centralised, commercial mills instead. To prevent resettlement of Eilean Mhealasta, a rumour also seems to have begun, that anyone born on the island would 'become an idiot'.

Processes such as these are the reasons why peoples of small boats have reputations as sufferers of many hardships who needed assistance from outside. This is a theme that's evident in the writing of many early visitors to Lewis. Martin Martin, whose writing on limpets, oysters, and seaweed was quoted above, had come to the island from Skye at the end of the seventeenth century. This was long after commercial inroads had begun to be made in the islands but before the advent of a monetary economy. Today, Martin's writing seems to be full of paradoxes. But these contradictions were so common in the literature of his age that they appear not to have been considered paradoxical at all.

His book, he claimed, had two purposes. One was to bring progress to the vulgar islanders, enriching them with the fruits of commerce and knitting them into a national polity. He wished, he wrote, to transform their current way of life into something more decorous and lucrative. His second purpose, however, was to praise the current islanders to the skies. They lived, he said, at one with the natural world. They were so exceptionally well versed 'in the Book of Nature' that their close observation of the plants and animals of land and sea gave them unique skills in making the most of their resources. 'They rather satisfy than oppress Nature in their way of eating and drinking', he wrote, and he gave this as a reason why 'not a few among them have a natural Beauty, which excels any that has been drawn by the finest [ancient artists]'. Islanders had medical knowledge, Martin insisted, that the rest of European society should learn from. His book is filled with details of the skilled use of cures and simples, and of the islanders' exceptional knowledge of methods to maintain good health. But for a few instances of poverty and hardship (which are now the most widely quoted passages of his book), what Martin described was a healthy, happy, population with sophisticated medical and environmental knowledge. Yet, still, his mission was to transform this culture by means of integration and commercialisation.

I don't know whether it's merely nostalgic to try to think of the histories of these coasts in ways that don't have the Enlightenment's vision of progress and transformation running through them – to imagine the lines of development they might otherwise have taken.

But it seems worthwhile, to me, to ask what it might mean to imbue our outlooks with a little of the coastal world views that Martin so begrudgingly admired.

III

If You Have a Sandworm, You Have Everything

Three places excelled as the boatbuilding centres of these coasts. The most northerly of them, Ness, stands alone. Here, in the nineteenth century, commercial development led a gradual evolution from oar to sail and resulted in the fast, elegant, and unique *sgoth Niseach*. These wide, undecked boats, with dipping lug sail, enliven countless early photos of the region. The other two centres – Great Bernera and Scarp – were special less for the distinctiveness of their boats than for the great renown of those who rowed them. In combining a sense of how boats were built and used in these three places we can understand the seafaring of a wide ocean zone.

The origins of all these boats are on the windswept beaches where these treeless shores had ready supplies of wood washed up from worlds away. While I stayed in Ness, a friend there embroidered a line of Gaelic onto the top I wear for paddling or rowing. It reads *Tha am muir ag iarradh a bhith 'ga thadha* ('the sea wants to be visited') and recalls the way islanders would wander to the sea before daybreak to seek wood for building boats. They looked for oak for stem and stern, red fir for keel, grey elm for gunwales, and larch for ribs and planks. Summer wood was worse than winter, because of the timber-worms and goose barnacles that flourished in warmer seas. Long days of work followed a find of wood, soaking it in freshwater pools, then steaming it over fires that cracked and sparked, so it would be ready to cut or twist into the smooth curves of bow and stern. The builder would need few tools. In many townships these weren't private possessions but made locally and shared between many crafts.

The small boats these communities built were dragged into the waves between sharp black rocks, and ridden through grinding surf to reach safe seas. This rough usage kept them small and light. Another local saying holds that *Cumadh an eisg cumadh an eathir* ('the shape of the boat is the shape of a fish'), and the form of boats made in 1800 was far narrower and sleeker than those that came later. It was more sharp-nosed mackerel than wide flounder, because these were boats built for rowing. Their return on rough days, clattering through the violence of white surf to golden beaches must have been quite something to behold. I've come ashore many times here, and only on the coast of Donegal do I feel I've received more bruises from rough landings.

Conventional wisdom holds that commercial use of boats on this coast was impossible in the early modern period, because monopolies on salt meant fish couldn't be cured for market on any scale. Yet there's evidence that some spaces in buildings used at this time, often labelled 'priest holes' and assumed to date from the Reformation, were nothing of the kind but were, instead, nooks for the illicit storage of salt. I have a strong, unprovable suspicion that its smuggling may have been a more expansive affair than we recognise. But terms such as 'smuggling' and 'illicit' make me a little uncomfortable. Time spent on these coasts – distant from the state and filled with natural resources – has made me consider that the efforts to control production of things like salt, and not the local attempts to evade that control, are the thing that's piratical.

The world of boats draws many examples of such state piracy. The close cousin of Lewis's rowing boats, the Shetland yoal, is one of the most vivid. In the sixteenth century, boatbuilding wood was shipped, ready cut, to Shetland from Norway. Families placed orders individually, till enough could be imported to make a voyage worthwhile.

Around 1575, however, an ambitious and piratical landowner, Lord Robert Stewart (who would later be made first Earl of Orkney and Zetland), saw a chance to profit at Shetland families' expense by imposing a charge on every boat imported in this manner. The measure backfired dramatically, however, when it drew attention from the Scottish state. The state rejected Stewart's right to a levy, but took this moment to impose official taxes. This was the beginning of changes that prevented families from living well from a single boat, and of the conglomeration of demand into commercial ventures. The Shetland historian Brian Smith estimates that only about half the boats imported in the period that followed were brought in legally and taxed. But I'd argue that, like those who smuggled salt in Lewis, Shetlanders importing boats in the traditional way don't come off badly from this story.

By the early nineteenth century, changes were underway in Lewis that permitted the builders of the *sgoth Niseach* greater scope to experiment with boat shapes. Beyond free access to salt, the most important change was the construction of large stone havens from the sea, of which the Port of Ness itself was the grandest and most elaborate. By 1850, these thick stone walls around a narrow sandy channel had made Ness a principal fishing station for hundreds of miles around, bringing in ling, cod, haddock, herring, and seafowl by the boatload. The *sgoth* became bigger, more difficult to row, and more suited to moving heavy loads under sail. In its heyday, late in the nineteenth century, over a hundred of these boats sailed from Port of Ness on long voyages to deep-sea grounds. They came in many sizes, from the seventeen-foot 'half *sgoth*', which would have been considered a large boat a century earlier, to the twenty-five-foot 'three-quarter *sgoth*', and the 'full *sgoth*' of thirty-three feet or more. In the terms boatbuilders favour, these craft were 'beamy' (wide) with rounded middles that make them look, deceptively, as though they'd be slow. With longer keels than many similar boats, they don't lean as they turn, so even the largest could sail without a deck. The result is that a full *sgoth* appears enormous inside. It was capable of carrying many miles of longlines and large quantities of fish. Depending on boat size, and the strength and skills of those aboard, a *sgoth* could sail with a crew of anything from two to twelve.

In April, the leading current advocate for the Ness boat, Ian Stephen, took me to sea in the half *sgoth Jubilee*. It was a joy to sail but a horror to row. He told me of all the places I should go to learn the lore of island rowers. The first port of call was Great Bernera and the archive of Seoras Chaluim Sheorais (George MacLeod). MacLeod was one of very few island oarsmen who saw value in recording his oral boat-lore in pen and ink. His father was one of Bernera's great seamen, whose boat, *Rhoda*, a half-deck sailboat, carried sheep to and from the Flannan Isles as well as fishing many miles of treacherous waters. George himself made his living as a dental technician, but combined his skills of seafaring and intricate craftsmanship to build small and beautiful model vessels, two of which now reside in the National Maritime Museum in Greenwich. When he recorded routes to sites such as the deep rocky expanse of Stearr, northeast of the Flannan Isles (a natural habitat for ling), he also recorded the sayings these places gave rise to. Any long thing on Bernera was labelled *cho fada ri langa na Stearr* ('as long as a ling from Stearr'). Macleod made delicate ling-long scrolls on which he drew navigation lines between seamarks and recorded the strategies that took seafarers straight to good fishing grounds. For ease of use, each scroll was wrapped round lovingly crafted spindles of polished wood. The names of his diagrams, such as 'Sinking Soray Island', sound almost like the names of folk songs. Following this instruction meant rowing or sailing out from Bernera while keeping a Lewis mountain, Mealaisbhal, perfectly in line with the Eilean Mòr lighthouse till the exact moment when, after many miles, the Flannan isle of Soray sinks below the horizon. To drop lines just then was to catch good fish.

By the time I was pointed to this archive I was nearing the end of my Lewis stay, so I took a final sea journey from Bernera, via the waters on Macleod's scrolls, to the rival isle of Scarp. Once there, I spent my last night in a sleeping bag on the island's highest point. At 4.20 a.m., I awoke to the first hints of blue light, and a golden eagle five feet away, looking me dead in the eye. As the sun rose, I wandered down the rock and heather slope and through the maze of croft houses and ruins that line the hillside. I recalled the 1930s photos that showed this slope covered not in rough grazed ground but in rich expanses of grain. The sun rose behind the mountains of Harris in a blazing golden dawn, and the tide came rolling, gleaming and fast, past the skerries in the sound below.

The past boats of Scarp are entirely uncelebrated: little wooden vessels whose style doesn't even have a name. Later in my travels, a Cape Cod boatbuilder (who had just described his own style as 'down and dirty') asked me what kind of boats were made in Scarp, and when I answered that I didn't think Scarp rowers really had a name for them, his response was a deeply satisfied 'Ah, just to them "the kind of boats we build"'. Yet the people of Scarp were celebrated far and wide for their profound sea skills and their strength in rowing these heavy, long-oared craft.

Since 1971, Scarp has been 'uninhabited', but this tells only a tiny fraction of its story: it's deeply integrated into communities in neighbouring Lewis and Harris, and there are islanders with a profound commitment to maintaining it as an active, working space, rather than the millionaire's playground that modern attitudes to islands lead so many to become. The small Scarp boat still goes out to tend the flock of hardy, stubborn little sheep, and the sense of community among those descended from Scarp's last residents is rich and strong.

Island memory is full of feats of rowing. One tale, for instance, recounts how an old woman on Scarp slipped on winter ice and hurt her leg. Four islanders leapt into one of the many small boats on

Scarp and, seated side by side with one oar each, rowed into the teeth of a gale to bring the doctor from Tarbert on Harris. It took them all night. The storm filled their vessel and saturated their tweed and oilskin clothes till they might have seemed more seal than human. They arrived in Tarbert with the dawn, shivering and spent. But, with just a bite of breakfast, they rowed the seventeen miles straight home with the doctor perched between them in the boat.

Almost all visitors relied on the islanders for boat passage. Even officials such as the school inspectors had to walk the long rough path to Huisinis on Harris, often after dark, and bellow at the top of their lungs across the half-mile-wide sound. If they were lucky, Scarp rowers would hear and ferry them over. One island memoirist, Angus Duncan, told how this situation frequently led islanders to imagine they heard shouts in every little buffet of the wind: 'How often have I heard our talk and laughter round the peat fire of a neighbour's house interrupted by someone saying, "Wheesht! I hear a shout!"' With no pier to disembark from, visitors might leave the boat by riding on the back of a rower in long seaboots. No complaint was ever recorded of the heaviness of people carried in this way, just of one or two being 'as slippery as seals'. Visitors' impressions of island rowers in their dark, wet clothes also relied on marine comparisons: 'They are just like cormorants.'

Duncan wrote that not just a few island men but every member of the community developed muscular strength from rowing and digging. Many of the most accomplished rowers were women. He told how, when he was young, his aunt was given the task of transporting a heavy load and chose to take him with her. A sharp breeze picked up and the water roughened till the boat was in real danger. Drawing on centuries of tradition, and the calm authority for which Scarp rowers were famed, his aunt made the lurching boat a schoolroom and taught Duncan, there and then, the specific skills with which respected rowers of the past had used their oars to combat raging seas.

As in many places, all this reliance on boats created a complex economy of vessels, of many sizes and functions. Beaches would once have been lined with them. The smallest, at eighteen feet, were used by crews of two to four to fish for lobster. The various middle-sized boats were for saithe fishing, often with five islanders aboard, and for travel to other townships bearing goods and livestock. The biggest boats of all had the shortest lives. Gone by 1950, they were used for offshore fishing. Their heyday, like that of the *sgoth Niseach*, ended with the world wars, but the fact that rarely is more than a sentence devoted to them in any writing on Scarp suggests they were never truly seen as part of the community. It was around the smaller boats that a vast array of daily activities was built. Duncan recalls taking them far and wide as a child, rowing miles with a friend, for instance, to find sweet blackberries on Harris because there were no brambles on Scarp.

When it came to boatbuilding, all work was done on the island. It's testimony to the multi-competence of islanders that it was the schoolmaster, Allan Maclean, who is remembered as the greatest of the last generation of boatbuilders. Twenty-three years before the last islanders left Scarp, Maclean penned a piece in Gaelic for the magazine *Alba* in which he discussed his multiple island roles. He praised the intelligence and adaptability of the islanders in making the tools of their trades, and furnishing their croft houses with elegance and neatness despite the condescension of outsiders who considered them backward and stupid. He recalled a subtle island saying that indicated the interconnectedness of all resources, *Ma tha luga agad, tha h-uile rud agad* ('If you have a sandworm, you have everything'). And he noted that this had somehow morphed into a blunt alternative, *Ma tha an t-airgiod agad, tha h-uile rud agad* ('If you have money, you have everything'). He believed that the advent of a monetary economy was making islanders less reliant on the skills they had all inherited, and risking those skills fading from memory.

Maclean explained that Scarp boats were mostly built by people like himself who inherited their trade without formal training. But there were also a few boatbuilders who travelled round the small islands every winter. These skilled individuals would take twenty days to build a boat, and for that time they would live with the person who requested their labour, working with the future crew to bring the boat into being. Maclean recalled seeing them work. He described their eyes, under stern and bushy brows, focused intensely on the lines they sawed. He watched the saw pour dust over their faces and beards, to the sound of its strange music. During the building process, privacy would not be a likely luxury: each action was closely watched, with running commentary about whether this choice or that was mistaken in fitting the new boat to local needs. Every resulting vessel would be different, but with enough in common that a visiting boat would instantly be obvious by its strange proportions. If a Scarp boat had a sweet running line from keel to gunwale, it would be a craft of which the 'brave, skilful, good-humoured' seafarers that Maclean knew and loved would be proud.

This article, published in 1948, described a living world. It reads now almost as an epitaph. It is far more weighted with emotion than maybe even Maclean intended. He spoke of the Gaelic culture of Scarp in terms that didn't permit despair: 'Though the wind is so much against us just now, who knows but that it may change again before the boat sinks altogether?'

Interlude

Of Clinker, Carvel, Birchbark, and Sealskin

I CHOSE TO introduce the structures of small wooden boats at this point in the book, rather than in its introduction, to emphasise the fact that technical knowledge of boats is not required for reading it. That said, there are a small number of distinctions between varieties of boat that are worth knowing as more of them begin to drift across these pages.

The boats in this book are built in four different ways. Some wooden boats, like those of Connemara and eastern Newfoundland, are made with an internal frame first. Then a shell is built from planks of wood that are placed side by side, without overlap, and nailed to the frame. Having no plank-over-plank overlaps gives these boats a smooth surface for the sea to move across. In these craft, the strain is on the frame rather than on the planks, so this allows the building of large boats. The term used for this approach is 'carvel' construction. 'Caulking' is extremely important to these vessels: this means using a material like cotton, reindeer hair, moss, or resin, to fill any gaps between the planks. The carvel method can be seen in the photos of the Galway hooker and the Winterton rodney.

The alternative approach to building a boat from planks is known as 'clinker' construction in Europe, or 'lapstrake' in the Americas. In this method, overlapping planks are put together first. Their overlap allows them to be nailed, lashed, or stitched to each other before a frame is built inside. This provides a strong, rugged hull without need for a heavy frame and is, in many people's eyes, the epitome of the beautiful wooden rowing boat. Clinker boats are found everywhere Norse influence was strongest, including Lewis, and can be seen in the photos of the Faroe boats and the Sámi boat.

The two other varieties of boat in these pages are made from tree bark or animal skin. Such vessels include birchbark or elmbark canoes as well as sealskin kayaks and cowhide currachs. All these form their hulls around a frame that's usually wooden, though they've sometimes involved antler and whalebone too. Such boats express their environmental origins in multitudes of ways: they're sewn together with materials ranging from pine root to reindeer sinew and sealed with substances from spruce resin to animal hair mixed with fat. These bark and skin boats have several advantages over planked craft. They're extremely light to carry between waterways, which means they suit transient ways of life. This lightness gives them agility: centuries of western travellers' jaws have dropped in envy when they first saw indigenous peoples negotiate seas or rivers in them. Some can be constructed in a single afternoon, from resources readily available, whereas building a good planked boat might take days or weeks. As well as making bark and skin boats ideal for mixed journeys by land and sea, these qualities mean such boats can be adapted to suit exact needs.

The most agile and sophisticated single-person vessels in history, Greenland qajaqs, were made in this bespoke manner. They were formed round frames cut from driftwood that floated from the forests of the Americas. While some in the community built wooden frames, others crafted sealskin shells into shapes inspired by seals themselves. With skilled builders, three harp-seal skins would stretch across the vessel. Whalebone would be used to protect the stern and stem, and tacks of reindeer antler would hold it all together. These animals were each hunted in different seasons, in different landscapes, and so a year's work by a whole community would be embodied in every qajaq. Each boat was shaped to its user, like a perfectly tailored suit. The length of the boat was defined by the length of its paddler's arms, the thickness of the paddle's shaft determined by the circle made when they touched their thumb to index finger.

The disadvantages of these boats include their durability. They need constant care, with skin – even more than bark – demanding regular replacement. There are also limits to the oceanic scope of skin boats. The skin of a traditional kayak becomes waterlogged after long spells at sea and loses buoyancy. But we know surprisingly little about the full range of treatments used on such boats and can't exclude the possibility that some might have ameliorated these limitations.

There is, for instance, archaeological evidence that Greenlandic kayakers reached Iceland. Most scholars today are highly sceptical of the frequent seventeenth- and eighteenth-century reports of kayakers arriving on the shores of Scotland and being labelled 'Finnmen' by locals. They consider these accounts to be rumours inspired by new commercial contact with Greenland. My view is that we have no reason to dismiss any possibilities as to what these reports recount. Because of the opening up of Russian archives in the 1990s, we now know of many more varieties of skin boat on Eurasian coasts than had been imagined three decades ago: circumpolar traditions were far more interconnected than previously imagined. And if Greenlanders did reach Iceland, then a route to mainland Europe via the Faroes is far from impossible. Right up to 1903, the North Atlantic Drift reminded Scots of these interconnections by pushing icebergs from Greenland to Cape Wrath and Orkney. Today, the drift still carries an occasional walrus. There's also a long history of scholars in western universities being proved wrong in their underestimation of past seacraft, whether Irish currachs or First Nations canoes. So I've come to favour erring on the side of an open mind.

Every hour spent using such boats reinforces that feeling. In the months that followed leaving Lewis, I took several well-made traditional boats on challenging seas, but the limitations I discovered were always my own. I'm used to sitting in a modern plastic or carbon-fibre boat and lamenting its clumsy lines and poor handling ('It's like getting in a bathtub,' one Massachusetts wooden-boater said on her first experience of carbon fibre). But I've never felt that way in a traditional boat. I've always been aware that their potential far exceeds the skill I have to make them sing on the water. They come alive for me in momentary surges. Only when I chance to get things right do I feel flashes of their power to cut a running sea. It's like I'm speaking in my second language and longing to be a native speaker with the fluency to communicate directly with the vessel I'm propelling.

This brings us back to the idea of a boat as a living thing. All four of the boat types described above are differentiated from modern boats by the way they move, not just in relation to their surroundings but plank to plank and shell to frame. Every part moves independently as well as in unison, with enough flex for the boat's shape to shift and breathe in crests or troughs of swell, but not so much flex that the power of the oars is dissipated. This combination of flex and tension is what makes seafarers refer to little boats with terms such as 'dancing' or 'lithesome'.

There's a deep form of connection to the natural world in the way the boat is animated not by some mystic divine spark but by the sea itself. This is often talked about as an alliance in which sea and boat celebrate each other's company. As one Maine seafarer put it, a freshly launched boat immediately bonds with the sea. The sea water rushes eagerly into its body to meet it, seeps into the cedar planks of its hull, and soaks into its great oaken keel, which will remain forever wet and with its weight serve to anchor the craft in heavy seas . . . salt water, like blood, moving freely throughout its body.

It's not at all unusual to hear this harmony of boat and sea compared to music, song, and dance. The shifting gaps between the planks of a carvel-built vessel determine whether its movements feel clumsy and stilted, or flowing and lyrical. These spaces aren't empty and anaerobic but as expressive as the breaths between lines of a song. It's these gaps, when wave meets boat, that shrink and expand, allowing the craft to bend and blend with the ocean. It's when the seafarer judges rhythms to perfection – so that rower, wood, and water resonate together – that the boat can truly be said to sing and the whole world feels integrated and alive. I know of no other experi-ence so connecting to the vast, living world in which we tiny humans make our way. This is echoed in the countless island songs that build whole choruses from shifting inflections on a single, simple line about the pleasures of a boat at sea, or end every verse with the same recurring phrase, such as, in the Faroes, 'the oars play at the thole pin'.

There are other ways in which these boats can be categorised. For instance, all the canoes and kayaks in this book are double-ended. Some of the wooden vessels are double-ended too, making them look like little Viking longships in miniature. Two pointed ends mean the boat can cut the sea in either direction. Many boat styles, however, exchange the pointed stern for a 'transom'. This is a flat rear end that can be almost as wide as the boat itself, cutting the vessel short near what would otherwise have been its halfway point. It can rise vertically from the water, but today is often raked (overhanging the sea, creating a space where a rudder or propeller can sit). Transoms strengthen the boat's stern, which is necessary if a motor is to be fitted. They have significant effects on the boat's performance, especially when rough seas bear down behind. Where the stern of a double-ended boat cuts waves, a large transom presents a flat surface that can be pushed rapidly forward by oncoming waves but with drastic reduction in control. The 'tombstone transoms' of New England dories are a celebrated compromise. These are small and narrow, named after their shape, and have none of the clumsiness of larger sterns. A following sea, short of a storm, will push the boat safely on. Since most seafarers in this book needed boats that gave them access to rough water, few boats here have transoms larger than a tombstone.

There are also distinctions between the ways boats are rowed. Some are suited to 'sculling', in which each rower holds two oars. Others are made for 'sweeping', in which every rower holds a single oar with both hands. This is less a regional distinction and more a feature of scale. For instance, in the smallest types of Faroese boat (twelve to eighteen feet) the rowers scull, while in larger sizes (twenty to thirty-two feet) the rowers sweep. Some boats also have an odd number of rowers, one of whom wields a single 'steering oar' like a long, handheld rudder. As well as differentiation by length, boats of many kinds are differentiated by the number of 'thwarts' (planks that run across the boat and are used as benches by rowers) or 'rooms' (the spaces between the thwarts). The smallest Faroese boats, for instance, have two or three thwarts (therefore one or two rooms), while the larger have four to six thwarts (three to five rooms).

Everything in a boat generally has its own specific name. Each thwart, each room, and each plank will have its own title, and these often vary by village rather than by region or nation. One of the striking qualities of these names is the frequency with which they're poetic rather than literal or functional, and they often evoke parts of human bodies (from feet to beards) or animals (from geese and ducks to seals and horses). This makes the language of boats immeasurably rich, especially because all observations about length, width, curvature, or weight carry implications of both aesthetic appeal and seaworthiness. A beamy boat for instance, will, in the absence of meliorating factors, suggest high carrying capacity but limits to velocity and turning speed. It will usually be a homely kind of boat rather than a racer or a work of art. Boats, like those of Connemara, that somehow pair breadth with great speed and elegance, are therefore legends afloat. Boatbuilders refer to a strong curve along the bottom of a boat, from front to back, as a lot of 'rocker'. This adds to its visual appeal, at the same time as making it easy to turn but trickier to row or paddle straight.

Most rowing boats today have 'rowlocks' (also called 'oarlocks'), which are metal horseshoe-shaped attachments into which oars are fitted above the strips of wood that top the boat's sides (called 'gunwales', pronounced 'gunnels'). But most craft in the past had 'thole pins' instead (either one or two small wooden shafts against which an oar is braced). Sometimes the shaft of an oar (called the 'loom') would have a widened section, with a hole through which a single thole pin fitted. On other boats, oars with round looms would be tied to a single pin with a cord made from sheepskin or whale fin. In some, the loom would be squared off to brace neatly and naturally between two thole pins at the perfect angle for the oar's 'face' (its blade) to propel the boat forward. In still others, skilled rowers would use a rounded loom between two thole pins. This is a feature of boats such as the Cornish pilot gig (which appears in this book as part of the rowing culture of Maine) and is a cause for nervousness among rowers who aren't used to it: it demands more awareness of the oar's angle and position than any other option.

But the construction of boats is something imaginative and artistic as much as technical. On rural North Atlantic coasts, it was often deeply improvisatory. Sometimes a boat began with a quest for perfect trees or items of driftwood, in order to form preconceived shapes of

OF CLINKER, CARVEL, BIRCHBARK, AND SEALSKIN

keel and planks. Other times, a beautiful piece of wood suggested the size and shape of a new boat. Either way, to see the boat's form in a tree trunk is an imaginative act that's followed by many more. The boatbuilder scrupulously assesses the grain of the wood, because the power of wooden boats comes from the immense strength of wood along the grain, while their potential limitations come from cross-grain weakness. The builder then bends planks, often by steaming them, into a shape influenced by the forms with which fish move through water smoothly. This makes boat forms as beautifully organic as anything in nature. Many boatbuilders, when asked how they learned, talk of watching older boatbuilders, with phrases such as 'mostly he wanted me to *figure out* how to do it'. They emphasise that their mentors often didn't have words to explain the intuitive intricacies of their craft.

The poet Robert N. Rose called boats 'the nearest things to dreams that hands have ever made'. His vision relates to the dream of perfect freedom that travel over water entails. Yet perhaps it also conjures these roles of imagination and intangible insight in every stage of boatbuilding. The boat's past in the forest and future on the water are constantly present in its builder's feel for how tree and sea will respond to one another, so that boats are, indeed, dreams given form.

These are all further reasons why boatish talk twists, like the torque of chestnut wood, back to story, song, and dream. This imaginative tendency defines the currents of meaning in which each boat is caught. It is why learning even a little about small boats can reveal so much about the world, and why looking carefully at a boat is a journey deep into a localised culture and its seafarers' dreams.

3

Sápmi

A Pine Tree at Sea

I

Forgetting the Sea Sámi

For six days, I was bombarded night and day by wind and water. Despite the grandeur of the islands I paddled beneath, the noise felt frantic and wearing. Then, one morning, I awoke to silence. I wasn't far from the spot that (despite the fact it's an island) is often called 'the northernmost rock in mainland Europe'. It occupies a liminal space between Atlantic and Arctic oceans and, with the world surreally stilled, my whole existence felt liminal too. After launching from the edge of a wide fjord mouth, I entered sheltered waters scattered with two hundred islets.

The previous week's paddling had taken me from 'the northernmost city in the world', Hammerfest, around the great headland of Nordkapp. I'd visited rugged islands such as Magerøya, and Rolvsøya in a quest to learn seas I'd never visited before. Rainbows and sunbursts had rendered bleak seascapes ravishingly beautiful. This was one of the biggest kayak journeys of my life and one of the most windswept. Swell, breakers, rain, and fog had defined my world, and it was hard to remember what it felt like to be warm, dry, or out of reach of waves.

Now, though, I was entering Porsanger Fjord: the heart of Coastal Sámi seafaring. When the winds dropped, the clouds cleared, so the water was glassy and blue. Within minutes, I was surrounded by fins. The gentle breathing of the largest pod of porpoises I've ever seen filled the silence as they passed back and forth. Some had tiny calves, barely bigger than salmon, who mirrored their parent's every move. Each time they seemed to have gone, they returned: haunting, persistently, a small zone beside the headland. I waited among them for half an hour, admiring the sleek black and greys of their smooth short backs. Then I set off along the 120 kilometres of this grand but gentle fjord, hoping to travel these waters with at least a hint of the quiet comfort of the porpoise.

The homeland of the Sámi, Europe's only people officially accorded indigenous status, is known in the Northern Sámi language as Sápmi. It stretches across Sweden, Norway, Finland, the Russian Kola Peninsula, and all their associated seas. But it's breached, today, by national borders, on both land and water, which drastically limit the free practice of Sámi life.

It's a place that ought to be rich with opportunity for good living: for all the time I was here, nature seemed bigger than I'd ever known it before. Millions of berries and mushrooms swathed island hills and valleys. Herds, shoals, flocks, and pods seemed always to contain multiples of the numbers I'd previously imagined possible. Otters ran from the water up into the thick foliage of the shores, while reindeer trotted deep into rivers and ocean. The profoundly living landscape, which has given Sámi world views their intense conviction in the vibrance and power not just of animals and plants, but of stone and sea too, was evident all around. Every section of this seascape is run through with ideas that are the roots and branches of Sámi life. Every porpoise, and every cliff face, is a person and more than a person.

As with many indigenous peoples, recent decades have seen a revival of Sámi knowledge and culture. Since the 1980s, in activism and art that have reached global audiences, the construction of 'the new Sámi society' has been channelling old world views into new forms, and Sámi film, music, literature, textiles and other crafts are all ascendant. They're rich with ways of understanding the human entanglement in wider worlds which can transform anyone's experience of paddling a coastline or walking a forest path.

More than ever before, however, the vision of Sámi life that's broadcast around the world is built on reindeer, mountains, and an inshore, nomadic way of life. In Sápmi itself, the visitor will see reindeer lodges, craftworks made from reindeer antler, and dozens of domesticated reindeer that wander through the villages: the bond between the Sámi and the herds will be inescapable. Academic articles written about the Sámi reinforce this association, saying, for instance, that since only 2,500 of the 65,000 Sámi in Norway are actively engaged in reindeer herding, most Sámi have similar jobs to the rest of the population. From such experiences and statements, it would be impossible to guess that the Sámi are one of the great maritime peoples of the world, connected as intimately to the porpoises of the fjord as to the reindeer of the mountains.

This sidelining of Sámi seafaring is a remarkably recent turn of events. For millennia, the diverse practices that made up Sámi life were part of all Sámi lives. Communities moved and lived at sea, on the shoreline, on tundra and mountain, by river and lake, and throughout the great pine forests and birch woods of the north. Ancient petroglyphs of Sámi sea boats are found in caves high in the mountains. The earliest commentators note that sleds, pulled by reindeer across mountain snow, were developed from these boats, dragged between watercourses until adapted to sail the land.

Only in the seventeenth century were distinctive niches labelled and consolidated. The Mountain Sámi were the most nomadic of three newly named groups. They were intimately connected to the vast herds of reindeer who wandered the tundra. Their lives, because they are the most different from the sedentary lifestyles of the city, became the image round which Sámi resilience rallied, seen as the simplest form of Sámi life to protect from pressures towards national assimilation. The Forest Sámi also lived close to reindeer, trapped ptarmigan, and caught salmon in the rivers. But they built sturdy homes of turf and wood rather than carrying light-framed dwellings long distances.

The third group were the Sea or Coastal Sámi, who took their ocean-going boats from fjord to offshore island, to practise the same mixed subsistence of herding, foraging, fishing, sealing, and fowling, just with a skew towards the sea, and greater involvement in long-range exchange of goods. Eighteenth- and nineteenth-century visitors describe Sea Sámi changing their residences twice a year. Their homes were often built from thick beams of silvery alder wood, and they left them standing rather than carrying everything from place to place. These three categories – of mountain, forest, and sea – always remained, however, just differences of emphasis. Boats, and not just reindeer, played parts in the lives of all Sámi.

The archaeology of this region is full not just of boats etched into stone but of centuries-old rowlocks and planks: the shift from paddling to rowing, and to larger boats than canoes, was made here early. Where Norse shipwrights used iron to join pine planks, creating the potential for boats on ever greater scales, Sámi sewed planks with root or sinew, favouring the lightness and versatility this allowed. When a vessel was needed but none could be found, these stitched boats could easily be carried between watercourses or dragged by reindeer over snow.

Some sources make the remarkable claim that Sámi communities could build such a boat from scratch in only a few hours. Just as significantly, they required no materials that were hard to find. Built with pine planks, stitched with pine root, sealed with pine tar, and caulked with moss, these boats are perfect expressions of the forests they came from. Through them, the forest permeated culture. Seams that echoed those of the boat came to play vital roles in Sámi ritual. For instance, at the time the coffin of a deceased person was sewn together, the seams of the clothes they'd owned were unpicked to prevent the departed's continued entanglement with the living. To sew a boat, therefore, was an act rich with many meanings.

By the Viking era, Sámi boats were famed for speed and lightness, revered by Norse sea lords. The thirteenth-century collection of sagas of Norwegian kings, Snorri Sturluson's *Heimskringla*, recounts this esteem:

> It is said that Sigurd made the Sámi construct two boats for him during the winter up in the fjord; and they were fastened together with deer sinews, without nails, and with twigs of willow instead of knees, and each boat could carry twelve men. Sigurd was with the Sámi while they were making the boats; and the Sámi had good ale, with which they entertained Sigurd.

The Norwegian king then composed and sang verses extolling his experience:

> In the Sámi tent
> Brave days we spent.
> Under the grey birch tree;
> In bed or on bank
> We knew no rank,
> And a merry crew were we.
>
> Good ale went round
> As we sat on the ground,

SÁPMI

> Under the grey birch tree;
> And up with the smoke
> Flew laugh and joke,
> And a merry crew were we.

Sigurd praised the boats for their lightness and dancing speed, so swift that no ship could overtake them:

> Our skin-sewed Sámi-boats lightly swim,
> Over the sea like wind they skim.
> Our ships are built without a nail;
> Few ships like ours can row or sail.

Snorri wrote at a time when the Norse frequently acquired their boats this way. When Norse settlers first travelled this far north, they made their homes on the bare peninsulas and shorelines, because the Sámi already occupied the pine-clad inner fjords and birchwood hillsides. A Norse seafarer, Ohthere, told King Alfred at the end of the ninth century that the wealth of northern lords was derived from tribute taken from the Sámi. Among the things the Norse gained were ships' cables made from the skin of whales and seals, which equipped Viking longships on their ocean journeys. But for the Sámi this was an early and ominous experience of the demands neighbours and colonisers would make of them.

Many later accounts also emphasise Sámi boat-craft. After the Thirty Years War, the professor of political science at Uppsala University, Johannes Scheffer, was despatched north to investigate Sámi life. In the resulting book of 1673, he wrote of boatbuilding as second only to hunting among Sámi handicrafts. He described the sewing of the planks, and the use of moss to make boats warm and comfortable. He recorded religious ceremonies in which boats played central roles, and speculated that this was because the people who brought Christianity to the north had arrived by boat. Sámi memory, however, holds that boats are significant because the Sámi people themselves found their homeland thousands of years earlier, when they arrived in skin boats, much like Inuit umiaq and qajaqs, with reindeer swimming alongside to pull their goods on floats.

Scheffer was followed by a flood of scholars. In 1732, the great categoriser of every form of life, Carl Linnaeus, drew two Sámi boats, in ways that emphasised their sewn construction and their virtue of lightness. Nine years later, another Swedish traveller, Arvid Ehrenmalm, gave one of the fullest descriptions of Sámi boats, describing a journey downriver to the sea. While he was further south, his journey was road-bound and terrestrial, but in Sámi country this hesitant water-traveller was forced into boats. Other inhabitants of these regions, he noted, were not the equal of the Sámi in the laborious and difficult arts of negotiating rushing waters by oar and paddle. He described the thin planks cut by hatchet, and the reindeer sinew fastenings. He described the boats as 'brittle' – 'a man might break them with his hand' – and so small that each could take only a single passenger in addition to the rower.

> But if the boat can only carry two men, one man is sufficient to carry the boat. When a Sámi meets with a water-fall, which he cannot pass by means of his oars, as he does not even possess any idea of sails, he puts the bowl of his little boat on his head, passes the oars into two wickers strongly fastened to the sides of the boat, takes his sack of provisions on his back, and places the boat above the bowl; then, by means of the hatchet, which he fixes to the stern, he preserves his boat in equilibrium, and guides it to the right and left through the trees. When he has passed on land above the level of the fall, he replaces his boat in the water and continues to row.
>
> However frightful to the eye be the rapidity of one of these

little boats descending a fall between the rocks, the great calmness of the Sámi amidst these perils induced us to attempt these passages with them, and when we had overcome several, we no longer wished to land, as we did before we had been inured to these dangerous ways.

The first book written by a Sámi author about Sámi ways came from a region of Sweden that's unusually far inland for Sámi life. It showed that by the start of the twentieth century something was changing in Sámi relations with their boats. Johan Turi's *Account of the Sámi* (1910) has been more powerful than any other text in shaping subsequent perceptions of Sámi life. It's full of beautiful passages that attest to the bond between Sámi and Sápmi, such as the paragraph that sets out the purpose of the book:

> I am a Sámi who has done all sorts of Sámi work and I know all about Sámi conditions. I have come to understand that the Swedish government wants to help us as much as it can, but they don't get things right regarding our lives and conditions, because no Sámi can explain to them exactly how things are. And this is the reason: when a Sámi becomes closed up in a room, then he does not understand much of anything, because he cannot put his nose to the wind. His thoughts don't flow because there are walls and his mind is closed in. And it is also not good at all for him to live in dense forest when the air is warm. But when a Sámi is on the high mountains, then he has quite a clear mind. And if there were a meeting place on some high mountain, then a Sámi could make his own affairs quite plain.

Turi's was emphatically a mountain world. Boats appear only once in the text, and they are the boats of outsiders who have arrived to steal from Sámi.

The twentieth century obscured and erased still more of Sámi seafaring history. In 1945, the boatbuilding tradition came close to complete destruction when retreating Nazi forces razed all they left behind. As well as buildings, they burned and broke every local boat they found. Unlike in Ireland and Scotland, where vessels I used had been on the water for a hundred years, all those I saw or used in northern Norway were part of the very recent revival of Sámi identity. The boatbuilders I met had begun this revival by constructing boats with modern tools, before introducing new layers of connection to the past with every boat they made. Each subsequent vessel is more fully an expression of coast and forest, and more distinctively Sámi. Yet this new tradition is still small and precarious, demanding care and advocacy.

The Nazi conflagration was just a flashpoint in a far longer history of marginalisation and silencing. Throughout the late nineteenth and twentieth centuries, the ideal of 'Norwegianisation' sought to bring all Norwegian Sámi into the modern state by the twin methods of crushing cultural identities and creating reliance on state structures. In discouraging use of the nine Sámi languages, Norway wasn't seeking simply to reduce linguistic complexity, but to diminish world views that provided alternatives to an integrated Norwegian way of life. The advent of modern state bureaucracies, and their increasing focus on the integrity of national borders, ended the ease with which small boats could cross between Russia, Finland, Norway, and Sweden, and made living Sámi life on Sámi terms impossible. New laws in the 1930s had required Norwegians to register single occupations, with severe implications: anyone, for instance, not registered as a fisherman could catch only tiny quantities of fish. The mixed occupations and sustainable practices of Coastal Sámi life were effectively criminalised and the seas were sacrificed to factory ships.

Where quality of life had been high, living standards fell dramatically. This decline was well underway by 1930, thanks in part to national schemes for economic development that improved life for

Norwegians but shut out Sámi. Loans to provide modern fishing boats, for instance, relied on credit institutions, formal deeds of land ownership, and facility with Norwegian-language bureaucracy that were all foreign to Sámi communities. The presence of modern boats transformed the nature of fishing for everyone: larger catches pushed fish offshore and dramatically increased the risk for small boats. The turbulence and traumas of the 1910s – from the First World War to the Russian Revolution and Finnish Civil War – had ended the exchange of goods with Russia, on which Sámi life had depended, forcing many into the same unsustainable way of life as urban Europeans: a monetary economy, commercial markets, and a rapidly globalising food system. Many Sámi lost their boats, fishing gear, and other elements crucial to survival, when the state began demanding tax in currency rather than as eiderdown or fish.

At the same time, the image of Sámi life swung dramatically away from the sea. By the mid-nineteenth century, Norwegian historians often drew stark binaries between sedentary Norwegians and 'true' nomadic Sámi. They built their image of modern northern Norway on the idea that the region had been populated before Norwegians arrived, but not 'settled', and that true history started with settlement and textual documentation. They depicted Sámi as wandering, 'timeless', mountain people, untouched by progress, in contrast to the thrusting modernity of Norwegians.

Two major international exhibitions help to illustrate these shifts away from boats. These were events much like the famous world fairs of Chicago or Paris, and they were held in Tromsø in 1870 and 1894. They had twin purposes: to display the diversity of Norwegian life, and, in the organisers' words, 'to tie this heterogeneity closer and closer together'. At this time, debates were beginning to shift from acceptance of cultural and linguistic difference towards demands for integration and assimilation. The 1870 exhibition presented these debates as central to the future of the nation. It left space for discussion, and organisers provided material in the northern Sámi language. The Sea Sámi had a prominent role in the displays but were given a specific narrative function. In supposedly embodying 'Civilisation's conquest of nomadic life', no longer 'true Sámi' but partly 'civilised', they were used to exemplify the idea that Sámi could be 'pupils in the schoolroom of the Norwegians'.

When the second exhibition was held in 1894, what small subtleties had been possible in 1870 were gone. There was no material in Sámi languages. There were no Sea Sámi to be seen at all. An ethnographic display depicted reindeer herding, but the displays for fishing presented the sea as an entirely Norwegian space. To be Sámi had become a matter of following herds through mountains, season by season, and the dynamic and complex Sámi past had been sacrificed for something simpler. Sámi were no longer Norwegian, nor to be celebrated for combining two value systems, but were an unruly 'other' within the nation's borders. There was no longer any space for envisioning Sámi as historic agents of sophisticated coastal trade with Russia, or as expert mariners who'd schooled the Vikings.

Today, a handful of people aim to restore Sea Sámi heritage. In works such as the *Coastal Sámi Atlas*, Camilla Brattland has begun remapping the inshore world of Sámi travellers and fishers. Other scholars, such as Konsta Kaikkonen, have published small pamphlets of Sea Sámi vocabulary, rich with species-specific words that convey the actions and attitudes of porpoises and seals. At Mearrasiida – the Coastal Sámi Sea Competence Centre – a small but committed group works together to learn and teach Sámi heritage. Hans O. Hansen, whose workshop is at the centre, is the only builder of Sámi sea boats in the whole of northern Norway. The Sámi parliament has devoted funds for him to take on an apprentice, but the quest for the right young person is still underway.

A few small festivals also aim to revive the memory of Sámi ties to their boats. In keeping with Sámi culture, these don't just recollect but re-enact, building practical bonds with living pasts. One such festivity happens in August, around the pilgrimage day of St Tryphon of Pechenga. It commemorates the forced removal of the Skolt Sámi from lands ceded to the Soviet Union in 1945. Passing from the Russian border through parts of Finland and Norway, pilgrims mark historic moments of loss and dislocation. In the 2010s, a root-sewn boat was added to this revitalisation of Sámi memory. Built collaboratively, it aimed to restore knowledge of local ecologies. Older women, skilled in the use of roots, taught young people how to work these tricky fibres, and stories were passed down of watching the boatbuilders of the past. After many months of communal building, the boat was launched, to much publicity, on St Tryphon's pilgrimage day in 2015. It was rowed from the border to the Sámi open-air museum. It is housed on the water there as a means by which Sámi people can physically renew their ties to waterways. There's something fitting that a boat built out of literal roots should be used to comprehend belonging as well as banishment. It was time for me to abandon my kayak and root myself in water.

II

The Sámi Boat

Mearrasiida is a large, low building crouched above a small bay on the western shore of Porsanger Fjord a hundred kilometres from the fjord mouth and the open ocean. Although part of Norway, this region has a population that's 48 per cent Sámi, 36 per cent Finnish, and only 16 per cent Norwegian, and so Sámi cultural centres are central to social life. I wandered into Mearrasiida one sunny morning and was greeted with freshly made waffles, brown cheese, and lingonberry jam. This is a resource and heritage space with its own boat workshop. It holds oral histories and documents, as well as traditional tools for such practices as cutting wood and stretching hides. It publishes books recording Coastal Sámi terminology and craft techniques, and organises collaborations with similar organisations around the Arctic. In the boatshed, for instance, there are sealskins stretched across wooden frames put together by visitors from Greenland. I was surprised when I arrived there to find everyone – except the boatbuilder – far younger than me and with a bright-eyed enthusiasm for learning historic crafts.

We talked about the past uses of specific islands in the fjord and about the conventions for the rights to pick cloudberries on specific hillsides. They told me about resistance to the building of trails that would lead to Sámi sacred stones and threaten to transform them from places of active belief into tourist sites. Ove, who runs the centre, and Hans, its resident boatbuilder, took me to visit the workshop in Mearrasiida's basement, where three boats stood in various degrees of completion. The space was dark and enclosed, and the smell among the cut planks, saws, and axes was heavy and resinous. It was more pine-fragrant than the forest itself.

The group at Mearrasiida began boatbuilding in 2017 and, at the time I visited, had constructed seven small Sámi boats, each a little closer to tradition than the one before: where those so far have been nailed plank-to-plank, the next will be fully sewn with roots. These boats are known in Norwegian as *spisse*, which means simply 'sharp' or 'pointed'. Hans showed me how all the angles of a boat are calculated and checked with a simple wooden 'spirit level' from which a lead ball dangles on a thread. The spirit level is a semi-circle, about thirty centimetres across, with a flattened edge that protrudes from its curved side. The curve is marked with pencil lines, with a letter to indicate a specific plank written next to each. When the flattened protrusion is flush against a particular plank, the ball should fall exactly at the corresponding pencil line. That so simple a tool is all that's required to form so beautiful a boat is hard to comprehend. I loved that when Hans used it he never seemed to follow its guidance exactly but made small adjustments built on long experience. He measured the gap between seams simply by the distance between extended thumb and forefinger. The same measure, which he called a *goartil*, was used to choose the planks that would be used as thwarts to sit on. Hans has a taste for boats whose upper planks remain wide till the last possible moment, so that their prows are thrown forward in a distinctive and graceful shape. Like all *spisse*, his boats are elegantly double-ended, built to a 'rule of thirds' in which the width is one third the length and the height one third the width: at four and a half metres long, a boat is therefore only half a metre tall. Such a shallow draught allows access almost everywhere. As the local saying goes, it needs 'nothing more than a wet lawn' to row across.

It was one of these boats that I'd been given the use of for my week rowing the fjord. It seems Ove and Hans are extremely free and easy about who can use their boats, but it still felt like an extraordinary privilege to be permitted to row these waters in such a vessel. Taking it through the labyrinths of small islands was a recipe for falling in love with Porsanger Fjord. I rowed all the way to the mouth of the fjord to feel the lithesome boat dance on a little swell. Here huge flocks of mergansers passed close by. Being caught in such a flock sounded like being in a sudden gale in woodland. In the past, islanders used these flocks for fishing: when mergansers landed in a bay, fish scattered to the seabed, taking shelter in any traps that had been placed there. Predicting where flocks would land was thus a well-honed island skill.

The only other boats I saw were seeking halibut, and my own little craft was suited to doing so. But building cooking fires on these small islands would have felt like sacrilege. In the past, the region's halibut and cod were salted and exchanged for flour, grain, and leather. Salt fish from northern Sápmi fuelled the Renaissance in Venice and the construction of St Petersburg: the ocean interconnected different worlds and built all our histories. Those were times when many whales swam in the waters I was rowing, before industrial whalers in the 1930s arrived from far away and purged the fjord.

I spent my nights outdoors in habitats ranging from tiny bare islands to thick pine forests that were home to wolverines and lynxes. The overstorey was busy with red squirrels and northern hawk owls. Three great salmon rivers run from the hills, passing through the northernmost pine forest in the world. Trees used for making boats were floated down these rivers to the sea. No larch, oak, or iron were required, because this northern pine is strong and supple enough to be keel, thwart, and strake. And the trees were used for far more than building. Pinebark was a valued foodstuff, used to enrich soups and ground for flour. Both pine and the birch that scatters slopes above the pines gave sap which was put to many uses. Later, I tried the birch-sap schnapps that continues this tradition.

Reindeer roam the shores in summer and move up through the forests to the moss-covered hills for winter. After centuries of living with the Sámi, many are semi-domesticated, and one afternoon in the fjord-edge forests I had the pleasure of one's company for miles of walking: since I set out from its home, it walked by my side all the way to the boathouses I was seeking, and led me all the way back (though it stopped for even more snacks than I did). At Mearrasiida, I'd learned of traditions of sharing resources with the reindeer. There are, for instance, many huge field mushrooms scattered across these hillsides, but Sámi have seen these as reindeer food, off-limits to human foragers. The sight of huge white-fronted reindeer, with antlers like trees, trotting straight down the middle of one of the great salmon rivers, water splashing high around them, is a moment I'll never forget.

It's the islands, however, that are the richest of all Porsanger's resources. This is because summer arrived there first and stayed there longest. Each island is its own warm, quiet ecosystem. Their intertidal zones and stony shores provide seaweed to enrich the earth and eggs to cook. But far more than this, they provide a substance worth more per gram than gold. As I rowed, I could locate the sites of such largesse by their names. *Fálástak* means 'down', and these feathers' importance was such that not just places around the fjord but a season of the Sámi year, Fálástakladdak, were named for it. In the early seventeenth century, ships from hundreds of miles away congregateded here for the warming down till, in 1631, the Norwegian king passed a law that no one else could buy the Sámi's eiderdown until the court had enough to stuff the soft beds of all the royals.

The islands' land was rich. Sheep and pigs were kept on some islands. Others were used for hay. The greatest number, though, were devoted to a practice central to Sámi life – the gathering of berries such as lingonberry, blueberry, crowberry, and the prized cloudberry ('the gold of the tundra'). Such foraging is highly esteemed in Sámi life, talked of as the realisation and renewal of bonds between people and place. Many urban Sámi who speak Norwegian in their daily lives return to family homes to take part in communal berry-picking and speak their ancestral tongue. It's common for such small communities to build a fire and fetch river water to make coffee together, as each member pursues a daily round of solitary picking and social breaks. Because of this, cloudberry foraging is intimately tied to the persistence and resilience of Sámi languages and is a practice of unrivalled cultural significance. One of the current research projects at Mearrasiida involves Sámi from different coastal regions joining together in berry-picking and egg-gathering in order to share views on the kinds of knowledge created and sustained by these activities. Taking small boats out to the islands, they start from the principle set out by Turi that Sámi knowledge exists in 'doing' and 'acting' and would be far more difficult to share and comprehend at an indoor symposium than on a breezy hillside. They work with Sámi languages to understand the concepts behind the task-oriented ways of naming places.

Part of the reason for all my travels is a belief that learning how to *be* in such places is among the most important work a human can do. I use the word 'be' because the usual language of English culture is so inadequate to this purpose. First, I wrote 'occupy', but even that is too loaded with ideas of human ownership to indicate the kinds of knowledge and experience I hope to gain. I knew that learning Sámi ideas *in situ* could be a step along the route I wished to travel. When I'd asked people at Mearrasiida what ideas I ought to know, they were unanimous in naming two concepts. *Meahcci*, they said, would teach me how to see the places the boat took me to, while *duodji* would help me to understand the boat itself. *Meahcci* is usually translated either with a word that misleadingly associates it with ideas of 'the wild' (for example, 'wilderness') or with specific cartographic spaces (for example, 'landscape' or 'outfield'). But *meahcci* is one of the action-oriented terms with which Sámi languages are exceptionally rich. Ove had shown me a small book, written by a friend of his, full of such action-focused words relating to other species. It contained specific words, with diagrams, for the actions seals and porpoises perform that combine to be each animal's *luondu* ('inner nature' or 'personality').

Meahcci itself is part of many significant words. A place where cloudberries are picked, for instance, is *luomemeahcci,* understood as a living landscape without fixed boundaries but determined by the activity of weather, plants, animals, and humans; where the berries ripen in summer, for example, is defined in part by the weather in spring, and Sámi learn to anticipate these patterns. Cloudberries grow on the kinds of nutrient-poor marshes that in other regions might be ignored or shown scant respect, and so their presence emphasises the deep significance of every fjord-side space and helps generate the sense that Sámi are caretakers of all of Sápmi. A person who has, since childhood, loved picking cloudberries might say berry-gathering is in their *luondu*, and their actions in the place where they do this are part of what makes it *luomemeahcci*. Other *meahcci* terms include *muorrameahcci* (where firewood is collected) and *guollemeahcci* (where fishing happens).

All mean that there's far less distinction between people and places, because places aren't conceived as static: place names are gained and lost as storms, dry spells, or the wandering of the herds affect the likelihood of success at foraging or fishing. Most importantly of all, though, people don't drive the agenda of *meahcci*. They are called to action by weather, plants, and animals. No activities in forests or at sea are ethically neutral – all are part of dynamic relationships through which the human place in a world of many powers is made. Christianisation didn't change this world view. As one current Coastal Sámi Youtuber puts it, 'I'm still more afraid of an angry cow than I am of the wrath of God.' To think with *meahcci* means to recognise the more than functional significance of land, sea, and species.

The anthropologist Tim Ingold visited Sápmi in the early 1970s and many of his most distinctive ideas were shaped by Sámi culture. He defined his concept of the 'taskscape' as the 'pattern of dwelling activities' which link people seasonally to place. The echoes of *meahcci* are clear. Ingold wrote of Sámi perceiving their history as 'woven into the landscape' so that land and sea are constant reminders of who they are. There 'can be no sense of longing for a lost past, no such feeling as nostalgia', he notes, when the past is manifest in places. Working thirty years later, another scholar of the landscape, Ingela Bergman, described similar things. Though Sámi are perfectly familiar with linear time, she wrote, moments of engagement with specific land- and seascapes generated something entirely different, allowing the past to protrude in the present and making distant events seem close: the past is brought to life when land and sea revive it.

Sámi arts enact these connections. The most famous of all, the *yoik*, is a chant-like song that can be directed towards a landform (such as a mountain or a bend in a river), an animal, person, or object (such as a boat). A *yoik* doesn't belong to its creator but to the person or thing it is gifted to and used to evoke or celebrate. The words of the song are only a small part of each *yoik*'s characterisation: many Sámi refer to *yoiks* as possessing 'more power than language' because they also resemble the river or whale they describe in terms of rhythm, dynamics, and melodic shape.

The purpose of the *yoik* is to fold time and space by making the thing described seem present. So, for instance, a *yoik* inspired by an enormous catch when fishing wouldn't aim to evoke the event itself, but might have rhythm, melody, and words to conjure the running water where the event took place. It doesn't tell the story, but transports its listeners to the site of the community's success. One highly respected yoiker, Ánte Mihkkal Gaup, described the relationship between song and place like this:

When I want to yoik a particular place in nature, such as a remarkable river or a special mountain, I travel to this place in my mind. We come there, we see the place for ourselves, and in a way, we are there.

The idea of *duodji* conjures similar attitudes to the entangled purposes of place and people. That the word could be translated either as 'fine art objects' or as 'basic tools of everyday life' reveals something of its essence. It denotes items lovingly crafted from wood, wool, stone, antler, or any other substance worthy of the act. The making of art isn't a special event that stands outside life and can be encased within the walls of galleries or museums. It is a style of existence and everyday habit. Every piece of *duodji* expresses the Sámi world view and its creator's connection to past, present, and future, as well as to the land and sea from which materials are drawn and in which *duodji* is used. The talent to make *duodji* does not belong to an individual creator but is an expression of family, community, and Sápmi itself. Most of all, *duodji* is as alive as Sápmi: its making is not an imperious act but a negotiation. It is to put something vibrant and harmonious, with its own will, back into the animate landscapes of the north.

I'd never come across the concept of *duodji*, or anything like it, till travelling to Sápmi. But suddenly the way that all boatbuilders talk about their boats made sense. The boat I was rowing was a living companion. The gentle creak of its oars each time I leaned my body back required attentive care. The more I listened well, and learned the boat's moods, the more it would care for me when the waves rose higher.

I spent the first two nights with the boat sleeping on small islands, where I could watch the life of the fjord unfold. As the sun set, eider settled near the shoreline and voles emerged from burrows. Flocks of cranes avoided lone eagles as they chose their roosting spots, and movements at the water's surface were salmon sliding by. Each dawn, as I set out, the golden-orange planks of the boat glowed in the first light of the sun. The thick pine grain, rough to the touch, was still a vivid connection to the forest. The olive-green gunwales, a convention of the *spisse*, echoed the foliage that topped the gold and silver islands. With no iron oarlocks, but simple wooden thole pins against which to brace the sturdy oars, each stroke felt like a link to the fjord's deep heritage. And each such movement pushed the boat into a long swift glide that made travel feel freeing and graceful. Sometimes, in the mornings, low white cloud clung to isolated areas of fjord or island, but no squally showers agitated land or sea.

I took note of the human things beside the shore. There was barely any iron on display, as there'd be elsewhere, but wooden winches for hauling little boats, large wooden frames for drying cod, and wooden boats upturned at the water's edge or dragged onto pebble beaches: each an item of *duodji*. There are images from as early as

1767 of Sámi in boats just like mine fishing for halibut and pollock at these spots. Those were times when owning a boat like this was to be secure and, in the terms of the region, wealthy.

My favourite night of all was spent on Kuommarsaari, an island the shape of a twisting eel in the middle of the fjord. As dusk arrived, easterly skies were a clear deep blue but for a few high bands of grey cloud. I set up to sleep at the island's highest point. To the west, the fjord's hills and ridges were black silhouettes, some obscured by low white sea-fog that billowed at the water's surface. The last of the sun cut through the fog's stray edges, reaching the water in brighter, colder tones than I'd ever seen at sunset. This made the barely ruffled sea look silver and heavy, like glistening mercury. The thin curve of the island, steep-sided and craggy, was also desaturated to silver. But to the north, the island was even narrower: just a sliver in the sea, with a beautiful shingle beach where my boat lay glowing on the pebbles.

The temperature was already dipping below freezing, and I was considering wandering around for a little warmth, when I saw a small dark shape fussing around the boat. I'd witnessed evidence of the curiosity of otters before, waking up on Hebridean beaches to find their footprints in the sand around my head. But I was overjoyed to see one weave across a Sámi shore, because of fleeting mentions of otters I'd seen in Sámi sources. Historians used to write of Sámi otter folklore as the stuff of myth, but seeing this one scour the beach, at its own leisure and seemingly less afraid of the boat than a creature like a horse would be, made me seek out the sources that soon confirmed that historians' scepticism had been misplaced.

I read of one Sámi elder, Ola Omma, interviewed by the ethnologist Yngve Ryd, who described her practice of collaborating with otters. There was one she'd given a name – Guollenjunnje ('Fish Nose') – who had learned to respond to whistles and spoken commands. She had found him a useful companion for fishing from the shore in winter, since he could reach a catch through very small holes in the sea ice.

Sources from elsewhere in Sápmi suggest this method was considered a good task for children, who could be sent wandering off with a tame otter years before they'd learned to fish with lines. Alex Andersson, whose papers are held in the Institute for Language and Folklore in Gothenburg, described otter-fishing from boats as he witnessed it in the decades around 1900: the otter 'dived for fish and brought them back to the boat. For each fish he caught, they gave him a part of the fish. This made him eager.' Other stories say that a person with a boat and a well-trained otter could sell their fishing gear but still become 'as fat as a wholesaler'.

With every day spent in the boat in Sápmi, I found myself spiralling away from the world I thought I knew. This was the first time, I think, when I truly felt what it meant for the boat not to be a shell protecting me against the ocean, but instead to be the connecting tissue that wove both its rower and its builder into a shared world of vibrant, living elements.

4

Føroyar/The Faroes
Down Comes the Puffin from the Cliff

I

Phoenicians of the North

I COULD QUITE happily spend a year or two reading nothing but Faroese poetry and fiction. These books evoke vivid green slopes, monolithic peaks, and glowing black sands with consummate love and care. Centuries of story and ballad have been built into writing that make these sea rocks into a small stage from which to see the changes that define our modern world. Hardly any Faroe Island writer or reader lives more than a mile from the shore, so boats and the sea are more than just motifs in tales of other things.

    The dancing little boats of island waters have come to play unique roles in modern Faroese identity, so you never need to read far in Faroese lore to come across the idea that island children are born with oars in their hands. Rowing and storytelling are said to come so naturally to the Faroese that eight people in a boat can share tales, chat, and laugh, while not one deviates from the perfectly timed action of their oar. Although some early photographs show a single rower ferrying passengers between islands, one-person boats in the

Faroes are rare. More than most places in this book, rowing was social and community-focused. The smallest boats don't even have the real names that larger vessels do, but are simply evoked by epithets such as *nalvi* ('navel') or *eggjakoppur* ('empty egg shell'). Faroese boat language is full of such visual analogies which, ready-made for literature, bind the domestic and intimate with wild worlds of oceanic drama.

Perhaps no book conjures this ocean theatre more effectively than William Heinesen's classic *The Lost Musicians* (1950). 'Far out in a radiant ocean glinting like quicksilver', this novel begins,

> there lies a solitary little lead-coloured land. The tiny rocky shore is to the vast ocean just about the same as a grain of sand to the floor of a dance hall. But seen beneath a magnifying glass, this grain of sand is nevertheless a whole world.

This North Atlantic outlook implies, for Heinesen, closeness to nature and deep awareness of the constant, world-defining roar of ocean. This is a book in which sea anemones have feelings, and in which the formative moments of a child's life might be their first sighting of leaping dolphins with the dawn glistening bronze on their skin. It is a book in which people are haunted by boats they once owned, in which ships at anchor listen to music from the land while they yearn for 'the unmatched freedom of the windswept ocean', and in which characters row out to tiny skerries to sing mystic hymns to welcome the rising sun. Critical of the 'radical individualism' of modern European world views, Heinesen believed the only way to build a foundation for understanding humanity was to step outside this atomistic present and bring the deep resources of the past to bear on a changing world.

I read this novel and much Faroese poetry in the long evenings of my first journey round the islands. This felt deeply fitting because the distinctiveness of this literature so often comes from its blend of ordinary hearthside talk, village politics, or dance halls, with the immensities of ocean elements. There's rarely a moment in some island novels when the two scales aren't present together, but the range of ways in which each can inflect the other is infinite. Every Faroese home I visited was full of literature, including Danish translations of British nature writing.

My plan, after a few days in the capital, Tórshavn, was to begin my journeying by experiencing the Faroe Islands' oceanic exposure. This is a sea that's never still, as the two great tidal movements, the east flow (*eystfall*) and west flow (*vestfall*) alternate their unpredictable dances. As if this wasn't enough, they wrestle with fierce southwesterly swell. I'd made a more detailed plan than usual – nervous about my tiny inflatable packraft – to paddle slowly from south to north along the archipelago's western edges, landing for nights and lunchtimes at key sites of Faroese life and history. I could learn in advance whether each had been beloved of past seafarers as a place with calm water (a *kyrrupláss*) or feared as a landing strafed by surf (a *brimpláss*). But I soon learned that the normal rules of the sea didn't apply here. The islands had almost no harbours until the twentieth century, and many places considered easy to land by the Faroese are the stuff of nightmares for other seafarers. I had to abandon several attempted landings and tackle different distances than I'd planned.

I'd made arrangements to end this journey in a small traditional rowing boat, a *tríbekkur* ('three-thwart boat'), in the gentle waters at the islands' heart. In the great inter-island sounds, towering mountain shores might be forbidding, but the waters are sheltered and welcoming. Here the island principle that the sea unites where land divides is discernible at a glance. It's these kinds of landscapes that mean boats were used for far more than fishing.

There is kinship but not commonality between the boats here and Norse-influenced boats elsewhere. I heard of one Faroese boatbuilder who was asked if his vessel was a Viking ship. He responded simply, 'It is not a ship, and I am not a Viking.' These boats are distinctive in their smooth upward sheer towards each end and the unique, shapely stem tops, some like stylised goose necks, that protrude over bow and stern (the gentle curve beneath the stem top is known in Faroese as *gasahálsur*, the 'goose breast'). There are also delicious little details to every boat. These often include unusually elaborate thole pins. The Faroese thole pin's parts are named 'foot', 'neck', 'beard', 'nose', and 'eye', so it becomes easy to imagine them as little people who help you work the oars.

Island literature and the accounts of visitors are full of descriptions of these boats plying to and fro across sounds and fjords. One of the books I carried with me was by the ornithologist Kenneth Williamson who spent much of the Second World War stationed here. He fell in love with the 'consummate grace' of the small boats, which went on with their time-honoured lives, barely changing through a millennium of threat, while the world beyond the sea was ravaged by warfare:

> Faroese boats are beautiful craft . . . Beside them the small rowing-boats of English shores would seem coarse and clumsy tubs; and although these natives of the northern seas . . . look delicate and frail, they are in fact very sea-worthy and well fitted for the heavy work required of them in the strong tides and changeable weather among the islands. The high, slender bow lifts buoyantly above the rollers; the stern . . . [divides] the attack of a following sea without shipping water as a boat with a transom stern would do.

He described, too, the resistance of Faroese mariners to the engine, 'this new-fangled evil for indulging ignorance'. This set me to musing on the full of range of knowledge that Williamson thought oars produced but engines undermined.

For all the pleasures of these bookish atmospherics, things didn't start smoothly. This was my first serious sea journey in the tiny packraft, and I learned on my first day's paddle that even a moderate adverse wind slowed my progress more than I'd bargained for. I'd planned only twenty kilometres for day one, but failed to make it. After setting off from close to the international airport on the island of Vágar, it took two days of high waves and stunning scenery to reach the village of Slættanes, whose population left in 1965 to take up residence nearer to the new road system. So, leaving Slættanes at dawn on day three, I was already a day behind schedule and still on the small island I'd started from.

On this third day, the wind stuttered into gusts, its dying and rising giving the sea weird and unpredictable shapes. My vivid red packraft danced a strange, lurching whirl across tall black waves while the land and distant sea were chequered by heavy cloud and fleeting shafts of sunlight. Whenever the light caught the boat, it looked, I thought, exceptionally bold and handsome. But the westerly swell, and the counterswell reflected back from the rocky land, left the boat's bright bow swinging and leaning like a drunk man's lantern on a stormy night. I would have given anything for a wooden boat's keel to keep me straight and true.

Dark cliffs gave the waves an extraordinary sense of silky depth, while waterfalls that seemed to extend from the sea to the heavens made the whole world feel like water, even when it wasn't raining. Cliffs and wet green slopes seemed to go on forever. The day's journey had looked from the comfort of home like a simple matter of a few kilometres. Now, in a flimsy little vessel with winds to fight, it felt like an expedition. Under the famous seabird cliffs of Vestmanna, my arms had to spin like turbines to make any headway at all.

Huge basalt sea stacks towered up from the sea, with sculpted overhangs and gouged arches that showed the raw power of the ocean. And seabirds swung between them: Arctic skuas, puffins, guillemots, shearwaters, and fulmars, all congregating at the start of their breeding season. Their numbers were testament to how much better the Faroese have stewarded their ocean than have other European peoples.

Once, it seemed a dark fragment of wave came loose, as a Leach's storm petrel (the only one I've ever seen) wheeled away from the ridge of swell it followed and passed just feet from my bow. But there was no chance to photograph these things while the sea tossed my little platform up, down, and sideways. As I passed black-sand beaches at the bottom of cliffs, I saw that some had climbing ropes hanging from the edge: accessible even though most islanders now don't travel their coast by boat.

I nudged my slow route north. Fat seals flashed past and flocks of eider bounced between swells. As this frenzy went on, constantly drawing my eyes from my route, I began to believe I'd missed my destination. But eventually, when I felt like I'd been paddling forever, a small discrepancy in the shadows cast by cliff on cliff revealed the mouth of a miniature fjord. As I turned into this passage, the weather was on my side at last, and I raced with the breaking waves into a scene of staggering beauty. The fjord was somehow both grand and pretty, both fiercely elemental and gently sheltering. I tumbled onto a black beach, called Út á Lónna, soaked to the bone but exhilarated. The guano-enriched hillsides glowed like emeralds. They seemed intensely oversaturated in their contrast with dark sands and white breakers. The smell was the clean, bright tang of oyster shells with no hint of seaweedy decay. I wondered if any city ever produced the bewildering sensory explosion this black-sand beach did.

Before deflating my boat, I carried it across the beach-edge shallows into a still lagoon and paddled a few hundred metres of extremely shallow water. Yet another waterfall poured from the cliffs, split into endless mist-like threads that made it, even in real time, look like a long-exposure photo. This took me to the destination of my mini-pilgrimage, the picturesque church on the hillside at Saksun. There was once a harbour here, with several boatbuilders, until a single storm blocked the entrance with black sand and created the landlocked lake. Early photos I'd seen in the museum outside Tórshavn had shown boatbuilding apparatus beside the Saksun lagoon, including stone-built pillars for the sawing of planks. None of this was visible as I paddled and wandered the bay. This absence brought home to me the extreme simplicity of means on which the Faroe boat tradition had been built. A few sawn planks, a little driftwood, and a handful of iron tools – not even so much as a carpenter's bench or any text or diagram – gave rise to the clean, elegant lines of boats that were suited perfectly to the tasks they were built for.

What was evident everywhere, however, were the marks in the landscape of past social organisation. The stone walls still stand that divided the infield, where hay and swedes were grown, from the outfield, where livestock grazed. *Bríkar* can also be seen. These were agricultural terraces in the infield, used to reduce the steepness of slopes and create ground that remains more fertile than elsewhere. This was one of many means, all time-intensive but with no need for outside resources such as fossil fuels, by which Faroese farmer-fishers used environmental knowledge to enrich their harvests from land and sea.

Perhaps because the tide had risen, threatening to swamp the path, no one that afternoon made it round to the stunning black-sand beach. I spent my long evening in this arena-like space beneath the mountains, watching the ducks, waders, and seabirds come and go. I sat down to read as night drew in, and found myself more sensitive than usual to the presence, in the older books, of terms such as 'rustic', 'peasant', and even 'primitive', which might have captured the means from which past Faroese life was built, but not the sophistication and elegance of the things those means made.

Over the following days, long hours beneath cliffs alternated with visits to tiny villages sandwiched between upland and ocean. Here island origin stories are written into the ocean-gouged rock. The crossing from the largest Faroese island, Streymoy, to its northeasterly neighbour, Eysturoy, is dominated by two great stacks, known as Risin ('Giant') and Kellingin ('Witch'). They tell of the oceanic orientations of the islands' past:

> In ancient times, when islands and countries, land and sea, and everything on our planet lived and breathed in a different way than we know of today, Iceland decided he wanted to own the Faroe Islands and have them moved all the way to his icy shores. To fulfil this task, Iceland sent the Giant and his wife the Witch across the sea with orders to drag the Faroe Islands across the ocean.

While the witch tied a rope around the top of a mountain, the giant stood firmly in the sea, waiting to pull, but the pressure of his hauling merely cracked the mountain. 'We can still clearly see the opening in the mountain where this rope was fastened,' says Faroese lore. They worked through the night with no more success in pulling the islands from their roots. As everyone knows, giants are sensitive to sunlight and will turn to stone at its touch. When the witch realised they'd been so distracted by their task that they'd failed to notice the approach of dawn, she jumped into the sea to be with her husband and both were transformed into rock. There they both stand, gazing longingly towards their home, as reminders of what could have happened had the sun not risen and the clouds not broken that day.

It's easy to see the echoes of history in this story. The islands' first inhabitants are thought to have been Irish monks, though they may just have easily been Iron Age Scottish colonists or pre-Viking Scandinavian explorers. Archaeological evidence shows that, for the centuries before the arrival of the Viking Norse, these communities relied heavily on the hunting of seals, whales, and seabirds, with a lesser reliance on the common grazing of sheep, cattle, and pigs. We know nothing of whether they moved further west across the ocean. Then began an era of subjection to greater powers. The early people seem to have been pushed out by the Norse during their *landnámstíð* ('age of settlement'). In that era, Norwegian Vikings settled every island group from Orkney to Greenland, establishing farms in the Faroes that would slowly become the islands' villages. They also shifted resource use away from the sea and towards livestock.

For nearly two centuries, islanders continued to live independently from Norway, establishing their own laws and customs. They owned their boats and traded with ports such as Bergen, exchanging wool and fish for timber and grain. But in 1274, Norway exerted increased control, under a unified law code, over the Faroes, Iceland, and Greenland. Trade was no longer an equal arrangement, but conducted on terms imposed by Bergen. Over subsequent centuries, overseas powers, from churches to Norwegian and Danish kings and vassals, made ever greater claims on Faroese resources. They took taxes, tithes, and fees in knitwear, sheepskins, tallow, down, ewe's milk butter, and fish. They claimed farmland and imposed their own rules for its inheritance.

In 1620, control of Faroese trade passed from forest-rich Norway to the Danish Icelandic Company. Access to boat timber became even more difficult. In 1709, Denmark proclaimed complete royal control over Faroe Island trade, marking the beginning of 'the monopoly period'. Like almost all languages of the edges – the tongues that contain in them the lore of boats and seafaring – Faroese was marginalised, while a metropolitan language, Danish, was enforced as the language of school, church, and state. The extravagantly rich oral literature of the islands went uncommunicated to the outside world.

But the possibility for Faroese perspectives on the world to flourish was gradually restored. In 1849, two seats in the Danish parliament were granted to the islands and three years later a new Faroese parliament (Løgting), was established, though it lacked the legislative powers of the old. In 1938, the ban on the use of the Faroese language in schools was lifted. Island governors, with increasing scope to practise a little independence, helped shift trade away from the woollens and agricultural goods that dominated the monopoly years back towards boats and the sea. In the 1810s, the islands' first resident governor recorded the number of island boats as 482; by 1903, that number was 1,463, and around nine tenths were small wooden rowing boats. Even when sailing sloops were introduced from Britain in the 1870s, they carried numerous little wooden rowing boats on journeys to Iceland and Greenland. After being used to fish from, many were sold to local people rather than shipped home, so Faroese boatbuilders served a transatlantic market.

The culture that emerged from this growing self-confidence was immensely diverse in dialect and outlook. This might be why there's so much literature. Exploring the tensions and paradoxes in island life seems to be a national pastime. Even when first paddling through, I was able to appreciate these combinations of unity and diversity. Villages could be described in superficially similar terms. Each is a little sheltered enclave amid landscapes where every plant that reaches ankle height is battered, gnarled, and windswept. There's a mix of modern homes and colourful old houses, many roofed with grassy turf. Almost all stand singly. These freestanding homes are often loosely clustered round a white church in which model boats commemorating lost seafarers hang from ceilings. Studies of island culture call these villages 'small, nucleated settlements', widely separated from one another but tightly knit in their own spaces. This, the studies say, is the perfect social structure for strong oral traditions to emerge.

Local differences begin in the way each village is built around its geology. This geographic structure – whether closed in by cliffs or or opening out into long curves of grassy slopes – shapes how a village feels and how its songs and stories operate. Tjørnuvík, on the north coast of Streymoy, is buried deep in a surf-filled cove and looks out onto oncoming storms. The sun struggles to reach the cliff-girt settlement. Its stories emphasise shipwreck and supernatural powers. On Eysturoy, just a couple of miles to the east, Eiði is set on a wide green hillside and feels open, sunny and outgoing. Boats run through many Eiði tales, and people from islands far and wide used to bring their biggest craft here, to celebrate occasions like Christmas. Gjógv, a little further in the same direction, sits by the shore in an amphitheatre of high ridges, with the mountains of Kalsoy Island visible across the sound. It carries the air of an Alpine resort in miniature, with stories expressing pride in its geological distinctiveness. All households here had shares in at least one boat and its catch of fish.

The emergence of well-known ideas about the characteristics of each village and its people was aided by the mobility of the Faroese. Among the most itinerant figures of all were the boatbuilders. Boatbuilding here was a more specialised trade than anywhere in the previous chapters, and a dedicated career began with an apprenticeship that often meant travel to a new village. It was also a uniquely social occupation. Most men in the islands laboured on the hills or on the sea. But boatbuilders worked outdoors in the centre of the village. Many loved their trade precisely because they became the social hub of each new village that hired them. Early photos of Faroese boatbuilders show curious children and teens gathered round them.

Islanders in outlying settlements rowed regularly to bigger towns to trade, with stops along the way, and gathered reputations as they did so. In the seventeenth century, for instance, the people of the small but spectacular island of Mykines are said to have had the biggest rowing boat the islands ever saw. It was so heavy it demanded

Hookers and currachs racing from Roundstone, July 2023

In the boat workshop, building a *púcán* which, before the mast is put in place, is as close to a *bád iomartha* as is to be seen today

The best-preserved *bád iomartha* on the shore (foreground), February 2020

Little boats below St MacDara's Chapel

The chapel on the cliffs at Filiscleitir

Setting out in the *Jubilee*, oars stowed and lug sail raised

Paddling towards Bearasaigh

Waking up to a golden eagle on Scarp

The view from Scarp to Harris, through the window of a crofthouse ruin

The Sámi boat I used for exploring the fjord.

One of a huge pod of Porsanger porpoise

The end of a 40km day in the Sámi boat

The 1kg boat amid spectacular worlds of vivid green hillsides and black sand

At sea in the Faroese boat

Some of the most atmospheric conditions imaginable: craggy, snow-topped peaks, still skies, bands of low cloud, and humpback whales everywhere

eighteen rowers. Threaded on its thole pins were unique iron rings, which are described as chiming like bells each time the oars were pulled. The result was that people ashore knew without looking which boat was entering their bay. Long after the vessel had ceased to exist, the character of a whole community was thought to be expressed by their once having rowed a boat as ostentatious as the bombastic puffin-covered sea cliffs of Mykines itself.

The same diversity appears in songs and rhymes. There are many genres of Faroese verse, most of which have never really travelled beyond the islands. There are traditional ballads, as well as the more modern *táttur*, or 'literary ballad'. In the most famous *táttur*, a *tjaldur* (oystercatcher, the symbol of the celebrated boatbuilder Nólsoyar Páll) protects the little waders and seabirds of local villages against powerful eagles, hawks, and ravens that prey on the islands from outside. But most songs are more local and everyday. There are relatively few themes – rowing, fishing, shepherding, preparing food, birdlife – but a vast diversity of patterns, tones, and meanings. In one, 'Down Comes the Puffin from the Cliff', a puffin marches round the islands, uttering social commentary and political complaints. The rhymes for children (*skjaldur*) are full of words for specific local coastal landforms or practices, such as *skor* (a place where sheep are grazed that can be accessed only by boat or rope) or *lunnar* (the wooden rollers on which communities with beaches would launch and land their boats). Communities created the cohesion that was so highly valued here by sharing neatly localised stories as they went about their tasks amid the land- and seascapes.

After passing Eiði and Gjógv, I had my longest crossing of this journey. This took me across inter-island seas guarded by the towering forms of Risin and Kellingin, until I was far from the Faroes' most populated regions and into the sparser worlds of the northern-islands. Many famed boatbuilding centres here, such as Blankskáli on Kalsoy, were among the villages abandoned in the nineteenth century. But the memory of the most renowned boatbuilding families remains alive. Other small villages survived their isolation from new road systems, and some, on the northern coast of the island of Kalsoy in particular, maintained a central status in Faroese boat worlds.

Indeed, early in the twentieth century it was isolated villages in the northern islands that kept many traditions alive. Their boats were generally smaller than those made further south, with many four-oared vessels. They were a counterweight to the southern villages at the cutting edge of change. It's even said that the ancient square sail, as simple as a blanket on a stick, could be seen here in the twentieth century.

This persistence of tradition might relate in part to the long lives of boatbuilders. There are a surprising number of stories in the northern isles of boatbuilders, such as Jákup á Biskupsstóð, who built more than forty boats after the age of eighty. It seems that the further from Tórshavn boatbuilders were, the more likely they were to be village elders and custodians of memory, shaping and preserving world views in ways more formal officials might further south in the islands.

I was fortunate for most of my crossing to Kalsoy. Although the skies were grey, and cloud hung low, the winds were soft so the sea was quiet. Coming directly from the west, the low breeze never worked against my progress. As I reached the island, stupendous cliffs towered high above, blending into cloud that hid the prickliest peaks. The views were barely believable: the northern end of Kalsoy is only a few hundred metres wide, but somehow it seemed to bristle with miles of crag and mountaintop. It looked, from the water, like a vast, jagged crystal cluster. In this still, sunless air, the cliffs cast an immense blue gloom on the water. But as I neared the headland itself, tidal movements ripped suddenly at the surface, unpredictable and loud as fireworks. The contrast of still sky with crackling, fizzing sea gave a surreal edge to the whole spectacular experience. I don't know whether the wind rose as I reached the northern side of the cliffs, or if I simply moved into the breeze's flow, but as I neared the end of my eight-kilometre crossing, gusts agitated the water all around and I saw there'd be more than a little surf in my landing at Trøllanes.

Waves slammed my little boat into a shore that felt shockingly hostile at first: its landing place was barely gentler than a cliff face. Only later did I read a description by the great eighteenth-century chronicler of Faroese seafaring, Jens Christian Svabo, which called this the most difficult village landing in the islands. I'd sought out Trøllanes, and the neighbouring village of Mikladalur, because of the fame of their past boatbuilders. But from the water it was barely possible to tell that I was reaching settlements at all, and it was certainly hard to imagine a long history of boats launching easily here. Only after a cold, wet clamber up black rocks did I find myself among the few small houses where I would spend the night. The population of Trøllanes is just fourteen and, since the village is enclosed in a cleft between mountainsides, it has never had the potential to be much larger. Yet these two settlements of Trøllanes and Mikladalur made Kalsoy as significant to the small-boat histories of the North Atlantic as Liverpool or New York.

Despite its dangerous landing, Trøllanes was beloved of seafarers because three hours' row from the village is a fishing ground of phenomenal richness. This made Kalsoy's settlements into ocean crossroads. They never produced large numbers of boats, but people travelled from Iceland, Denmark, and every Faroese island to learn the skills of their boatbuilders. Because of the local swell, boats here were short-keeled and limited in speed, but strong and exceptionally seaworthy. They were famed as the boats you'd most want to be in if caught in a storm. The proximity to fishing grounds encouraged the villages' role as boat schools. On their way out on week-long fishing trips, boats from villages far to the south or east, would drop off a boy or two, still too scrawny to haul the nets, to learn to work with wood among Kalsoy's famed builders. Some teenagers returned every year, others stayed just one winter month. Remarkably, lines of familial or professional descent can be established from boat-builders in these two villages to almost every other boatbuilder in the islands. To travel the coasts of the Faroes feels like following these webs of influence, with boats as spiders that span silken lines, village to village, over centuries.

One of the most remarkable things about paddling these islands was the extent to which being offshore felt like still being on the cultural map. Most modern societies aren't good at representing shores. Land maps (whether road atlases or Ordnance Survey sheets) leave the sea blank, while sea maps (such as Admiralty charts) leave the land empty. The strange result is that everything that takes place across the shoreline is unmappable. Because so much of the coastline is vertical, the bird's-eye perspective of our maps also hides large areas of profound cultural significance, such as Faroese sea cliffs. In the Faroes, more than anywhere else, I felt the sea to be continuous with the land: a roadway into past and future. This continuity appears in poems and stories which insist the richest land in the islands lies under the sea. The bearings by which little boats navigate are thought of like cables or rigging that tie Faroese land above the surface to the wider Faroe Islands below. It's impossible, in such situations – even when out in a tiny packraft far from anyone else – to feel alone.

II

Rowing Out for Fish

The central roles of boats in Faroese life lasted longer than in regions easier to cross by road. Only in the last few decades, with the building of long undersea tunnels, have cars surpassed little seacraft as the means of island movement. The Faroes is still unique in the degree of official recognition afforded to old boats: the best spaces in the docks at the heart of Tórshavn, for instance, are reserved for traditional Faroese boats, so that all visitors can admire them and residents never forget the extent to which the town was built on their efforts.

One of Faroe's unusual characteristics is that the unpredictability of the fjord winds makes sailing more treacherous than rowing. To cut the wind, rowers wield long, thin storm-oars, completely different from my wide-leafed oars in Sápmi. Rowing is often more communal than sailing, because it doesn't lend itself to roles such as skippers or captains who command each adjustment of rigging or rudder. So boats built a remarkably egalitarian society in the islands. Boatbuilders, alongside the blacksmith, were particularly esteemed, while boat crews were a fundamental unit of social structure. Where Christmas lunch elsewhere might be organised round nuclear or extended families, in the Faroes it was structured round the boat crew. Rowers were thanked for their year's work with caramel potatoes, salt lamb, sausages, and Christmas pudding. Because of a tradition in the islands of writing *bygdarsøgur* ('village histories') it's possible to reconstruct these crews, and the names of 161 late nineteenth-century boatbuilders have been collated by the Faroe boat's leading historian, Morten Gøthche. Nowhere have the names of past boat people, as well as terms for boat parts and boat practices, been better preserved than in these islands where their esteem was highest.

Each crew and their boat had to be capable of handling powerful tides, risky shallows, treacherous whirlpools, and towering swells if Faroese life was to thrive. And amid risk, lore abounds. The idea of *útróður* ('rowing out'), for instance, grew to be rich with meanings, though its use always denotes commitment to traditional, subsistence, rural ways of life, in which small crews rowed out for community boiled fish feasts. Both natural and supernatural seafarers haunt the lore. To succeed at sea, a rower needed many contrasting competencies: these included science (built on skill), art (derived from intuition), and faith (rooted in omen). The figure who balanced these capabilities best was the *miðamaður*: a semi-mystical seafarer whose ability to find safe passage or good fishing exceeded rational explanation. A 1987 poem by Sigurð Joensen sets these qualities out:

> But what is never lifted to the surface,
> is the best half of Faroe Land
> And to explore land that the ocean covered
> Became the life and science of the miðamaður
> . . .
>
> So, every spot where fish are swimming
> was attached to Faroe Land by bearings.
> And the Faroes expanded in scope and glory
> With the work and science of the miðamaður.

I rarely fish. Perhaps irrationally, or paradoxically, it doesn't usually seem to fit with the ways I want to experience the ocean. But I felt this project would be incomplete without casting a line in at least some of the waters I wrote about. I liked the idea of doing this in the Faroes because of the detailed understanding the islanders have cultivated of the world beneath the waves. I was reminded of *meahcci* when I heard people speak of fish: cod weren't treated as a single species, but as beings whose qualities and habits changed so much with the seasons that they required completely different names.

Torrafiskur was cod caught on oceanic fishing grounds in January and February. It was large and fat, perfect for drying as stockfish (any *torrafiskur* too heavy to hold by the tail with one hand were used in this way). Big winter boats brimming with fat fish are the stuff of many songs. The roughest grounds, west and north of the islands, were avoided in winter, but in March and April attention could turn to them. *Várfiskur*, only slightly less fat than the winter cod, and fast as tuna, shoaled around the grounds. Then, in May, the cod spawned and focus turned to the *summarfiskur* (or *landfiskur*) within the fjords. These cod were plentiful and easy to catch but far less rich and plump than those that were in the open fishing grounds at the same time (which were known as *miðafiskur*). *Summarfiskur* was for eating fresh. In the next season, the relationship between the cod in the fjords and in the fishing grounds was reversed: the fjord fish, known as *heystfiskur* ('autumn fish'), grew much bigger than the *miðafiskur*. As with everywhere I travelled, these many kinds of fish were spoken about not as a mere resource but as though, in the subsistence life of the islands, they had inner worlds and intelligences that deserved respect and care.

I met with Samson Højgaard, who keeps a small three-thwarted Faroese boat deep in the network of sheltered fjords known as Tangafjørður. This was one of the most shapely boats I've ever seen, its curves elegant and subtle. Longer and deeper than the Sámi boat, but no less agile, this craft was suited to bigger swells. The pale yellow of its unpainted planks gave it a friendly air that belied the Viking origins of its form, while the swirling grain of spruce ensured it always felt organic. Even without ballast, this felt like a boat that would be easy to row long distances.

With a crew of four, we headed into the sheltered summer fishing grounds. Even expecting richer seas than I knew from home, I wasn't prepared for the plenty a single rod could yield. Within an hour, I'd caught pollock, ling, cod, haddock, and saithe (the fish of choice for salting in many a Faroese household). My fellow seafarers concentrated their efforts on cod and saithe alone. Had we fished all afternoon, we would have had enough to feed a large family for a week or more. But instead we lit a little stove, drank coffee, and ate apples. Used to hearing of small boats going out from Scottish coasts today and catching a handful of mackerel or nothing at all, this plenitude emphasised yet again how rich with resources coastal spaces once were.

My share of the fish went home with the boat's owner to be preserved for his family's later feasting. In drying or fermenting cod, saithe, and mutton, Faroese cuisine makes full use of the climate of sea and hillside. The wind speeds, humidity, and temperature in which foods are hung out to dry all shape the conditions that create local delicacies, as does the distribution of the micro-organisms that cause fermentation. Salt was far more rarely used than it was elsewhere. It's as though communities re-immerse their food in the natural environment before consumption. This is sometimes done outside, and sometimes in *hjallur*, wooden buildings with gaps between their slats for wind to blow through. Any islander who loves local food will tell of how flavours vary by location, and might assure you that they can easily pinpoint the origin of produce treated in this way.

As we ate our apples, we discussed how conflicts between the islands' transnational industrial ambitions and deep commitment to local traditional community shape all debates about the future. And I learned of the changing patterns of fish stocks, including the decline of halibut and the current prevalence of the strange, muscular, breed of cod that turns bright red from its habits of grazing the iodine-rich kelp on the seabed. I was told of one fisherman who had recently gone out and, instead of bringing in the hundreds of red cod he could have netted, had managed to land a single halibut and haul aboard a sheep that had died falling from a clifftop. This catch of surf and turf was spoken of as a great event to be celebrated.

The long resilience of Faroese boat traditions means that a great deal is known about the customs surrounding a row-out two centuries ago. We know that each crew would have travelled with a food box, filled with dried lamb and rye bread. Cows held a central place in village life, so rowers drank milk when at sea. Despite this, the large barrel of fresh water in the middle of every boat was so central to a day's activities that it was tended with almost superstitious care. There were well-known conventions for carrying goods in different weathers. And we know much about the evolution of the beautiful Faroese woollens that were developed to keep seafarers safe.

There were four primary roles in a fishing crew. One was compass bearer and navigator. To be given the honour of holding the compass, Svabo noted in 1782, was 'a medal or badge of honour'. The navigator planned the day's journey in accordance with the tides. People ashore knew when to expect a crew's return and light the cooking fires, because the decision of what tide to come home on would have been made the previous day. Without clocks, all relied on tide and compass, and the whole community would be ready to prepare a fish feast when the crews were swept home. A single boat, Svabo said, could bring in as many as three hundred cod, and several boats might launch from a single village.

The next role was the *andovsmaður*. This was often a member of the crew who was either yet to reach full strength or whose strength was waning. Their task wasn't to haul lines but to sit with two oars on a central thwart and keep the boat in the best fishing places. Since crews fished while drifting with the tide, the *andovsmaður*'s role was often to slow the drift, keeping the boat over the fish for as long as possible. The crew would then all row back to the start of the tidal movement and begin the drift again. The *andovsmaður*'s other duties included making sure the boat was properly equipped and in good working order.

The third role was usually shared by two people. These were the watchers, and one of them had the task, disliked by most, of waking people in time to ride the day's first tide out to a fishing ground. Watchers took charge of launches and landings, sometimes jumping into the sea to help bring the bow ashore, then ensuring the boat was safely out of reach of rising tides.

In this way, authority was shared between the rowers, and everyone knew who would take charge at each moment. There were perks with each role. The *andovsmaður* was entitled to the largest ling of the day, for instance, while the watcher who woke people up got the largest cod or halibut. But other than this, the catch was shared equally between all aboard, with one additional share going to the boat's owner if it wasn't communally owned. In some eras, a tenth of the catch was taken as tax, to be used for export as stockfish. If there was anyone on board who wasn't part of the crew – a child, clergyman, or teacher who might be using the fishing trip as transport between settlements – they didn't share in the catch, but kept what they caught themselves.

As in Lewis and Sápmi, the mixed resources of the sea were blended with those of hillside and shore in intricate systems of what sociologists refer to as 'communitarian and kin ordered food production'. In the Faroe Islands today, extensive work is being done to understand how these systems worked and how their best features can be perpetuated in a world of resource-intensive imports and exports. Ragnheiður Bogadóttir is a human ecologist at the University of the Faroe Islands. Her work uses the idea of 'social metabolism' to measure societies' rate of resource use. She analyses the low social metabolism and 'quiet sustainability' that occur in island economies, where the continued exchange of subsistence goods such as yarn, hay, barley, swedes, fish, butter, and mutton still affects islanders' lifestyles. These practices of 'informal provisioning' account for more than forty kilograms of annual food consumption on average for every person in the Faroes; by comparison, the figure for many other European populations is close to zero.

Over the past half century, however, there has been a drastic rise in social metabolism because of the vast energy usage of export-oriented fishing and aquaculture. The Faroe Islands now have some of the highest GDP per capita in the world, despite nearly 95 per cent of their exports being fish. But Bogadóttir shows that there has been a strong reaction against the export–import economy, involving conscious efforts to reconnect island life with its distinctive past uses of natural systems. This has happened at every level of society, from tiny villages reclaiming their history of non-monetary exchange and local production, to fine-dining restaurants drawing on past techniques and attitudes to give diners local alternatives to the transnational tasting menus of the Michelin-star circuit. Bogadóttir emphasises two very different economies coexisting in the islands today. She shows that 'alternatives to unsustainable resource use patterns and strategies are already (quietly) present in society' and that more than 70 per cent of the Faroese population are engaged in the informal economy. This economy, she argues, shouldn't be seen merely as alternative sets of practices, but as worlds built on 'different logics and moral principles'.

All this is complicated by the fact that the non-monetary economy, the very heart of Faroese culture, is unrecognised in official statistics. It is perceived by the state simply as people's hobbies. Money is seen as the single measure of reality. Bogadóttir's purpose is to show that we need fuller understanding of the workings of community-based production, recognising the survival of informal spheres of the islands' economy as 'both a bio-physical process and a cultural process'. Returning Faroese cattle-rearing to a sustainable and resilient practice, for instance, would entail rejecting imported industrial feed and reviving the historic cultural landscape. Infields would be returned to hay pasturage, and the gathering of hay would be restored as a seasonal marker and social occasion full of meanings. In this vision, the future doesn't need inventing but rediscovering. Bogadóttir's use of the phrase 'quiet sustainability' conjures the way in which answers to problems of resource exploitation are often cultural more than technological. To think with small boats is always to think with time that isn't linear and pasts that are at least as alive as the present.

As I pulled my pair of long, thin oars to bring the Faroe boat back towards its dock at the harbour in Kollafjørður village, I could see an extraordinary range of different landscapes, from sheep-grazed hillsides down to shellfish-swathed shores, settlements with infields, and the fish-filled open fjord itself. A long road now winds round the bay and returning to harbour meant moving back into the sound of engines. Because of these roads, rowing out into the fjords is now a minority experience. The waters we'd just travelled flow over huge new undersea tunnels and even the world's first underwater roundabout. The tunnels were opened in 2020 and only then did the practice end of locals seeking out boat owners to travel between settlements that had long been connected by water.

I wondered, as the noise of cars grew, how far the restoration of the Faroese cultural landscape could go. If it's possible to imagine infields returned to pasturage in order to end the resource-intensive import of feed, is it possible to imagine the water too as part of the future-focused recourse to tradition? Might the practical as well as symbolic place of the small boat in Faroese life also be restored? Everything is in place for small-scale subsistence fare to see resurgence: from revival of practices such as fermentation to new interest in foodstuffs once dismissed as 'peasant food'. What would it mean for the skills of Faroese rowers and boatbuilders to be a purposeful part of this movement?

It might already have been surprising, to some, to see Faroese culture praised for its care of the ocean. In recent years, the islands have received little but bad press in English-language culture. This has largely been shaped by the perceived incompatibility of the *grindadráp*, the pilot whale hunt, with modern global values. Boycotts of Faroese goods and tourism have been accompanied by direct action. There have been media campaigns – multi-million-pound endeavours – to make the worst excesses of whale hunting global knowledge. This activism has almost never attempted to engage with or understand Faroese culture, in all its environmentally conscious richness. Its leaders and participants have often expressed their total rejection of that possibility: 'We don't compromise . . . We're not here for cultural exchange.' For that reason, despite all the resources in wealth and fossil fuels devoted to them, these movements have been spectacularly ineffective at saving whales.

Indeed, by radicalising a small portion of Faroese youth, activists have led to gradual reversals of what many Faroese had expected would be a terminal decline in whale hunting. The last ten years have seen a few hardliners play fast and loose with the values of respect and care that previously governed Faroese interactions with the ocean. Some older islanders, who believed they'd be the last generation to hunt whales, find their children spurred by anger at the actions of campaigners into taking part more energetically than any generation in living memory. Wooden boats are replaced by jet skis and – in stark contravention of Faroese custom – the pursuit of whales beyond local bays.

To some islanders, activists are representatives of the urban societies that are most enmeshed in destructive global food cultures. Those cultures, they argue, embody the unsustainable consumption that traditional Faroese life, with its informal, communitarian provisioning, has worked so hard to resist. As one islander put it when addressing activists, 'It is you who polluted the whales and now you come here and impose your lifestyle upon us!' Activists accuse islanders of 'ecological imperialism', while islanders accuse activists of 'cultural imperialism', and both generalise each other's attitudes as either 'evil' or 'naive'.

These clashes are not unique to the Faroes. Many western environmental campaigns of recent decades have failed to recognise the cultures of low environmental stress – and the ritual respect for ecologies – in societies whose ways of life they've attacked. In some instances, this lack of cultural awareness has forced whole communities, even whole peoples, to abandon sustainable living for lifestyles that are costly both for individuals and the environment. Perhaps the most famous such examples are the campaigns against seal hunting that began with Greenpeace in the 1980s. Aimed at industrial seal hunters in Newfoundland, and deliberately excluding small-scale indigenous seal hunts, this initial campaign nonetheless caused a precipitous drop in the value of sealskin, which ended the ways in which Inuit communities could acquire necessary resources by exchanging or selling seal-related products.

The result was a collapse in Inuit living standards: thousands of Inuit living independent and sustainable lives were forced into the destructive and dependent economic logics of global food systems. This came at a time when indigenous peoples were being idealised as environmental guardians, so that many were shocked by the sudden switch to demonisation and the new conflict with western environmentalists. This moment remains a flashpoint in Inuit perceptions of western 'environmental imperialism'. Films such as Tanya Tagaq's *Tungijuq (What We Eat)* (2009) and Alethea Arnaquq-Baril's *Angry Inuk* (2016) tell the story from Inuit perspectives.

Though much of this debate was carried out in tones of unthinking outrage, Tagaq (who received numerous death threats) led some coverage towards meaningful discussions that are relevant in the Faroese context too. Key among these was whether it was possible both to love animals and to survive off them. This question creates paradoxes for western values. For instance, the cultures of the North Atlantic, particularly in those enclaves that maintain subsistence-focused household production, possess more environmental knowledge and stronger ethics of care than mainstream western culture, yet their respect for the natural world, and the homage they pay to its active intelligences, is focused around acts of hunting and killing creatures whose environment has been profoundly degraded by western ways of life.

In the Faroese conflicts, one set of voices, that of Faroese people against whaling, has been almost entirely sidelined. Their concerns, including ones over the pollutants that run through the bodies of whales and are harmful to humans too, might have been enough to end the *grind* by now, had the backlash against outside activism not brought dozens of new converts to the practice. Those I met in the Faroes had a wide range of attitudes to traditions such as the whale hunt, but all had deep ecological awareness and understanding, created by living close to the ocean and its fragile resources.

My experience of paddling and rowing the islands led me to believe that Faroese culture has much to teach western society about living well and sustainably. That the demonisation of the *grindadráp* threatens to prevent us recognising and respecting Faroe's oceanic knowledge is one of the great tragedies of the current North Atlantic stand-off.

Interlude

Crossings and Connections

IN THE SHAETLAN language, used on the islands of Shetland, the word *shoormal* indicates, in the words of the poet Robert Alan Jamieson, 'the space between the tides where the moon weighs the density of the ocean . . . a symbol for the flow and ebb of language and culture'. This term for the intertidal zone is used as one of a set of resonant images explored by island poets and artists as part of the current Shaetlan revival. One such writer, Roseanne Watt, writes of language and culture as drenched with seawater, as in the poem 'Saat i da Blöd' where one Shetlander admonishes another for having 'parched dy tongue' by 'propering' words into English and losing the 'langwich . . . dat cud captir da percussion/o waves apo its consonants'. The speaker reminds the listener that

da saat dat courses trowe	The salt that courses through
dy veins is da lifeblöd	your veins is the lifeblood
o an aulder converseeshun	of an older conversation
wan dat ebbs and flöds	one that ebbs and flows
joost as da tide.	just as the tide

In the poem 'Raaga Tree', Watt explores the idea of Shetland history as a rootless tree. Shaetlan emerged as a literary language in the 1860s, while Shetland's Nordic language, Norn, had died a century earlier, leaving fragments of vocabulary but barely a literary trace. This means that to try to write Shetland's history is to be adrift in a world without traditional textual sources. The language, shaped by loss, is driftwood, its roots worn away by ocean:

Ta see me	To see me is to see
is ta see	an absent world
	caught between
a vodd	seaweed and old nets.
wirld, shakkeld	You will not
	find me there –
atween tang	not as I once was.
an auld nets.	See, I was
	brought here
Du winna	by storms,
fin me dere –	the sea voyage
	made me strange;
no as I	made black tentacles
wance wis.	Of my roots,
	crossgrained my body
See, I wis	with the green
browt here	of sharp porphyry.
	What I was
by rees,	I hardly remember.
de sea-vaege	Don't ask me.
	Leave me.
made me uncan;	I have no time
made swart	for your lost gods.
	My boughs shall not

AFLOAT

be gallows here.
taentacles
o my röts,

twarterit
my boady

Wi de grün
o thunderbolts.

Whit I wis
I hardly

mind myself.
Dunna axe me.

Laeve me.
I hae no time

fir dy wilt gods.
My boughs

Sanna be
gallows here.

At first, Watt was intimidated by the absence of these linguistic roots, but gradually came to recognise this condition as rich with potential: not just a void but a creative space. It's notable that, throughout her work, objects of wood, stone, reed, and twine are conjured as things to fill the void. The evocative image of the *raaga* tree is a thing that drifts across ocean, connecting Shetland with east and west at the same time as it defines the islands' history.

CROSSINGS AND CONNECTIONS

Everywhere around the North Atlantic, it is poets more than historians or archaeologists who have reclaimed marginalised histories. Everywhere, understanding the world of the maritime north means reconceptualising voids as creative spaces and feeling our way to what might have been and what still could be. Tim Robinson described his method in similar terms, arguing that recovering the past of Connemara wasn't compatible with the Enlightenment idea of illuminating the past or constructing an authoritative narrative. Instead, he said, his tales 'mark some points of attachment of the historical web from which one can grope back along the strands into the darkness'. The long memory of oral culture, which doesn't work in narratives of cause and effect, and doesn't always think with linear time, is where the meanings of the sea reside.

Moving from the Faroes to Greenland in the middle of this project felt like a major leap, from ice-free waters warmed by the Gulf Stream, into a world of glacier, floe, sea ice, and the cold-blue bergs of the frigid Labrador current. This was the jump from east Atlantic to west, and from Europe to the Americas. But this step is less dramatic than it might seem and, despite our perception that globalisation has made the world smaller and more interlinked, would have been still less abrupt in the past. The condition of living in the *shoormal*, or of pasts that resemble a *raaga* tree, spans the northern circumference of the world.

This is a theme that can be shown through boats as well as language. In the early 1960s, Edwin Tappan Adney and Howard Chapelle published a classic study of indigenous American watercraft, *The Bark Canoes and Skin Boats of North America*. Adney had been taught, at the age of nineteen, to build birchbark boats and speak the Maliseet language by an Algonquin boatbuilder, Peter Joe. He spent the rest of his life creating a vast archive of photographs, drawings, and descriptions of indigenous boatbuilders, their cultural practices, and the vessels they crafted. After Adney's death in 1950,

Howard Chapelle built the material he had collected into a book that manages to be history, ethnology, and boatbuilding guide all at the same time. This work found an unexpected audience: of everything ever published by the Smithsonian Institution, this is the book in print for longest.

Since then, traditional canoes have become symbols for the resurgence of indigenous thought and the dismantling of colonial influences. They've come to symbolise the cultures of North America so fully that many would consider them phenomena of the Americas alone. Yet seventy years after Adney's death, Harri Luukkanen and William Fitzhugh published a kind of sequel to his work which many once assumed could never exist: *The Bark Canoes and Skin Boats of Northern Eurasia*. This fiercely ambitious study took in the canoe histories of every Arctic region from Scandinavia via Siberia to the Bering Strait: 10,000 kilometres of tundra and boreal forest that were once opened up to human access by technologies of birchbark and sealskin. The range of peoples whose boats Luukkanen and Fitzhugh describe is vast, from Sámi, Karelians, Khanty, Mani, and Komi in northeast Europe, to Nenets, Enets and Nganasan along Arctic coasts east of the Urals, as well as the peoples of the Yenisey, Lena and Amur river basins, Lake Baikal, and the Chukchi Peninsula.

That book would have been impossible before 1991 and the collapse of the Soviet Union. Then the opening of Russian archives and archaeological sites revealed hosts of boat traditions previously unknown beyond Russian borders. Indeed, despite the fame of the Irish currach, northern Europe is the region Luukkanen and Fitzhugh cover that has the smallest and most limited archaeological record of canoes and skin boats. Throughout their book's regions, the use of canoes and skin boats began no later than the end of the last Ice Age, 12,000 years ago, and has adapted through many stages of continuous tradition till the twentieth century. My response when I first read the book was to question whether I should be more bewildered at the scale of cultural diversity on Arctic coasts, or by the intertwining of waterborne histories that generated strange parallels across vast distances. The text drives home the truth that, in the Arctic even more than elsewhere, distinctions between Europe, Asia, and the Americas make no sense. The ceaseless traffic of little boats bound all the north's cold-water worlds together long before Columbus.

There's a striking difference, however, between the American study of 1964 and the Eurasian book of 2020, which is that the former featured living traditions and so could describe construction techniques and paddling methods in detail. The latter had to rely for these elements, and indeed for images of many boats, on travellers from previous centuries. In this way, the iconic roles canoes and kayaks have come to play throughout Greenland and North America, as well as the extent to which they've been adapted into new boat traditions, has few Eurasian parallels. Luukkanen and Fitzhugh's work instead points to open questions: a host of voids and creative spaces.

One of the greatest such mysteries is the frequency of close similarities in boatbuilding approaches between apparently unconnected peoples, such as Koryak skin boats and those of the Aleutian Islands, as well as Koryak and Greenland kayaks. These unexpected echoes are complemented by centuries of cross-pollination, including stories of European states learning boat-craft from the Americas. In the eighteenth century, for instance, many Swedes and Finns, from small-scale farmers to the King of Sweden himself, paddled indigenous North American birchbark canoes on Finnish rivers and coasts. In 1747, the king, Adolf Frederick, had sent one of Linnaeus's protégés, Pehr Kalm, to North America. Kalm saw hosts of birch canoes, and journeyed in one of elmbark, quickly coming to the belief that this technology could spur the Swedish rural economy into an era of ascendancy. He and his pupil Anders Chydenius, whose father had been a priest among the Sámi, then toured northern Europe to seek European alternatives to North American materials. They learned that the birch of northeast Finland made the best substitute for American birch, and that spruce could stand in for hickory. The indigenous technologies of the Americas have been used by Finnish farmers ever since.

The nature of the Atlantic, as connective tissue not uncrossable abyss, is expressed in a multitude of ways. From Ireland and Scotland to Greenland and Newfoundland, the fauna of the shore is remarkably similar. As I travelled, auks, sandpipers, long-tailed ducks, and ospreys were regular company, even if some species had names like 'guillemot' in one zone and 'murre' in another. The humpback whales I would see in Greenland could be the very same individuals I watched in Barbados or Ireland. On his North American travels, Kalm even described much the same techniques for fishing with otters that I'd learned of among the Sámi:

> I have seen some which were as tame as dogs, and followed their masters wherever they went; if he went out in a boat, the otter went with him, jumped into the water, and after a while came up with a fish.

Much of this transatlantic affinity dries up on land: even a hundred yards from the shore, the bird species, mammals, and insects are dramatically different. Yet naturalists' understanding of the exceptions to this phenomenon have recently been transformed. One example is found in the ornithological idea of 'vagrants'. Birds appear on the 'wrong side' of the Atlantic with great regularity. A lifetime watching American great blue herons, whether on the shores of Nova Scotia or in the marshes of Nantucket, could easily include accidental sightings of grey herons just like those that can be observed on park ponds near Nuneaton or Nairn. This was once interpreted as the freakish result of storms and hurricanes, and the term 'vagrant' labelled these birds as accidental interlopers across an imagined Atlantic boundary.

Fuller data, however, has shown such movements to be not strange deviations but ordinary occurrences. Every year, grey herons use the conduits of wind and weather to cross the Atlantic by northern routes (Europe to Newfoundland) and southern routes (Africa to the Caribbean). They appear in Greenland, Iceland, the Azores, and Bermuda. They're engaged in the normal ways in which species' territories shift and flow. They're not, as birders have long assumed, 'lost', defective in their orientation or victims of bad weather. Grey herons are just running about half a century behind the cattle egret, which shifted its range across the Atlantic from Africa to South America in the 1950s, and many millennia behind the puffin, which once took the reverse route, from the Pacific via the Caribbean, to populate northern Europe. The idea of 'vagrancy' is one of countless ways in which the Atlantic has been conceptualised as breach or boundary rather than a space just as continuous as pasture, moorland, or highway.

To move from Europe to the Americas, though, is to cross vast gulfs of power in the dynamics of history. In the eighteenth century, the global economy was formed round Atlantic weather systems, as Europeans used trade winds and Gulf Stream to expand the 'triangular trade' in which enslaved peoples were forced to labour for the coffee and sugar that stained and rotted European teeth. These dynamics shaped settler expansion in the Americas and the dispossession of their peoples. Humans had crossed the Atlantic countless times before Columbus, but the century after he made getting lost into a world historical event marked a new scale of ambition in the building of European fortunes upon the exploitation of the Americas' resources, from silver and salt fish to human lives.

The Caribbean basin, in this era, became the centre of the world:

the histories of Africa, Eurasia, and the indigenous and settler Americas were woven into one story of wealth and subjugation. The making of the modern world occurred in the transformation of 'the masterless Caribbean' of freebooters and buccaneers into the settler colonies of plantations and enslavement. These were histories of large, many-masted coffin ships and seas policed by schooners. But they were also histories of small boats.

Some of the most significant and beautiful reinterpretations of modern history, such as Julius Scott's *The Common Wind* (2018), have been the result of bringing the perspectives of the small boat, rather than the schooner, to the forefront of the stories. Some of the most profound philosophies, such as Édouard Glissant's *Poetics of Relation* (1990), have arisen from the question of how the world looks from the little open boat of an African in the Indies rather than a European commanding the deck of a sailing ship. To move into the Americas is therefore to add layer upon layer of significance to the stories small boats can tell and to find a host of new ways for envisaging the power structures and politics of the modern world from within Atlantic waves.

One of the most emblematic rereadings of the Americas' past from a small-boat viewpoint comes in the work of the Canadian Cree artist Kent Monkman. In 2019, Monkman designed two paintings that put small wooden boats and their paddlers at the centre of every visitor's experience of the Metropolitan Museum of Art in New York. Called *mistikôsiwak (Wooden Boat People)*, this diptych re-envisages the arts of the Americas through the indigenous and non-binary lenses that Monkman's work is famed for. The two huge and colourful paintings were hung in the Met's imposing Graeco-Roman Great Hall, on either side of the entrance with its four grand Corinthian columns that symbolise the museum as a neoclassical temple of fine art.

The first of the paintings, *Welcoming the Newcomers*, shows the arrival of settler cultures in North America. Various figures, in the garb of French, English, or Spanish colonists scramble onto a rocky, verdant shore, where indigenous men and women save them from the rough sea. Four men cling to an overturned wooden rowing boat and a shark's fin passes between them and the safety of the shoreline. Spotlighted by the rising sun, Monkman's alter ego, Miss Chief Eagle Testickle, looks straight out of the canvas at the viewer. Dressed in nothing but a long red sliver of silk, high heels, and pride earrings, she helps a manacled African from the sea. She represents, Monkman says, the Cree values of *sakihitowin* ('love') and *wahkohtowin* ('kinship').

The second painting, *The Resurgence of the People*, depicts the displacement of indigenous peoples a century or two later. On a small rock surrounded by high swell four men wield guns. A wooden boat overflows with brightly dressed people, several holding traditional paddles. The enslaved African from *Welcoming the Newcomers* is now a doctor assisting those who flounder in the water. Miss Chief Eagle Testickle stands in heroic pose, gazing forward to the boat's destination and holding an eagle feather, while a figure by her side holds an indigenous coup stick as though it were a national flag. In this painting, Monkman explains, Miss Chief represents 'a certain strength that comes from our teachings' which show us 'actually how to get along with other cultures and get along with each other'.

Monkman began the process of conceptualising these paintings by wandering the Met's galleries and absorbing the scenes of encounter they held. These included European visions of romanticised indigenous people on the edge of extinction, 'vanishing' as bygone tradition gave way to heroic modernity. They also included myths of nation: the founding moments of the settler Americas. Monkman transmuted all these inputs into a wholesale rereading of the history of North America. And it's telling that this alternative vision should be constructed from the perspective of the small boat.

As the art historian Sasha Suda has written of these paintings,

Miss Chief 'find[s] power in claiming the boat as a means of transporting Indigenous peoples and their values into the future'. Symbolic boats populate many more of Monkman's paintings too: steam paddleboats represent modernity in scenes of displacement, and canoe paddles stand for indigenous values.

These wooden boats therefore become symbols for assessing what ideas such as 'nation building' might mean in the modern world. Where the older paintings in the gallery presented mastery over land and people as the measure of victory, Monkman uses the weather-blown wooden boat to reject this. He places oceanic migration and displacement as the foundational events of the modern world and shows viewers that the nature of the societies we build is predicated on whose perspectives we choose to take on them.

Monkman also stresses the ways Miss Chief and her wooden boats subvert the linear pasts of history writing and western art, presenting instead a vision that bounds acrobatically through centuries:

> When I inhabit that character of Miss Chief it allows me to be present in history and I think that's something that I can't do just as Kent Monkman the artist. I can really place Miss Chief deep, deep into history hundreds of years ago, thousands or millions of years ago. I've created her as this legendary being that's existed for millions of years. By putting Miss Chief into these historical moments it makes history come alive by making it personal, by making it human, and so I have Miss Chief living in these different time periods as a way to just connect people to the humanity, to the emotional experience of what it means to live through these historical experiences.

How we choose to interpret water, shores, time, and the small traditional boats in which many peoples have navigated all three, is, Monkman shows, key to making sense of what our world has been and could be.

CROSSINGS AND CONNECTIONS

From Greenland sea ice to blazing Caribbean heat, rowing and paddling the shores of the west Atlantic meant exposure to ways of conceptualising the relations of past and present, and of people and power, that are remarkably different from those I'm most familiar with. Small boats have a symbolic significance there that they've often lost elsewhere, and so the revivals and resurgences of the early twenty-first century have had a particular potency. Everywhere, however, these boats express values at odds with the ideas of progress and conformity as universally good. Every small boat expresses alternatives. Every oar- or paddle-stroke ripples with possibilities.

5

Kalaallit Nunaat/Greenland
Home Is Where the Umiaq Is

I

Qajartuarpoq

THROUGHOUT THE VAST Inuit world, poets make qajaqs into symbols of resilience, change, and the passing of time. One of the most evocative examples, dg nanouk okpik's 'Inupiaq Women' (2022), conveys the joys and hardships of living in transitional times. A kayaker paddles out past salt flats to find still fishing waters. Her sun- and wind-chapped cheeks show her status as a woman subsisting for her young family:

> In body, in Inuit, she thrives on the
>   bleakest
> ecstatic love. Here on her knees,
> in her seal skin buoyant boat,
> her duties of her village complete,
> she knows her place among the caribou
> women.

KALAALLIT NUNAAT/GREENLAND

Her children, who'll eat her catch, are indoors, gaming, with their headphones on. They live in the timeframe of the transnational networks of gamers and gaming forums. They don't live in the timeframe of tradition or the sacred time of local rivers. They

> will not follow her in the knowledge of ice,
> dressing a caribou, preparing dry-fish,
> jarring jellies, dip netting hooligans,
> purse netting whitefish, tracking
> and setting traps for marmot, squirrels,
> arctic fox and wolverines.

In Greenland, on the other side of Inuit space, several leading voices explore these same themes. Katti Frederiksen – kayaker, marathon runner, poet, and former Minister for Education – makes the qajaq a central image of this negotiation between old cultures and a new global order. In Frederiksen's Greenlandic-language poem 'Ijaajjajjaa' (2006), a respected hunter is made to relocate to the city and loses his qajaq paddle. He forgets the details of his birthplace as he negotiates an urban world that he can only experience as if through fog. He attempts to live according to the old values, securing shelter for his family, and expecting care from them in turn 'like the days of old required'. He makes the parts of his qajaq into toys for his daughter's baby but soon afterwards is haunted by dreams of capsizing. It is always things that happen to his qajaq that signify the struggle to adapt. Frederiksen interprets the threats to Inuit culture in terms of industrialisation that took place too quickly to permit cultural adaptation.

All qajaq poems seem, in one way or another, to be about loss: framing the distance between today's children and their ancestors. But they are also almost always about the joy and freedom of being on the water. This is a venerable tradition. One poem, already old when recorded by a 1920s Danish expedition to the most northerly Inuit settlements, described how, when out on a 'small adventure', a kayaker realised a rising offshore wind spelled danger. Everyday worries, 'that I thought so big', suddenly faded into realisation that

>there is only
>One great thing,
>The only thing:
>To live and see in huts and on journeys
>The great day that dawns
>And the light that fills the world.

To be in a qajaq amid the most spectacular fjords in the world, beneath vast ice floes, with the crack of bergs and the breath of whales the only things to punctuate the sunlit silence, is to test your capacity for joy to the extreme.

In some parts of Greenland, the living culture of the qajaq is now two or three generations gone. But in others it has been protected from the inroads of industrialised fishing by both strong local commitment and sea ice so persistent that the old ways of sled and paddled boat remain the best ways to negotiate this ever-shifting icescape. This local safeguarding of a non-mechanised small-boat tradition, persisting as a complete way of life, is unique in the North Atlantic. It persists despite the pressures to modernise that long contrasted 'outdated' Inuit tradition with European industrial progress and, in the words of Katti Frederiksen, succeeded in making Greenland's Inuit 'ignorant of how advanced they really were'.

In the heyday of those pressures to progress, in the mid-twentieth century, qajaqs existed in their thousands in remote rural settlements, but in the thrustingly modern capital city, Nuuk, where Greenland's politics and identity were formed, there were almost none. Yet, by the 1970s, something remarkable was underway. The qajaq took centre stage in a rediscovery of Greenland's past and a determination to reinterpret that past through Inuit, rather than Danish, eyes.

At the heart of this rediscovery were events of a century earlier. In the mid-nineteenth century, two Danish art collectors, Hinrich and Signe Rink, had befriended an Inuit artist called Aron, from the islet of Kangeq, two hours by qajaq from Nuuk. Aron was skilled in all the things valued on a small island. He was a renowned kayaker, who also worked with wood and stone to build everything from boats to houses. And he possessed an equally esteemed talent for passing down island stories through generations. Current Inuit memory holds many centuries of local family story, and Aron's own cache of tales reached back far into pre-colonial times.

Interested in Aron's narration of Greenland's past, the Rinks encouraged him to write and paint the stories of figures from history and myth. This, naturally, included many of the great kayakers. He made several images of one particular paddler, a kind of patron saint of kayakers, famed for his skill in a towering sea. In this story, the seafarer was caught in a storm, but was saved by a seabird who taught him the song the gulls used to glide through chaos. With this more-than-human insight he became the greatest of all seafarers and spent so much time joyously paddling the storms that he lost his hearing and left the world of human conversation behind. There were beautiful elements to the story, but also grisly ones (the seafarer's wife threw herself in the ocean because he refused to fulfil his land-bound duties). Much about the Greenlandic passion for the qajaq seems to be captured in this tale.

The Rinks took Aron's work and gave it to the National Museum of Denmark. There, his stories and paintings were buried and forgotten, until they were rediscovered in the 1960s. Only after years of pressure were 160 of his works returned to Greenland in 1982. Suddenly he began to be called 'the national artist' and 'the father of Greenlandic art'. Over the next few years, there were exhibitions, broadcasts, and films based on Aron's painting. Twenty-four of his pictures became an Advent calendar, while a band was formed to record settings of the stories he passed down.

Until this point, no qajaq from before the twentieth century was displayed in any museum in Greenland, while many that had been taken by European whalers were on show in Denmark, the Netherlands, Scotland, and England. It's still the case that someone researching the boats of the Inuit world is as likely to have to visit London as Labrador. But, in 1983, three older qajaqs were returned from Amsterdam, and they became part of the same quest for cultural reclamation that spurred the celebration of Aron's art.

Few could have predicted the wide-ranging impact of the display of these historic vessels. A group of young Greenlanders became so fascinated by them that they formed a new organisation called Qaannat Kattuffiat (the Greenland Kayak Association). Their aim was to make the leap from admiring the qajaqs of the past to promoting the qajaq as a practical part of everyday city life. They hoped to encourage Greenlanders back onto the water and revive the skills of historic sea travel. Soon young people could be seen wandering Nuuk in T-shirts emblazoned with *Qajaq-Atoqqilerparput*, a typically efficient slogan that translates as: 'The Kayak: We Are Starting to Use It Again'.

For forty years, Qaannat Kattuffiat has championed far more than just a boat, showing how qajaqs are tied to the ways in which Greenland was known and navigated by millennia of Inuit peoples. One widely repeated slogan adapts local myth to emphasise that a qajaq is an extension of a paddler's limbs and a link between a Greenlander and the seasonal ebb and flow of sea ice:

> In ancient times, Greenland's hunters wanted to learn how to walk on the sea. The only spirit that allowed that was the winter spirit. The summer spirit gave them the qajaq.

KALAALLIT NUNAAT/GREENLAND

Qaannat Kattuffiat has now built a global presence, with chapters around Greenland, in the USA, Denmark, and Japan. They coordinate gatherings, expeditions, and days out, as well as world championship races and qajaq-rolling contests that are held in Greenland every year. At their 'Paddlers' Retreat' festivals, small numbers of people meet to build qajaqs, fashion paddles, and craft *tuillit* (the one-piece hooded suits worn by traditional kayakers).

The range of skills these events preserve is astonishing, and is embodied in the way the famous Greenland rolls put other kayakers' skills to shame. Whenever I set out to battle waves, but a wave wins and knocks me in the sea, I have a single clumsy roll with which I right myself, achieved not with an elegant flick of the hips but a crude yank of the paddle that's regularly mocked by better kayakers. An accomplished paddler might know a handful of different twists to achieve this manoeuvre. In the rolling competitions run by Qaannat Kattuffiat, there aren't just two or three, but nearly forty different styles of hip-flick roll in which a Greenlander will be proficient. Contests to test kayaking skill don't just happen on the water, but in virtuosic displays of balance, timing, and dexterity on suspended slacklines.

I'd booked myself a session in the sea at Nuuk to try to learn some of these rolls. My instructor seemed bewildered by the lack of flexibility in my hips, and in practical terms all I gained was a greater sense of how much I didn't know. This session, though, was profoundly useful as an introduction to qajaq terminology. I wrote down lists of words for qajaq-related acts. I particularly loved those individual terms which would require whole sentences to express in less boat-oriented languages: *qaannerivoq* means 'to do maintenance work on a qajaq'; *qaannivoq* means 'to haul a qajaq onto land'; *qajalukaq* means 'to begin to learn kayaking'; while, best of all, *qajartuarpoq* means 'to kayak simply for the joy of it'.

II

The Ice Fjord

On a small Danish island, in the middle of the nineteenth century, Carl Rasmussen was the eldest of eleven children of a master tailor. At fifteen, he went to Copenhagen to learn hosiery, but instead he fell in love with the paintings he saw in the big city and began training as an artist. He was in love, too, with the sea, and took passage as a cabin boy on a ship destined for Scotland, painting the ocean along the way. By 1863, he was exhibiting these paintings, but he was eager for a wider range of ocean worlds to work from. By 1870, he raised the funds to travel to Greenland and make the sketches on which his short career would be built. Twenty-three years later, on the return journey of another trip to Greenland, he and his easel were swept overboard while he tried to sketch a stormy sea and they were never seen again.

Rasmussen's most famous paintings show wild historic seas filled with boats, whales, and icebergs, or snowy mountainsides where families await a sealer's return. But one that particularly caught my imagination was a scene of an Inuit community in Nuuk Fjord in 1871. This picture was beloved of 1870s Danes, and turned into an engraving that was widely circulated in magazines.

The painting shows flat seas and blue skies, with the mountains in the fjord serenely snow-clad. In the foreground are two large Inuit family boats: umiaq. Each is being rowed by four women seated one to a bench in the boat's bows. They're smartly dressed in white, red, and blue, with a variety of snug and colourful hats. In the stern of each umiaq is a person with a steering oar, and in the middle of the boat are more women and several children. The children's depiction, in particular, is beautifully casual: one has their legs dangling freely over the gunwales. There are at least two men in the umiaq as well. One shows a curious child a tiny object of interest. The women are engaged in conversation between the two umiaq, their characterful faces angled to the viewer. Light glows through the stretched skin of the boat, its translucency revealing the detailed structure of the frame beneath. In the middleground, four qajaqs depart across the glistening fjord. The paddlers' faces are turned away from the viewer, and the emphasis is on their sealskin hoods and the inflated sealskin buoys stowed behind them. Their paddles are thin driftwood sticks, as was the Greenland standard.

The name of the painting is *Spring Day Returning from the Hunt*. It depicts a stage in the seasonal movement of Inuit people from settlements at the ocean's edge, where seals were hunted in winter, to the camps by the open fjord where spring fishing took place. They'd then take mobile summer camps to the tundra and high fells. These were more than a hundred kilometres deep into the fjord at the edge of the ice cap. They were where people met the migrating caribou. Some Inuit, by the time their annual round was complete, would have travelled many hundreds of kilometres to reach these caribou grounds. The cheerful faces of the seafarers in Rasmussen's painting sit neatly with many accounts from the eighteenth and nineteenth centuries that described the anticipation with which Inuit communities looked forward to the spring voyage into the inner fjords.

The goal of my first Greenland journey was to follow these routes from Nuuk to the edge of the ice, exploring the many histories of one of the largest and grandest fjord systems in the world. I arrived in storms, and passed five days waiting out the weather, before Nuuk Fjord transformed into the blue-glazed idyll painted by Rasmussen. Knowing the dangers of failing to stay dry through nights at Greenland's low temperatures, I'd chosen to travel a little less light than usual, with a tiny pole-less one-kilogram tent to protect my waterproof sleeping bag. But the sun, rather than the cold, was my main cause for concern: trying to sleep through bright Arctic nights in this thin yellow tent, which seemed only to accentuate the glare of the midnight sun, felt the kind of misjudgement only someone who'd never been to Greenland before would have made.

For most of the first sixty kilometres of Nuuk Fjord, the shores are bare and abrupt. They're walls of grey rock, with veins of snow that reach sea level, and ice-clad peaks that often look impossible in the drama of their pinnacles and overhangs. On long stretches of unbreachably cliffy coast, my breaks would be spent on little shelves beneath precipices, rather than on beaches I could have walked inland from.

Within an hour of leaving the city, I was looking up at the exact spot that was the backdrop for Rasmussen's painting. The charismatic mountain Sermitsiaq dominated the vista, while the last remnants of the morning's sea-level cloud were fading into nothingness. Suddenly the first humpback whale of the day broke the surface. My view to the north wasn't of the fjord's far shore, but of the great narrow islands that crouch at its heart. Some of these islands are themselves vast: twenty to forty kilometres long and ridged with layer after layer of pewter-grey mountain.

The islands are significant for the human uses of the fjord since they create narrows where the arrival of humpback whales, narwhals, seals, and shoals can be observed. Such narrows are scattered with historic sites above and below the waterline. Many are extravagantly ancient, but some were settlements within living memory. One such site is Qoornoq, a village of pretty, colourful houses, with church and fish factory, which was emptied by government decree in 1972. Descendants of its residents still keep the houses looking bright and clean.

As I passed the southern end of the first island, a US Coastguard boat raced up, convinced I must be here by accident, but willing to let me paddle on once I assured them my course was intentional.

KALAALLIT NUNAAT/GREENLAND

Other than that encounter, my progress was slowed only by the whales, whose sudden slounges from the sea looked impossibly grand beneath stupendous arrays of rock and ice. Their great black backs and white, barnacled tails rolled past repeatedly and I found it impossible to tell whether I was seeing significant numbers of different whales or being accompanied by one or two. In general, though, I could make good pace, the shelter of the fjord and the gentle breeze at my back speeding me along.

For my first two and a half days, I paddled parallel to a peninsula that runs from Nuuk in the west to the ice cap a hundred kilometres to the east. There are no real paths on that long landmass, but a series of tiny mountain huts dot a route across the peaks and bays. Occasionally people trek this trail, though they often find one hut or another derelict and filled with snow. Hikers are warned to plan on taking at least an hour for every kilometre, such is the challenge of the terrain. This meant that in just a morning with the tide I could cover more distance than a hiker in two days. It's no surprise that, before steamships, it was the 'qajaq post' that took letters and packages between settlements. Hundreds of paddlers crept along thousands of miles of shore, and a complex society was sustained by exchange of information in one-person sealskin boats.

As I edged my way along the mountainsides, and camped beside the stones of ancient tent rings, I did all I could to imagine the annual umiaq voyages and the visions of life they were crucial to. Inuit thought knits people into this sea in many ways. Hila, the goddess of the natural order and of human thought, binds nature and consciousness together, so that weather and health, sea-state and mood, are always entangled. After death, the souls of humans and animals return to the bottom of the ocean for assignment to new physical forms by Sedna, the sea goddess. One Inuit proverb holds that 'the great peril of our existence lies in the fact that our diet consists entirely of souls'. Not knowing whether humanity or sealhood was your future fate was an unrivalled recipe for respect and coexistence despite the need to hunt.

The umiaq was a product of this deep environmental knowledge. Where the qajaq was historically used for journeys of a single day, the umiaq was the true connecting link over distances. In the inner fjords I was travelling, many place names have 'umiaq' elements, tying place and boat together even after the vessels have long gone. The umiaq was defined by its huge capacity: the greatest of any historic skin boat. On hunting trips, it was the station at sea where the catch was prepared, and the vessel that allowed the community to travel together. In West Greenland it was a steep-sided boat, with a large flat bottom, in contrast to the more gradual flair of the bowl-like East Greenland craft.

In Barrow, in Alaska, traditional umiaq are still used for moving camp, for hunting in the spring, and for racing in July. They're dragged by dog sled to the far edge of the sea ice and launched into what is essentially the heart of the deep open ocean. Current residents maintain their belief that these are the best boats to have around ice. Descriptions of them emphasise the absolute silence with which a well-coordinated crew can paddle, building speed while barely breaking the water. But they emphasise robustness and convenience too. As one Barrow resident puts it:

> You just can't beat a skin boat. They are fast, light, and tough. Some crews do have canvas boats, some fiberglass. This year a fiberglass boat had to go back because they hit the ice and got a hole. You can't beat a skin boat.

The sheer scale of the umiaq demanded great ingenuity in working the products of the shore. Driftwood was shaped into complex joinery, with hook scarfs and mortice joints. Pegs of tusk or antler, alongside strips of baleen, held joints fast. Even fish vertebrae were put to use, sliced to form the rings that fastened straps together. Sealskin lashings held the shell of skins to the wooden frame. Each lashing was fed through dozens of small holes cut in the wood with bone-tip drills. The extremely time-consuming task of drilling would, in many cases, have simply made the vessel ever so slightly faster and quieter on the water; that such great effort was put into this marginal gain shows the significance of the boat. Umiaq shells could be made from as many as thirty sealskins (in contrast to the three skins that formed many qajaqs).

No instance has been found of an umiaq with intensively cured or treated skins, which means that all those we know of were exclusively coastal boats. Keeping them seaworthy, without danger of waterlogging or disintegration, required their removal from the water every night. They needed to be cared for like a living thing. But such requirements were naturally turned into advantages. The umiaq didn't go unused while it dried out on land: with the windward gunwale on the ground, and the other held a few feet high by poles, it became the perfect tent-like home. A lamp, in the form of a wide soapstone bowl filled with whale oil, was lit at the centre. At the same time as making the upturned umiaq into a cosy home, this sped up the overnight drying process.

The further into the fjord I paddled, the more often steep cliffs gentled into fertile slopes. Every area of flat land had its historic remains, whether Inuit camp, Norse farm, or Danish outpost. Many sites had been all these things and more. At the edge of the ice cap, thin bands of rough, flowering tundra run for hundreds of kilometres. My target, by the third day, was a spot where mountain, fjord, and tundra meet at a staggeringly picturesque settlement called Kapisillit. Here the houses slope upwards from a shapely bay which sits below the lake and river that give the place its name. The name simply means 'salmon' in Kalaallisut, and the species of salmon that breeds at this spot exists nowhere else on earth. From here, there are craggy mountain views in all directions.

During the twentieth century, several island communities from around Nuuk Fjord were relocated to Kapisillit in an effort to commercialise the region, but villagers still feel their ties to the old places, so their knowledge of the fjord ranges wide across both space and time. In 1939, a trading station for cod and fox fur was built by the shore, and from 1948 to 1960 a school, fish-preserving factory, and church followed. By this time, there were 302 inhabitants on a spot that had become a town.

The population today has dropped to fifty-three, but I was taken aback by how bustling Kapisillit felt. On this calm, sunny day, the little jetty was busy with local people, and the central play area was used by an improbable number of children. A sea eagle hopped around the village and little birds, mainly Lapland longspurs, flitted between willow shrubs. A man in his eighties who was walking with a stick sat beside me on steps that had been used that morning for cleaning fish. He asked about my plans, and when I told him my route he marked on my map the hunting trips he took to trap Arctic foxes fifty years ago. He pointed out where the ice used to be thickest for walking across the ice fjord to the traps on the opposite shore, but said that no one did that any more. He told me the meanings of some places on the bay, such as Neriunaq, the 'Place of Opportunities'. I asked him about boats and he said his family used to row an umiaq westwards in summer, loaded with tents for camping and fishing, but that only motors were used now. I hadn't realised until this conversation that the move to seasonal settlements for fishing cod and Arctic char continued within recent memory. When he mentioned a church camp where Nuuk children were brought each summer to experience life away from roads and cars, he made Nuuk sound unthinkably distant – he might as well have been talking about Los Angeles or Tokyo.

Opposite Kapisillit are structures left over from the drive in the 1950s and 1960s to commercialise the bay. The biggest are from an attempt to farm reindeer commercially, which between 1953 and 1961 had 3,000 animals, though the cost of raising them was always higher than the price they could fetch. The largest venture since that time is currently being planned: the region's first hotel, which the people I spoke to welcomed as a step towards securing the village's future, rather than as a threat to its community. Kapisillit is sometimes written about as though it's an invention of twentieth-century economic experiments. But it felt entirely unsurprising, while standing at this meeting place of tundra, mountain, river, and sea, to learn that the spot had been chosen by peoples of small boats for four millennia or more. It had been known to Inuit as Nunaqarfigssuaq (the 'Great Settlement'), and there are remains of many old winter dwellings and tent rings around the modern village. The bay here would once have been filled with umiaq as soon as the sea ice melted each spring. And at the height of summer they would have journeyed around the peninsula from which I was about to hike into the heart of the inner fjord.

The earliest archaeological evidence nearby stretches back to Greenland's beginnings. It was left by the Saqqaq people, who hunted seals in open water. In those warmer times, the ice margin was between thirty and eighty kilometres inland from today's glaciers. A lock of hair from one West Greenland site was used in 2010 to confirm the Saqqaq as a migratory culture, which crossed via Baffin Bay from Siberia five millennia ago. Though most Saqqaq sites now lie below sea level, two of the most significant are on the shores of the fjord, not far from Kapisillit. The Saqqaq loved to work with a grey metamorphosed slate called *killiaq*, which they carved and drilled. This slate is found at just a handful of West Greenland sites, where quarrying happened on a staggeringly large scale. They also worked in stones such as agate and quartz, and tools have sometimes been found at immense distances from the places these were quarried, revealing huge networks of exchange. Saqqaq works also show great skill in carpentry: they had no shortage of driftwood for tools and fires, thanks to Greenland's raised beaches where the seas dumped tree trunks. Their hunters used bows, and their middens show a diverse diet of berries, molluscs, and at least forty-five species of vertebrates, including deep-sea fish and seabirds.

Until the 1980s, there was no direct evidence of Saqqaq boats, and some even doubted their existence, but in 1988 excavators published the discovery of fragments from two very different wooden frames, which they interpreted as a slender qajaq and a sturdy umiaq. Fragments of driftwood paddles were also found. This was a transformative moment, which extended the history of the region's boats by millennia.

Around the ninth century BC, however, temperatures in Greenland dropped and ice crept west to engulf the coast. This meant the Saqqaq approach to open-water hunting lost its efficacy, and Saqqaq tools soon disappeared from the archaeological record. Evidence of one of the great creative cultures of the ancient and medieval worlds, known as the Dorset, begins to appear in these same coves a few centuries later. Their small communities, often no more than twenty people, were profoundly well adapted to the cold. The Dorset culture spanned 2,000 years and tens of thousands of Arctic miles (it's named after Cape Dorset, the colonial name for Kinngait in Nunavut, where the artefacts that led to the identification originated). They manufactured prodigiously, making snow knives, sled shoes, and soapstone lamps. Soapstone was among their most valued resources, though it could be quarried only at a few Greenland sites. A small island near Kapisillit, called Umanaq (the 'Heart-Shaped Island'), on which soapstone runs deep, was a major site of Dorset industry. Soapstone lamps were crucial to cold climate living. They allowed families to stay warm, cook, melt ice for drinking water, thaw meat, and dry clothes. It's likely that lamps were kept permanently alight, burning blubber and animal oils, their wick tended night and day and shortened or lengthened to lessen or increase the heat and light they offered.

It has been argued that Dorset people pulled their own sleds, since no evidence has been found of dogs, and this led some commentators to see their lives as gruelling and unhappy. But there are many reasons to question this. Research around the world has shown that the kind of small social units they lived in produce exceptional senses of purpose and belonging. The anthropologist James Woodburn has written of the small hunter-gatherer groups he spent his life researching that members value their way of life to an exceptional degree, seeing it as a 'wonderful life' because 'they have a living which makes sense'. But rather than speculative comparisons, the best evidence that Dorset people's lives were not brutal and harsh is the artwork they produced. They were among the great aesthetic makers of the pre-modern world, no less accomplished than the sculptors of Greece and Rome. Their artefacts can be found in almost every museum within 500 miles of the Arctic, and scholars of the Dorset culture have long insisted that specialist artists existed even in the tiniest communities. This implies a surplus of food and goods, not to mention extensive leisure time and a highly trained, and shared, aesthetic sense.

The earliest scholarship, from the 1960s, recognises humour and 'creative joy' in the exquisite carving the Dorset conducted, but assumes its purpose to have been entirely shamanistic and magical. Some carvings are naturalistic visions of seals, others are stylised polar bears, while still others depict as many as sixty faces in a single antler tine. Recent interpretations argue that the use of terms such as 'ritualistic' to categorise the functions of this ancient art risks failing to recognise the improvisatory brilliance of its creators and the rich diversity of their culture. The appreciation of these artworks also suffers today because of our habits in relation to art. Artworks tend to be seen in photos or behind glass, but Dorset works have no single viewing angle and are intended to be handled, turned over, and observed in all dimensions.

As with Saqqaq culture, scholars long insisted that the Dorset had no watercraft but hunted through holes in the ice the marine creatures that they ate. To this day, no items that are unequivocally parts of boats have been found at Dorset sites, though some scholars have made strong cases for qajaq ribs and even toy qajaqs among their goods. This absence of physical evidence of boats is not unusual. The ancient 'Red Paint People' of the Maine coast, for instance, traded with Newfoundland and caught large numbers of swordfish. Their diet could only have been caught from boats, yet not a scrap of evidence for their vessels has ever been found. They don't seem to have possessed the tools to make birchbark canoes, and their climate was too warm for skin boats of the Arctic kind to function. If it wasn't for the swordfish bones, scholarly authorities would surely insist that these people too had no watercraft of any kind.

It's a remarkable feature of research in the Arctic that oral history provides as much evidence of eras a thousand years ago as does archaeology. Inuit memory is long and is frequently confirmed by subsequent discoveries. Throughout Inuit culture there are memories of 'Tuniit', a people much like the Inuit except taller, who were already in Greenland and other Arctic regions when the Inuit arrived. They were able, the stories say, to lift a walrus almost as easily as an Inuk can lift a seal. Many old songs and stories feature the Tuniit, or are said to have been written by them. These stories recount largely peaceable relations in which the main focus of conflict was the Tuniit love for qajaqs, which they frequently 'borrowed' from Inuit, often without asking. One legend of why the Tuniit disappeared tells that, after an Inuit boy killed a sleeping Tuniq for stealing his qajaq, the Tuniit feared the more numerous Inuit would kill them all. They bundled up their goods, tied their long hair into topknots, and set out, never to be seen again. From 1955 onwards, several scholars have come round to the possibility that 'Dorset' and 'Tuniit' might be two names for the same culture.

The warming seas of the tenth century AD brought new interest in Nuuk Fjord, and, in an innovation sometimes described as the greatest marketing slogan in history, the new arrivals dreamed up the name 'Greenland'. This name was first used in the 980s by a Norse settler, Eric the Red, to persuade his compatriots to join him in settling the vast island. But the description was more apt than is often imagined. When Eric arrived, at the start of the Medieval Warm Period, the land truly was green. The Norse recognised the shores of Greenland's fjords as better prospects for farming than the lava-strewn earth they'd left behind in Iceland. There were birch groves, juniper, and willow scrub for fodder and fuel. There were plants such as lyme grass, rarely used as human food but whose grain was relished by the Norse.

Sweeping out from the main expanse of Nuuk Fjord are many smaller waterways, each a mighty fjord in its own right. These provided huge, sheltered arenas for Norse fishing and the raising of crops and livestock. This sheltered zone was well placed, too, for risky summer expeditions into the icy north, which gave access to unspeakable riches of walrus ivory, narwhal tusks, polar bear pelts, and gyrfalcons as well as resulting in encounters with the Thule (the ancestors of modern Inuit). The Norse use of these geographies was the reverse of every other culture: where others primarily drew on the resources of oceanic regions and treated the tundra and caribou of the inner fjords as supplementary, the Norse used the inner fjords' flora as their staple and the ocean for their surplus. As long as the value of walrus ivory in Europe remained high, Greenland could make its Norse settlers wealthy.

The biggest farm the settlers built, Sandnes, was a short distance south of Kapisillit, but around a hundred sites of Norse farms have been identified around the fjord, including two on the outskirts of the village itself. Many of these are still visible to the paddler. Since I had no connection to the outside world while I travelled, it was only later that I could check my guesses about such sites. When I did, I learned that if a coastal site looks a likely place for the Norse to build a farm, it's pretty much guaranteed that they did. Streams and lakes, formed by ice-melt, gave plentiful water, while herds of reindeer provided hunting not unlike that in Scandinavia. This rich little enclave thrived for 400 years, until the climate cooled once more, bringing encroaching ice and shorter summers. At the same time, the value of walrus ivory in Europe plummeted. With these combined misfortunes, even these skilled farmers couldn't keep their settlements afloat, and the little Norse enclaves faded away like the Saqqaq and Dorset peoples before them.

From this time until the eighteenth century, the Thule and their Inuit descendants, had the island to themselves. In their early centuries here, Thule peoples moved into every major fjord system and made use of the many opportunities the cooling climate created, proving more adaptable than the settled Norse could ever have been. Over these centuries, Inuit knowledge of the island's icescapes, and of how to live well in them, flourished into a profound and diverse body of knowledge captured in the phrase *Inuit Qaujimajatuqangit* ('what Inuit know'). It will surely never be equalled.

But, in 1721, the large wooden ships of Scandinavian seafarers returned to Nuuk Fjord, this time not just as farmers but as evangelists and empire builders. When the missionary Hans Egede failed to confirm the idea that had brought him here – that he'd find centuries-old Scandinavian communities deep in Nuuk Fjord – he set about converting Inuit instead. For nearly two centuries, the Danish Royal Greenland Trade Department oversaw the incorporation of Greenland's small islands and villages into European commercial society. Amid the sweeping industrialisation that followed, many small Inuit communities were lost. Islands such as

Aron's Kangeq were abandoned. But Kapisillit stands today as a place that straddles the commercial present and the pasts that remain legible in its environs and meaningful to its residents.

I rolled my packraft into my rucksack and set out from Kapisillit on foot to cover the few short miles to the ice fjord. I'd moved now from mountainous coast into more fertile tundra and found a landscape to fall in love with. I was now forced to travel swaddled in unbroken clothing: my skin had turned a sunburnt pink and the skies were relentlessly clear but for the splayed wings of soaring eagles and distant forks of geese.

The sensory experience of this trudge through tundra was astounding. The smell of vegetation was often so intense it could be tasted like honey on the air. Swathes of thick lemony herbs released their aromatics underfoot, and wildflowers and flowering mosses lined the watercourses. Grey willow shrubs in dense thickets sometimes reached waist height and slowed me to a stumble. One of the most plentiful and pungent herbs was a plant I found myself sleeping on that evening, and its smell shapes my memory of the bright Greenland nights. These plants have long, thin leaves with pointed ends and so are called *qajaasat* ('qajaq lookalikes'). They're used here as a spice, as tea, and as a cure for colds. There were saxifrage, alpine azalea, Arctic thyme, and small buds of angelica. Greenlanders eat angelica, called *kuannit*, raw with sugar, as people elsewhere eat rhubarb, and rhubarb itself is *kuanniisat* ('angelica lookalike'). Many other flowers are used by Greenlanders in ways I'd never eaten elsewhere, in delicacies such as harebell jelly.

After wading the Kapisillit River, past Norse remains so close to the bank that the farmers must almost have been able to snatch salmon from their doorway, I climbed onto a small ridge, from which the gentlest of slopes stretched north and east down to the ice fjord. This large space, referred to locally as 'the meadow', was a botanist's dream, each fragment a miniature world of different flowering plants. A lone Arctic fox ran off in the distance, and a pair of reindeer, perhaps a remnant from the failed farm, watched me with suspicion. Lapland longspurs flitted from low foliage like pipits might in Britain. Beyond this slope, the ice fjord extends some fifty kilometres from northwest to southeast. At several places on its eastern shore, the ice cap sags down to the sea, calving slowly into the ocean. At others, lush glacial tunnel valleys rise from the water's edge and climb gently through the mountain ranges beyond. This is an entirely different climate from the world of bare rock and ocean just a few kilometres away: it's a place hospitable to anyone.

 I set up my little tent on a knuckle of land on the western shore where broken blocks of drift ice ground past on three sides. I was beside the ruins of structures identified as a *qarmaq* village from the eighteenth century. These were transitional settlements, used in spring and autumn when the weather wasn't warm enough for tents, but the snow not heavy enough to require winter homes. It's likely people came to the one I camped beside just as the ice fjord melted, seeking the harp seals that fed there. The *qarmat* themselves would once have had solid earthen walls but skin roofs (sometimes double layered, with heather in between for insulation).

 Until coming here, I'd never seen an ice fjord and had never paddled with icebergs. I was full of anticipation for the next day's paddle to the ice cap. My excitement seemed matched to the night life of the ice fjord which was noisy and joyous. Once the sun was behind the hills and the glare reduced, I could gaze into the water and see thousands of invertebrates flit beneath the ice. They were the food which brought everything else. Coos, squawks, wingbeats, and scratches issued from between the bergs and faces of diving birds would, from time to time, pop up behind the ice. But my favourite sights were the little flotillas of black ducks, often sleeping, which would float past on their flat white platforms. Some were just feet away, but oblivious to my presence. From long-tailed ducks to mergan-

Midnight by the ice fjord in the inconveniently yellow tent

Ready to launch into the first ice fjord

The charismatic longtailed ducks that were constant company between icebergs

As I look up from the water, a fulmar wheels in front of an iceberg, half a mile long, as though it was a seacliff

Bay punt and asters

The little red boat
beneath the boat house

A rodney in Jerome Canning's workshop, Winterton

Taking two rodneys into Trinity Bay, with hundred-year-old make-and-break engines

Rowing up to the front of Lowell's Boat Shop, the home of Maine dories

In the legendary workshop

Fall at the shoreline

Egrets in salt marshes, protected by sandbars from the surf

A night sleeping on the sandbar

A great blue heron crosses the sea

Danny and family taking out pots he'd built in their Moses boat

A Moses boat tops the swell on the fishing grounds west of Six Men's

sers, these species were all familiar, but their appearance was not. In full summer breeding plumage, in these nutrient-rich waters, black feathers were rich with shimmering iridescence, while white down was dazzling. Red and golden eyes and bright bills gave every waterbird a regal air to match their haughty willingness to stare me down.

There was no true dark, but a world purpled. At midnight, the ice took on new shades of pink and gold to contrast its turquoise hues in daylight. On my soft bed of foliage, at this stunning water's edge and with the promise of another sunlit day ahead, I felt safe, secure, and as warm as I could ever have wished. I didn't know whether my little boat and I could paddle the miles of ice I'd planned next day, but I felt no pressure to succeed. If all I learned was that I lacked the tools and talents of past kayakers, then that would be lesson enough in this achingly beautiful seascape.

The next morning did indeed reveal the challenges ice can pose. At 4 a.m., but with the sun already riding high, I launched among the little bergs. Exercising extreme caution at first, in case sharp ice should tear my vessel, I negotiated my way through narrow, mazy channels, each paddle-stroke sending icy lumps spinning through the water. The fjord is a consistent three to four kilometres wide, and the ice cap and the places I was aiming for were on the opposite shore some ten kilometres upstream. Though there was tidal movement that made my morning easier than my afternoon, the downstream flow outweighed incoming tides so that I always had to work against the drift of ice. In this way, the journey was very different, and far harder, than my icy ventures further north would be. The first thing I learned was that although the watery passageways are evident from an elevated vantage, they're far harder to follow from below the tops of the bergs: I never knew what routes or blockages might lie beyond the next hulk of ice and so I often found myself back-paddling while ice closed in around me, like the walls of a shrinking room in a horror film. The enclosed space of the fjord also made the ice loud: the grate and crunch of moving ice on stone or against other bergs was constant.

I took my time experiencing the ice. Twice, though only when it was extremely safe to do so, with icebergs grounded in shallows a few feet deep, I climbed up onto them to check out routes ahead and take photos of these scenes. With a surprising lack of rivers running into the fjord, beyond a few silty runnels, I found that breaking off small chunks of iceberg, as many Kalaallit Inuit do to make coffee, was the best way to quench my thirst. I spent most of the day negotiating a very short distance, but was forced to land a kilometre or so before my target, when the ice thickened too much to paddle through. Eventually, on foot, I reached a venerable landing site at a flat place called Umivik. This is the kind of site famed as a gathering point between camps, where the umiaq would be left and old friends would meet. There are stories of disputes being solved with singing contests at sites like this, and the communal building whose roots are still visible might date to as early as 1650.

I'd reached a region called Nunatarsuaaq, formed of wide, fertile river valleys and high, lake-strewn fell tops that hold out against the ice that climbs their backs. *Nunataq* is one of several Greenlandic landscape terms (it means a 'summit or ridge protruding from a glacier') that, since the 1870s, have gained international usage: now there are *Nunatat* in Antarctica and other distant places. Along the fell tops and up the valley that I hiked there are several ancient trails that link winter and summer encampments, some marked by the *inussuit* ('waymarker cairns') that mapped Inuit space.

With just a little sense of where waymarkers and paths had been, it became possible to visualise the Arctic hunting landscapes that were once central to cultures of qajaq and sled but are now easy to misinterpret as remote. The valley I was in has few boggy patches, but is run through with countless life-giving and clear-running streams. These are just a quick leap for caribou or human and allow the region to feel like a continuous realm of uninterrupted running space and fertile ground. The meat caught by hunting would be eaten through the autumn and stored in winter caches. But the skins were valuable trade commodities and travelled thousands of miles, exchanged for the produce of walruses, narwhals and baleen whales further north. I'd been told I might find an old caribou-antler arrowhead or two in this region, but didn't spot any such remnants underfoot.

The story encountered so often, that the history of a place begins with pioneering travellers who become the 'first settlers' and start traditions of record-keeping, taxation, and documentation, is undercut dramatically by a place like Nunatarsuaaq. Here history was dramatically diminished by settlement, because the turn to permanent residences in towns and villages ended the millennia-old idea that home and history are where the umiaq is. As my conversations in Kapisillit had shown, the umiaq remains within living memory. This fjord made the possibility of small-boat ways of life seem more immanent than ever.

III

Icy Silence

Many Inuit songs and poems start by setting out over sea ice or water. They celebrate encounters in vast windswept spaces of dazzling ice or iron-dark ocean. Most are characterised not by the sounds of snow flurry or seaspray but by silence. One song, first published in print in the 1920s, is typical of this stilled start to a tale of trial by sea hunt:

> I could not sleep
> For the sea lay so smooth
> Near at hand.
> So I rowed out . . .

Until my second journey in Greenland, I hadn't registered the prevalence of dead-smooth seas in what I read. Only by learning first-hand how ice and snow transform the rules of water did I begin to understand the irresistible lure of silence in the songs.

If my first journey had been about exploring Greenland's pasts just beyond the edges of the ice, my second sought out the historic significance of ice itself. I set out from the modern town of Ilulissat in Disko Bay with winds rising, and skies of grey, but fairer weather forecast for the next two days. After that, however, the forecast showed ominous signs that made me eager to explore before storms closed the seas.

Across the vast space of Disko Bay, hundreds of kilometres of broken bergs still the sea's surface and blanket all sound. No artificial barrage could be more effective at cutting out swell and breakers. Once I'd launched from just below the Ilulissat Qajaq Club, I was travelling through flat calm on a day when other seas would have risen and fallen to the wind's command. When travelling by paddle or sled, occasional rifle-cracks of breaking sea ice and percussive bursts of whale breath, might be the only sounds you encountered all day. The silence often felt so intense that the arrival of a whale was like a world-rending eruption.

Because of these mazes of broken ice, and the need to carry a qajaq long distances to unfrozen seas in winter, Disko Bay qajaqs were traditionally the shortest in the whole of Greenland. As well as their usual qajaqs, communities from here northwards also had a type of boat called the *maqittagaq* ('portable qajaq'). This lacked the robustness of most qajaqs, having very few ribs or crossbeams, and thin sheer boards. It was made to be carried upside down on both shoulders, with the kayaker's head in the cockpit. This method was known as *maqinneq*, and, for those with experience, it left both hands free for action.

I paddled south, among bergs that were hundreds of times bigger and more dramatic than those near Kapisillit. This was an entirely different kind of seascape: vast openness in contrast to the other ice fjord's noisy, crunching closure. Yet I soon learned that I couldn't trust my eyes. I'd been briefly surrounded entirely by ice, nudging slowly through a few of the many channels that opened and closed between bergs, when a headland suddenly loomed off my bow, travelling towards me at great speed. This was the most disorienting of moments. I'd seemed to be travelling slowly only because the whole icescape was swiftly moving with me. Tidal undertows were carrying the bergs at such speed, as if swept by rivers, that it was bewildering that they could seem so still. This combination of constant movement with vast silence is an experience like no other. It makes knowledge of tides, as well as of the behaviour of ice and water, an even more powerful tool for living well than in any other seascape I'd travelled.

Fortunately, I'd read enough to plan for the implications of this combination of ice and tidal power. I knew to expect to have to follow a lunar schedule. The fact that ice is dragged by the pull of the moon is one of many reasons that Inuit time has long been measured by daily lunar transits and monthly cycles rather than by arcs of the inconstant sun. I'd had to check before I left that my journey wouldn't coincide with a full moon, because that time each month is treacherous: the differential melt below and above the waterline is briefly combined with the tug of spring tides to cause big bergs to break and flip. The high waves that ensue are unpredictable in the extreme. They engulf beaches and seafronts, so that the coast bristles with signs to warn of the danger of death from tsunami.

By the afternoon of this first day, I was paddling across the mouth of the second biggest ice fjord in the world, and some of the bergs I passed beneath were half a mile long. Their tops were like whole landmasses, with peaks, valleys, ridges, and escarpments. The low sun cast huge shadows that accentuated every gorge and geo in the towering turquoise crags. Having seen the waves caused by the tipping of a berg a millionth of their mass, I wondered what would happen if these shifted and spun while I paddled beneath. But with the moon just a sliver in the daytime sky, I could assure myself the chances were remote.

Not just icebergs but animals contributed to this sense of oceanic scale. Countless gulls and fulmars flew past the sides of the bergs, looking as tiny as if they passed a cliff-girt coastline. And I don't think I went a single waking hour without hearing whales. First sighting was often just a pillar of thick mist rising between the bergs, these breaths audible for miles on these ice-stilled seas. Fin and bowhead whales kept their distance, but, every single day, humpbacks came close enough to make me think I was a cause of curiosity. Occasionally one emerged just feet away, showering me in a plume of its eye-wateringly pungent breath. There's an appreciation of scale that comes with the realisation that the creature by your side is 30,000 times the weight of the little boat you're in.

Though whales are everywhere in Arctic waters, it's at the mouths of these great ice fjords, where meltwater stirs up nutrients and awakes invertebrates inert since last summer, that they gather to feed and sing. The sea's wealth is expressed most appreciably in this whale song, as well as in seal whistle and walrus growl. But these are also waters rich with fish, such as halibut, capelin, and Arctic char. It's the combination of nutrient-laden ice and vast ocean currents that make these the most northerly resource-rich waters in the world. Because fresh water is lighter than salt water, iceberg-melt leads to columns of nutrients rising through the sea, like waterfalls in reverse. The ocean's sustenance pools in sunlit surface waters where plankton bloom in vast numbers and feed grazers and predators of every size and shape. This is why a huge range of life, including humans, can thrive north of seventy-six degrees while some regions at seventy degrees offer only frigid barrenness.

KALAALLIT NUNAAT/GREENLAND

By the time I'd crossed the ice fjord, I was paddling through dizzyingly beautiful worlds of sculpted ice. There were great caverns gouged in the sides of land-fast escarpments and stalactites twice my height hanging overhead. Most bergs were bare-topped but, on some, gulls huddled in little colonies. They seemed to favour small, low blocks of ice, perching just a few feet from the sea and entirely covering their berg with a little feathery enclave. These gulls included snowy white Arctic species I'd never seen before, including three beautiful Ross's gulls, so narrowly confined to these northern reaches that some ornithologists used to argue their existence was mythical.

Even gentle movement through the ice required an intensity of focus equal to paddling in the chaos of a gale, and, by this point, I'd been pushing myself hard for days. It was still just mid-afternoon when I decided to climb up onto shore-fast ice and make myself a cosy place to rest. I couldn't quite believe the grandeur of my surroundings. Ice mountains rose all around, run through with vast crevasses that made them look like mighty ranges. Icy islands filled the western horizon, and plumes of whale breath rose regularly. The banded grey skies of the morning had been slowly separating for hours, till the whole world above and below was pristine blue and gold. I left my little boat inflated, knowing that past travellers on sea ice always erected tents on top of their sleds for speedy departure should the ice begin to move.

When I talked about sea ice with those I met ashore, all were at pains to emphasise its familiar domesticity, but I noted divergence in the tenses people talked in: 'it means freedom', 'it's like a garden', or 'it was home'. I read interviews conducted over the last twenty years with community elders who worked the frozen oceans of northwest Greenland, Nunavut, and Alaska. There was enormous emphasis throughout on the warmth and homeliness of the ice and its stark contrast with the hostile land. 'On the land in winter,' Jacopie Panipak explained,

a seal oil lamp, even when it is fully lit, it doesn't get very warm
... On the sea ice, it is much warmer ... You tend to get homesick to the sea ice when it has been a while since you haven't been. There are also more animals on the ice ... a good home for all things. Foxes, polar bears, humans.

When the ice is fresh, before it has been topped with snow, it's the polar bears' domain, slippery to less ice-evolved feet. Late in the season, when lakes have formed, huge flocks of birds arrive to make the sea ice home. To everyone, thick, strong sea ice meant the chance to travel: where crossing coastal mountains was close to impossible, the ice was truly 'the freedom-bringer': the only kind of solid surface that could be travelled with ease. The ice might be ephemeral, but the trails across it are ancient. It is different every year, but the geographies of tides mean it always possesses some familiar patterns. In some regions, the trails are actively maintained by consolidating pressure ridges with ice picks and shovels. As the Inuit editors of a beautiful collection of interviews and photographs, *The Meaning of Ice*, put it:

> Being on the ice means being free, alive, ready ... The sea ice season is a time of traveling to different camps across the ice, helping the long nights pass, sharing stories old and new, joining in games and songs and dances ... The ancient trails we retrace ... are places themselves. Traveling sea ice is a part of our individual and family stories and histories, which we continue to tell and add to.

The anticipation and excitement concerning all these things are fundamental aspects of the meanings of ice.

In places that have strong tides in summer, the winter ice is more liable to endanger life by cracking. Even in the thickest ice, when winds align with strong tidal movement, large icebergs that seemed fixed in place for winter awaken and grind their way onwards. Where holes opened in the ice, such spots would become feeding sites for polar bears. Icebergs, pools, and ridges were the main navigation points that punctuated the wide frozen miles. The language surrounding them is intricate, with multiple words for icebergs, whether pointed or flat-topped, floating or grounded. There are different terms, too, for ridges formed in different ways, and for ice surfaces made of broken blocks, depending on whether dogs could (*maniilaq*) or couldn't (*maniilarraq*) pass them.

When there are low, dark clouds, the sky acts as a mirror for the ice, so an experienced navigator can read the sky to see patterns of ice and water, including movements of floes, at huge distances. Knowing how ice would behave requires immense knowledge of wind and tide, and so the sea knowledge of good kayakers was crucial even when living on the frozen surface. Boats were essential. The edges of the ice floe were celebrated places, bringing humans, narwhals, walruses, and seals into close conjunction. In the far north, using engines or guns in such places is still strictly controlled, and so, in the depths of winter, the qajaq remains the major mode of transport.

Where communities relied on winter travel by dog sled, and on the resources the ice opened up, the impacts of climate change have been many. The communities of northwest Greenland have sea-ice experts, including Qaerngaaq Nielsen, who have mapped the shifting patterns of its formation.

> The forming of sea ice in the fall is coming much later. It does not form until November in the fjords . . . we used to hunt for seals at the floe edge bringing our qajaq [in October]. There was still daylight when the ice had frozen like this. During those times when the sea ice forms at first we called it *quasammik* because it was very slippery . . . Today when we think of our settlement, the sea ice is forming

later and not forming until the *kaperlak* (winter solstice) and the weather is much more unstable. The forming of the sea ice is not as easy as it used to be. Hunting from the floe edge and from the *quasaq* (newly frozen ice) is now only something we can remember about.

Two of Nielsen's maps depict the extent of northern Greenland sea ice in the late twentieth century and in the 2010s. Changes that began to be seen in the 1990s left the old hunting grounds inaccessible but also meant that large numbers of polar bears now passed by his village every winter, where once they never used to be seen, and often ate the caches that were a traditional way of keeping food fresh.

Many of these interviews involve descriptions of catching winter food from the edge of ice floes by qajaq, and using qajaqs in the summer on open water when past calm weather was far more predictable. 'We call it *qajartululluni*,' Nielsen says of this summer calm that was ideal for kayaking, 'and that was real fun.' 'I don't want to replace this kind of life,' he adds. Toku Oshima describes the moment when the sea ice becomes thick enough to build the fishermen's wooden huts far out on the frozen sea. She describes, too, the tents constructed on sleds by those hunting mammals. These hunters like to camp near icebergs because observing a berg gives clues about changes in weather and sea ice. But all these uses of the ice provide the opportunity to 'feel the silence and the peace, the clean air and the purity'. It's not just food but all the other essentials of life that come from the ice: polar bear trousers, sealskin boots, and fox-fur parkas.

The ice forms different geographies every year, creating new contexts for the old established trails. In darkness, in the depths of winter, reliance on sled dogs with their far superior night vision was intense. Through weeks of night, it was they rather than people that navigated this fleeting landscape. To guarantee the ice skills of the

KALAALLIT NUNAAT/GREENLAND

species remain undiminished, there are strict rules here against the keeping of any kind of dog other than the Greenland sled dog. These working dogs have immensely high status since their health and strength are crucial to communities; many interviews stress the 'strong working relationship' that families must have with their dog team. Every year, the number of days when dogs are idle because there isn't enough ice to take sleds on either land or sea increases. In such circumstances, the number of active dog teams falls, as people resort to engines instead.

After my night on the ice, I turned back northwards and paddled through the morning with the tide on my side. When the tide turned and impeded my passage through the ice, I landed within the ice fjord, just southeast of the old village of Sermermiut, which was left behind in 1850 when the last residents moved to the burgeoning town of Jakobshavn (now Ilulissat). From here, I could join the official ice-fjord trail and walk back to town across the bustling hillsides where dog teams are housed and exercised. All the talk in town was now of the oncoming storm, and my hopes of travelling still further north unravelled as the calm spell ended. I settled myself into a cosy room with an ocean view, and watched the weather front sweep in.

Such storms have been a feature of sea-ice life since its inception, but Arctic cyclones have intensified in frequency, power, and scale in recent years. Becoming as large as Mongolia as they sweep the Arctic Circle, these storms cause huge surges that threaten coastal villages, either directly or through mudslides. Several of the settlements most famed for their kayakers, such as the village of Illorsuit, have been lost to avalanches in the last decade alone. In the words of the team of scientists currently studying the feedback loops between cyclones and sea ice, storms are said to 'chew up' vast areas of the ice surface. Rough ice, instead of dragging wind speeds down, actually serves to stabilise storm cores, leading vast, ferocious weather systems to run on far longer than ordinary storms. Even the best scientific modelling today fails to predict with any precision the ways in which these storms develop, in part because it's impossible to guess the proportion of a storm cloud that is whirling ice shards rather than water droplets. This is a far cry from the predictability of smaller historic storms, which Inuit culture was well adapted to predict and guard against.

By the time the storm I sat through cleared, the ice I'd slept on would no longer exist: 'chewed up' and swept in chunks into the sea. The ice caves I'd photographed would have been gouged away, and whales would rise into entirely different labyrinths of bergs and floes. The predictability of past sea ice is gone forever. Greenland faces challenges on scales never seen before: it is drawn increasingly into the temperate world of urban industrial development and resource extraction. Only Inuit knowledge of the living Arctic and Greenlandic self-determination will ensure that new forms of co-existence with this stupendous ocean world can come to be.

6

Ktaqmkuk/Newfoundland
London Is a Ladder up the Cliffs

I

The Bay Punt and the Burying Place

MANY STUNNING STRETCHES of Newfoundland's coast acknowledge their own beauty in names that don't err on the side of modesty. One afternoon, with a wonderful Newfoundland family, I took out a little wooden boat called a 'rodney' from the outport of Heart's Delight towards its neighbour, Heart's Ease. On a different day, I rowed into a tiny cove called God's Pocket. It was everything its name suggested: bright, sun-trap beach, crystal-clear waters, and perfect shelter from any storm. I still dream of my night there whenever I have to spend too long indoors. But there was one place I found more beautiful, affecting, and paradoxical than any other. It lies beyond the scars of the asbestos industry, which disfigure much of the Baie Verte Peninsula, where spruce woods meet the seas of Notre Dame Bay.

I reached this cove on foot, setting off from an outport called Snook's Arm, which itself demands a long sea journey or a considerable drive down bumpy, dusty gravel roads. Snook's Arm is a narrow cleft between thickly forested hills, where the sea runs between tall crags to a tiny beach that feels like the only flat shore for miles around. The village itself is vertiginously steep and its fourteen houses are perched on hillsides in the shadows of thick spruce and fir. I'd read that the population of ten had been voluntary relocated in 2018. After the cod and crab fisheries ended, the authorities had been reluctant to send snowploughs to so little a sea-girt slope. When I arrived, early on a sunny September morning, I was surprised to find local people cutting wood and preparing to launch small boats. Their presence was lucky. I would never have found the overland start to my route without their help.

I joined two men, in their sixties or seventies, who stood chatting outside the highest houses in the settlement. We mainly talked about squid, but they also told me how good life still is here in summer, though it had become impossible in winter. There was no melancholy or nostalgia in their voices, until the moment I mentioned the place I wished to head to. Then they told of times when the path across the wooded coastal ridges was in regular use and easy to find. The whole community, they said, walked its five-kilometre stretch each summer to the bay at the other end. They mentioned specific picnics, decades ago. After wandering down the hill with me, they pointed up a steep, pathless slope where the forest was no thinner than anywhere else and told me to start by scrambling up the ridge. I was bound to see moose, they said, and possibly black bears. I ducked under a bush and clambered upwards, using hands as much as feet. And I wondered if a joke was being played on me. Soon, though, I found ropes hanging down the hillside to ease my climb and prove this was a route well (comparatively) travelled.

I clambered, sweating, over the first ridge and through narrow valleys of dense foliage. The trees included species that could block the way at every height, from tall balsam fir and black spruce, through elegant white birch and trembling aspen, to twisted shrubs of mountain alder and sheep laurel. Occasionally, hints of path were visible, but always overgrown. Eventually, on flatter, higher ground, the landscape opened out into sudden idylls: standing surreally in green and golden clearings of knee-high grasses were hundreds of huge heads of the province's official flower, the Newfoundland pitcher plant. These wine-red blooms stand high on scarlet stems above jug-like hollow leaves in which they catch their insect sustenance. They looked like alien intrusions amid the gentle colours of the marshes, but gave the whole scene an impression of impossible lushness. Soon I reached a long string of lakes and slow, silent rivers, which would lead to my destination. On the opposite side of one lake, a huge moose faded into the treeline; it had been aware of me long before I saw it: my every footstep cracked the fir and spruce twigs underfoot, while its slow, heavy movements were impossibly silent.

Eventually, after edging my way back down to sea level, I reached an open space that was surreally flat and fertile amid this craggy world. This had once been a large sports field, but was now thick with fen plants. Shoulder-high saplings showed that all of it would soon be reclaimed by forest. I passed through one last stand of trees, where a moose skull lay among the leaf mulch, and a huge view opened out ahead. Some fifty kilometres away, the eastern shores of Notre Dame Bay broke the horizon, each low hill and island a distant little smudge. The cove I was entering was bounded by rocky cliffs and scree slopes, but it was bursting with lush foliage, including multitudes of raspberries and hops.

The most striking aspects of the scene, however, were the large wooden homes, fishing stores, boathouses, and flakes (fish-drying platforms) on all sides. The first tall, square house had been built by Emma and John Adams in the 1790s, and the other homes that soon sprang up were some of the most beautiful imaginable. Most look directly east onto the ocean: dawns seen through their windows must have been spectacular. Their architecture, built from overlapping spruce planks, was more boat-like than any other homes I've seen.

Much of these buildings' style and atmosphere can still be seen and felt. Each window had white lace curtains that complemented tastefully airy decoration within: light greens, vivid reds, sky blues, clean fawns, and whites. They seemed calculated to catch the play of morning sun streaming in. The clear paths between doorways made it similarly easy to imagine the social life of the settlement. A population of forty was sustained by a close sense of community and by oceanic links to dozens of outports just a short row away.

The community's boathouses were large and impressive, with ropes and lobster traps still scattered round. These are the buildings that were known as 'fishing rooms' and were the fundamental unit of settlement in the early centuries of European activity: outports happened in the places wherever it was possible to build such rooms and land boats beside them. Newfoundland has been labelled a 'true sea province', 'blown adrift' against the shores of Canada and 'always straining back', and these fishing rooms were like moorings between land and sea.

The wide flake beneath the fishing rooms is made of sun-bleached spruce trunks laid on high stilts. From here, a pebble beach leads to the stunningly clear waters of the gently curved bay with not a piece of modern plastic to be seen. A large wooden bay punt rests upside down near the tideline. Beside it are bursts of intense colour: dozens of mauve and yellow asters and many varieties of pink and purple wildflower. The whole scene fits its geography perfectly, constructed with care at a site ideal for using little boats to access the resources of island and sea.

But the vista is made extremely odd by its dearth of right angles and straight lines. Houses tilt, as if rocking on a rough sea. Roofs sag, pulling walls inwards, so that whole buildings look fluid and seasick. The punt, too, has lost its lines, its keel as undulating as the ripples of water where two tides meet. Step inside the houses and the contrasts are disorienting. Some of the large stoves, which were used to heat homes as well as cook, still have their accessories, such as tinderboxes and frying pans. They look almost ready to cook on. There are sofas, as well as smaller, handmade benches and tables, and there is a wringer washer from the era when the settlement got its first electric generator. Bright linoleum, sometimes used on shelves here as well as floors, has held its primary colours perfectly. But floorboards have collapsed, and doors have fallen from their hinges. Wood has fared less well even than upholstery as the buildings have begun to droop and subside back into the valley's earth.

Before launching and paddling east into Notre Dame Bay, I ate lunch in front of the ruined punt, with the gentle water lapping at my feet, and imagined this bay bustling with people in the very recent past. But the heyday of this settlement, from the eighteenth century to the twentieth, ended abruptly after Newfoundland joined Canada in 1949. The national government and the leaders of the newly formed province embarked on a rapid effort to 'modernise' the island and diversify its economy away from the sea. This bay and those like it were labelled 'dour, demanding, rural without being pastoral, industrious without being profitable ... everyone's half forgotten past and no-one's future'.

Crucial to the modernising project was the project of centralising the population as a workforce for hundreds of new factories, making everything from heavy machinery and cement to batteries. Urban society, insulated from the effects of weather, was seen as more efficient and manageable than communities beholden to the whims of ocean and the price of cod. Reliable work in factories and mines was presented as a brighter future than family seafaring and small-scale agriculture. Fishing, too, was consolidated into industrial fleets sailing from large ports and promising huge volumes of cod for high profit without monopolising the island's labour. Just as industrialisation on land would lead to the catastrophic bust of the asbestos mining industry in the 1980s and 1990s, this industrialised fishing was the very thing that would result in the cultural and economic shock of the total fishing bans in the 1992 cod moratorium.

It was during this time of upheaval that a literature celebrating these outports was born. Arthur Scammell was raised in an island outport where, as a child, he penned songs about small boats and fishing. One of these, 'Squid-Jiggin' Ground', is still regularly performed. Later, Scammell wrote dozens of appreciations of the settlements' culture. These were driven by resentment at outsiders' criticisms, and by bewilderment at their failure to see both what was good in the communal life of small settlements and how much satisfaction could be gained from facing the challenges of an oceanic environment.

'If you have ever lived in a Newfoundland Outport,' Scammell wrote in the *Atlantic Guardian* in 1945, 'be proud of it.' He praised the 'daily lessons in co-operation and kindliness, taught by rude fishermen who wouldn't know a vitamin if they met one, but who did know that "man doesn't live by bread alone"'. These were lessons, he insisted, 'that all the inventions and discoveries of modern civilization cannot lessen or cheapen'. Scammell spurred a new genre of authors attempting to provide an alternative world view to the state rhetoric of 'develop or perish'. Many were outporters pushed away to cities such as New York who wrote of their desperation for the day when pension eligibility would mean they could return from atomistic urban worlds to small, close-knit, coastal fishing spots.

When the government's centralising project began, there were more than 19,000 little rowing boats dotted throughout the outports. By 1975, 300 outport communities, amounting to some 30,000 people, had been moved into towns and cities. In many instances, the whole community moved abruptly in a single year, forced to adapt suddenly to new ways of life. This entailed the abandonment of whole islands and a drastic shift in the human geography of Newfoundland. Spectacular photographs from the time show intact houses strapped to rafts of boats and barrels. They were carried by sea from small coves to the bigger bays that had been chosen as 'growth centres' and which were more accessible by the roads that were coming to dominate trade and travel. The demographic shift this caused was dramatic: one historian of Newfoundland, Harry Hiller, has calculated that where '83 percent of the labour force was engaged in fishing in 1891, only 8 percent were so engaged by the late 1970s'.

While some welcomed these changes, others felt manipulated into leaving. It soon became clear that the promises of progress were, as usual, not quite what they seemed. Urban growth centres didn't have enough employment to accommodate all resettlers, the costs of relocation turned out to be far greater than the assistance on offer, and many of the new industries went bankrupt in their first few years. Most grimly ironic, perhaps, was the situation in Placentia, where those who relocated were promised jobs at the coastal boat terminal; the coastal boat service, however, now had fewer outports to serve and so faced immediate cutbacks, leaving Placentia with fewer possibilities for work than ever before. The new 'floating factories' of industrial fishing, which rapidly replaced family-owned activities, were also recognised as drastically destructive of fish stocks, community, and place: as dredgers swept the bays, fishermen lamented their lobster pots and fishing grounds, destroyed along with their homes and 'old ways'.

Soon the burgeoning literature of complaint was matched by new folk songs expressing shame at having accepted the government's money to relocate. Bud Davidge's 'Outport People' (1985) is written from the perspective of his father, who was resettled in 1968. He sits on the dock of his new home and dreams of a life where he'd told officials 'to go straight to hell'. The weather as he sits and dreams is perfect for fishing, 'But his boat's full of weeds and there's tears in his eyes.' Although the houses had been rowed out to sea, the song continues, 'home' itself had stayed exactly where it was:

> Don't take a man from the life that he knows
> And tear up his roots and expect him to grow
> Cause if he's unwillingly forced to decide
> He'll move without leaving and never arrive.

Much of this new song and literature doesn't present the outports as some kind of timeless idyll but 'the best and worst of places at the same time', in the words of the poet Tom Dawe. But what the songs all attest is that, even when people 'chose' to accept state funds to leave, many lived to believe that the promises of 'progress' were unfulfilled and unfulfilling, and to be haunted by the memory of outport life. For a long time, all of this was dismissed as 'nostalgia', sometimes referred to as the 'Newfcult phenomenon', which created an origin myth for urban Newfoundland. But accusations of 'nostalgia' and 'romanticism' are, I find, often convenient labels to justify the dismissal of uncomfortable truths.

Two of the great voices celebrating outport life in the mid-century, Farley Mowat and Harold Horwood, had taken on bleak tones by the late 1960s. Mowat lamented that he had 'failed to glimpse the heart of darkness beating black within the present hour', and described the 'sinister sea-change' that had engulfed the island. Horwood depicted 'a people caught in the most painful stage of transition, a people whose roots have been destroyed so recently that they have been able to make no new sustaining growth'.

In *Moved by the State: Forced Relocation and Making a Good Life in Postwar Canada* (2019), the historian Tina Loo offers an even-handed analysis of the Newfoundland government's aims and their impact. She explores the economic theories the state drew on, with their clear statistical assessments of what constituted poverty and how quality of life should be measured. But she suggests this was a very different vision of what constituted the common good than existed in the outports themselves. Residents there

> were enmeshed in an informal economy that not only gave people a living but also contributed to the social cohesion and health of the communities they lived in. From the beginnings of permanent European occupation in Newfoundland, settler families sustained themselves through a combination of work in the seasonal fishery, subsistence production, and cooperation among kin and neighbours. Firewood might be traded for potatoes, moose meat for help repairing gear.

All this was invisible to the state whose vision, despite all the statistics it generated, was driven by an unevidenced idealism far more simplified and romanticising than any kind of outport nostalgia.

Refusing to heed state discouragement, a few families did return each summer to the settlement I'd walked to. Their visits over several decades account for the extraordinary preservation of the tilting buildings. As one former resident, Vey Stoodley, explained to the photographer Scott Walden in the 1990s, knowledge of the good fishing grounds was too hard won and significant to give up. Stoodley took a little boat to the bay as soon as his sons acquired a GPS. He used his old methods of navigating by seamark, then saved the sites of the best grounds to the GPS's memory in order that the knowledge would be passed on.

The cemetery in the cove records the occupants of these houses. The artist Angela Baker has used paintings of a few resettled outports to ask, 'What must it have been like for people to leave their loved ones and ancestors in these graveyards, destined to the loneliness of winds and encroaching nature?' A few surnames are repeated on the headstones. It's striking that all of them are ones I could meet with in the cemeteries of an English or Irish village, including White, Ryan, and Bowers. Some can be traced, via the marriage registers of the settlement, to origins in Hampshire and Devon. Others married into the community from nearby towns. On this sunny day, it was easy to imagine their wedding parties among the trees, and this felt like a place that must once have been homely and happy. Other records show that some residents worked in a mine at Betts Cove, three kilometres to the southwest. There, between 1870 and 1884 (by which time the mine was depleted), copper was dug and shipped to Swansea, where it was made into wires for the first commercial phone lines in Wales. These transatlantic connections, in a spot that felt profoundly rural and remote, seemed surreal.

But the name of this outport reveals its connection to deeper histories. It was called Indian Burying Place. The peninsula it lies on forms the western edge of the great bay that was the heartland of the Beothuk people, who had populated northern Newfoundland for more than a thousand years when the first post-Norse European landings began in the fifteenth century. Local memory holds that the name of the settlement came from settlers' experience of finding birchbark-wrapped burials while building their homes. Coves such as Indian Burying Place and God's Pocket were the reason these shores had been so attractive to many First Nations peoples whose lives were mobile and coastal, centred on small islands, protected bays, and estuaries where smelt and salmon ran.

II

A Bay of Birchbark

If the state in 1949, when Newfoundland became part of Canada, was hostile to the outports, it was brutally dismissive of the cultures of the canoe. 'There are no Indians', the province's premier Joey

KTAQMKUK/NEWFOUNDLAND

Smallwood infamously claimed, 'in Newfoundland.' Yet Mi'kmaw canoes have made a comeback, and can now be seen on several island coasts. Mi'kmaw elders, such as John Nick Jeddore, describe their Nation's 'distinct maritime orientation'. When I asked one elder, Calvin White, why he chose as the cover for his memoirs a canoe from a community far from his home, his response was that it symbolised the unity of people bonded by their seacraft.

East of Indian Burying Place is one of the world's great arenas of historic ocean canoeing. Although Newfoundland's Mi'kmaw presence today is most strongly connected with the south and west of the island, particularly Conne River where the Miawpukek (Middle River) First Nation is located, many of the places I passed as I paddled Notre Dame Bay are centres of Mi'kmaw culture. Not far from Indian Burying Place, for instance, is Halls Bay, the birthplace of Mattie Mitchell, renowned as 'the greatest and most resourceful woodsman who ever lived'. Mitchell's family was instrumental in the development of the Qalipu (Caribou) band, which has grown dramatically in recent years. The large Exploits River pours through a maze of small islands into the eastern side of Notre Dame Bay. This huge estuary hosted many Mi'kmaw camps and settlements. They are listed in every census since Newfoundland's first. Every time I looked on my maps and saw places named for people, those people turned out to be Mi'kmaw trappers or guides. Two of the streams which feed the Exploits, for instance, are Noel Paul's Brook and Tom Joe's Brook.

The historical marginalisation of the Mi'kmaq in Newfoundland has taken many forms. One relates to the idea of the 'extinction' of the Beothuk. The last Beothuk died in 1829, this story says, and after her death these bays were 'empty'. Their defining feature, in these narratives, was the absence of their indigenous people. Even some of the richest writing on these shores generates this imagined emptiness for settlers to fill. As the introduction to Michael Crummey's novel *River Thieves* (2001) puts it, 'Only the land is still there'; Scott Walden's beautiful photographic record of the resettled outports, *Places Lost* (2003), strikes a similar tone with the claim that empty coves such as Indian Burying Place 'called out for human habitation'. Ironically, the Mi'kmaw trappers who gave their names to nearby places lived in exactly this post-Beothuk era of supposed emptiness. More fundamentally still, Beothuk and Mi'kmaw intermarriage challenges the idea of extinction. Such intermarrying meant that no one, let alone the young woman Shawnadithit, whose tragic life ended in the European town of St John's in 1829, could be identified as 'the last Beothuk'.

A second technique of marginalisation is the unevidenced assertion that Mi'kmaq had not 'inhabited' Newfoundland until European settlers hired them to exterminate the Beothuk. Mi'sel Joe, who was, until 2024 Chief of the Miawpukek Mi'kmaw nation, based at Conne River in southwest Newfoundland, recalls what he was taught at school about the Beothuk:

> It was a very short paragraph, about us being brought from Nova Scotia by the French to kill the Beothuk people. Of course, when you get home, you ask your grandparents, and they say, 'No. Who else are you going to blame it on?' We weren't writing the history. There was always someone else writing the history. So we grew up with that. And you know, actually, at a time I think I might have even believed that.

All attempts to make the case that Mi'kmaw were a new presence on the island were based on narrow assumptions concerning what it meant to 'inhabit' a place: the watery mobility of dozens of interlocked First Nations peoples was unaccountable to European reckoning.

These erasures began to be challenged at the end of the 1960s. This had been a particularly bleak decade, with provincial authorities employing new vigour in applying the rules and regulations of a settled, urban society to the very different world of Mi'kmaw life. In an infamous 1969 white paper, the Trudeau government proposed getting rid of the category of 'Indian' altogether and signalled its intent to push assimilationist policies harder than ever before. The backlash this provoked has been labelled the 'Great Awakening'. Across Canada, a National Indian Brotherhood was formed to preserve and revitalise threatened aspects of indigenous cultures, arts, sciences, and languages. But the situation in Newfoundland was unique, because the official denial of Mi'kmaw existence hampered organisation and activism. In 1973, the Native Association of Newfoundland and Labrador was founded to advance the interests of all the indigenous populations of the island.

Every decade since then has brought watershed moments in reclaiming First Nations life. In 1985, for instance, education in Mi'kmaw communities was reclaimed from the church. Mi'sel Joe recalls being

> asked quite bluntly by a priest, 'If you get your hands on education, what are you going to do with the money? Are you going to buy cigarettes and booze? Because you know absolutely nothing about education.'

Forty years later, thanks to this reclamation, there are Mi'kmaw scholars, like Tammy Drew and Shane MacDonald, of whom Mi'sel Joe says

> those are the people that are going to make the difference in the world. Those are the people who are going to continue to tell the right story. They're our scholars. And we are writing our history now.

There remains a strong memory, however, of just how much the authorities seemed to want to set Mi'kmaq up to fail, believing that the 1985 handover of education would reveal inadequacy, and end in failure, rather than resulting in the flourishing movements that exist today.

It might sound like exaggeration to say that when the building of birchbark canoes was restored to the island in the mid-1990s, this was a development of almost equal significance to the restoration of Mi'kmaw schooling. But building a canoe is an enterprise involving a vast range of traditional skills that run parallel to more formal education. It requires engagement with the land just as closely as growing and harvesting food does. Each boat built is an opportunity to re-establish a deep connection to place.

As well as sheets of birchbark, a single canoe might use as much as 1,000 feet of spruce root. This root is boiled and split in ways that give it great strength. It's these tightly wound roots, rather than the bark itself, that make the shell robust. Harvesting roots involves significant woodcraft, and a canoe builder must learn how to dig them up in ways that encourage further growth rather than damaging a tree. The collecting of roots is thus one of the most evocative practices in Mi'kmaw culture: it's an occasion when canoe builders often speak of their connection to the past. As Derek Stride puts it in a short 2022 film called *Gwitna'q* (the Mi'kmaw word for travelling by canoe), 'to realise that my ancestors done this. And to be able to do what they done years ago, hundreds of years ago, well to me it's an honour and a blessing.' He continues by stressing that 'it's very important that our young people realise what our ancestors done and how they done it'.

The form of these Mi'kmaw canoes has been gently adapted through millennia to generate a boat that is at home on the ocean as well as the river. Its bow and stern are tall, but the sides also rise in the middle of the boat to protect the canoe from side-on swell.

KTAQMKUK/NEWFOUNDLAND

The genius of these vessels comes from the fact that the green-wood frame is not inert or passive. It stretches the shell into high tension, making the boat a spring-loaded, dynamic work of art with the pliability of a living tree. Such stretched smoothness means these boats glide like few others. Every commercial builder of canoes would surely concede that no industrial technology compares when it comes to the in-the-moment feeling of sliding through the sea in bark from a birch tree.

As well as possessing layers of cultural and symbolic meaning, these canoes were the vehicles of life itself. Their invention 3,000 years ago was a dramatic technological transformation from the heavy dugouts that preceded them, and their speed revolutionised travel through the woodlands and islands of the boreal subarctic. By the time the second wave of European settlers arrived in the fifteenth century, First Nations people in Newfoundland had developed this technology to the highest degree of ocean-going sophistication it has reached anywhere in the Atlantic. Boatbuilding sites were situated where gravel beds allowed wooden stakes to be driven into the ground, and here communities would gather, bringing all that was required to build the boats. Construction was labour-intensive: boatbuilders today devote at least thirty days to the construction of a canoe. This was also a uniquely specialised and virtuosic skillset: because canoes were the hardest of all items to make, those able build good boats had uniquely high social status.

Throughout North America, the late twentieth century saw boats become objects of intense political contestation. When explaining twentieth-century institutions' history of viewing First Nations people as 'less than human', Mi'sel Joe gives the example that 'we weren't allowed a boat until the 1960s'. Where Mi'kmaq were forced into reserves, in regions such as Nova Scotia, their geography deliberately discouraged boat use. Many reserves hemmed coastal peoples in to entirely landlocked spaces, but even in coastal reserves large fences were often erected to block access to the water. In Newfoundland, as elsewhere, the pressures to conform to sedentary western lifestyles pushed birchbark canoes almost to extinction.

It was therefore a resonant moment when, in 1996, Mi'sel Joe, his brother Billy Joe, and Derek Stride invited a canoe builder from Quebec to visit Newfoundland and teach them to work with birchbark and spruce root. The boat they built was an opportunity to undo centuries of forced alienation from Mi'kmaw tradition, to re-establish a deep connection to the island's forests and coasts, and to demonstrate the technological sophistication of traditional life. After the building of this first canoe, the Miawpukek band council realised it could be used to make a statement to the outside world. Billy Joe led a team that paddled the twenty-six-foot boat on a traditional route across 300 kilometres of ocean. Over previous decades, several writers had expressed doubts concerning the stories of bark-built boats crossing ocean, and it was a matter of deep pride in Mi'kmaw woodcraft and seafaring for this canoe to prove them wrong.

It was also a matter of pride to make this a continuous tradition that would never again be lost. In subsequent years, huge canoes, thirty-two feet long, and tiny ones of only twelve feet, have been added to the community of little boats. Every style that's revived is a new step in the reclaiming of culture. Today the First Light organisation based in St John's supports and celebrates the recovery of indigenous practices and its embrace of canoe construction. This has involved sharing Billy Joe's and Derek Stride's canoe builds on Facebook Live, allowing people to share techniques and ask questions. It felt odd to join one of these on my phone while encamped on a beach where these boats, and those of the Beothuk, have been the pinnacle of ocean-going prowess.

Many documents that mention the Beothuk begin by stressing how scarce the evidence concerning them is. Yet as I edged eastwards towards the mouth of the Exploits River, it seemed that sites of encampment, encounter, or burial were everywhere. These are the most perfect canoe coasts imaginable: rich with marine resources and full of tiny, pretty coves where canoes might land but no bigger boats could follow. The thickly greened sea rocks and islets support few large trees, but lots of stunted shrubs, and other vegetation, while the river mouths would once have run with otters, muskrats, and beavers, as well as salmon. Before the introduction of moose to the island in 1904, the largest grazers were herds of caribou that once wandered the wide Exploits estuary. I looked through the discussions of local history groups to find their views on probable past locations for *mamateeks* (Beothuk tents made from spruce poles overlaid with birchbark and caribou hide), but it was easy enough to make guesses based on the lie of the land, and the Beothuk once used every inch of this coastal space.

I stopped on Big Island in a stretch of water called Pilley's Tickle (meaning 'a narrow passage between islands', tickle is one of Newfoundland's many local terms for a variety of waterway), where islanders out berry-picking in 1886 had stumbled across the burial place of a Beothuk child: a local boy, the newspapers reported, had put his foot straight through a 'slight covering' of birchbark that veiled the bones. They took the dead child's head and 'some trinkets' to a local merchant, who then visited the spot and discovered an array of grave goods: neatly wrapped pieces of dried fish, a child-sized bow and arrows, a wooden doll, and three miniature birchbark canoes.

The body was soon displayed in the museum in St John's, which was housed inside the post office. The few surviving photos from the time show the skeleton of the child laid on a bed of birchbark, alongside two of the miniature canoes, a model qajaq with paddler in Inuit dress, and jars containing squid and fish. By the 1970s, these remains had become a focal point of dispute. Mi'kmaw representatives mounted complaints to officials that indigenous bodies were 'put on display like animals'. Gradually, in the late 1970s and 1980s, they were removed from public view, but many older Newfoundlanders still remember them, and the narratives of 'extinction' that surrounded them, as formative for their understanding of the island.

As I headed through the dense maze of islands concealing the eastern shore of Notre Dame Bay, the clear weather broke. A full-scale subarctic storm was heading in. My final stop would be a Beothuk site called Boyd's Cove, where the most thorough excavations of Beothuk life have taken place. It is also the setting for an annual outdoor celebration of indigenous life, 'Voices on the Wind', which I'd timed my journey to arrive in time for. Usually Mi'kmaq, Innu, and Inuit from around the island gather here, but this year the incoming storm prevented travel. The Mi'kmaw drum circle who would have led an outdoor ceremony didn't make the journey, and I didn't get to meet the iconic figures of the Mi'kmaw cultural revival who attended the ceremony in many other years. But I wandered, in the fierce winds, down to the most heavily studied and best-preserved Beothuk site of all.

This camp's discovery was the result of a large-scale project. In the late 1970s, finding Beothuk sites was made a priority because although extensive early written descriptions relating to most First Nations existed – often because European missionaries had lived among them – there were no such detailed texts relating to the Beothuk. In June 1981, a team of archaeologists began to survey Notre Dame Bay by boat. They identified sixteen settlement sites, ranging from the prehistoric 'Maritime Archaic' culture to the eighteenth-century Beothuk, but Boyd's Cove is the most sensational of their finds. It's a large field atop a gravel platform left behind by the last Ice Age. Beothuk homes were dug a little into the ground, so required the kind of drainage this glacial moraine provided. Within the hollows that they dug, a wigwam-like *mamateek* would be erected and covered with bark and turf to a create a warm, watertight room.

KTAQMKUK/NEWFOUNDLAND

The footprints of eleven such structures were excavated at this site, once home to a community of around thirty-five people. A stylised carving of a bear was found here, as were repurposed metal items from European fisheries: 1,157 iron nails had been fashioned into tools; fish hooks had been straightened into awls; and lead was made into ornaments. Since Boyd's Cove lay between a French fishery to the northwest and an English fishery to the southeast, it's even possible that easy access to nails when the Europeans returned home in the winter was one factor behind the choice of this site. Occupation seems to have begun before 1650 and ended around the time of the founding of the town of Twillingate, thirty kilometres away, in 1730.

At the edge of the settlement, the field runs down through a thin stand of trees to the perfect shore for pulling up canoes. In May, the river is a plentiful breeding ground for smelt. The number of bones of these small fish show them to have been a key attraction of the site for its seasonal, spring occupants. Such bones wouldn't normally survive in the archaeological record, but the Boyd's Cove Beothuk ate large quantities of clams whose shells preserved all other remains from the acidic soil and left an unusually clear picture of their past diet: beaver, caribou, goose, cormorant, flounder, sculpin, harp seal, harbour seal, and even polar bear were all eaten here.

A replica Beothuk canoe sits inside the interpretation centre near the site. Its construction was based on models such as those found in the burial in Pilley's Tickle and on research done by scholars like Ingeborg Marshall who, in 1985, published her dissertation on these boats. It's a striking vessel: similar to Mi'kmaw canoes in construction methods, but entirely different in form and behaviour on the water. The most striking element is the canoe's extreme flare, from a sharp V-shaped hull into large, almost wing-like edges (which might be referred to as 'humped gunwales' with 'dramatic sheer'). The V-shaped hull would have made these boats extremely unstable if not for the use of substantial ballast (an unusual phenomenon in

First Nations boats). With rocks to weigh the boat down, however, these canoes were perfectly adapted for manoeuvring through high swell: the 'wings' kept out the waves, while the lower sides fore and aft meant paddles could be wielded unimpeded. The combination of hull shape and flare would also have created enough secondary stability to allow heavy catches to be hauled aboard. Some of the islands the Beothuk frequented are forty-five kilometres or more offshore. European travellers who saw these boats noted that even with just two paddlers they could outpace a European longboat bristling with oars. They noted that their shape, with its tall stern and bow, was 'as beautiful as a crescent moon'. These were among the most unusual vessels ever to have negotiated oceans, and there's no doubt their striking appearance has contributed to the mystique of the Beothuk in Newfoundland culture.

Near the interpretation centre stands a statue of Shawnadithit, the person sometimes labelled 'the last Beothuk'. After her capture by settlers in 1823, and in the tragic last years of her life, she sketched the fullest record of Beothuk society that exists. A major feature of this account was her mapping, by memory, of journeys, including those once undertaken by her family. Her maps present a canoe-bound world view, with lines marking water-travel and the overland portage of boats. Early descriptions of her work criticised her supposed inattention to scale. Later authors, however, have recognised her understanding of the shifting nature of her landscape, characterised, for instance, by the transformations of freeze and thaw. Her images are not so much linear representations of distance but of the time it took to travel rivers and seas that changed hour by hour. In this way, aspects of a Beothuk outlook, at odds with European habits, emerge (however hazily) from her work.

It's a strange feature of Newfoundland life that where there are hundreds of books, articles, reports, novels, and poems featuring Beothuk canoes and archaeology, publications on Mi'kmaw canoes or archaeology are so few in number as to have been, until very recently, almost non-existent. Mi'kmaw people in Newfoundland have had to fight so hard for recognition and representation that this scholarship long took a back seat. In an edited collection called *Visioning a Mi'kmaw Humanities* (2016), Marie Battiste puts the new Mi'kmaw movement in global context. She shows how 'in this time of fragile, vulnerable and tragic environments, humans are going to have to redefine and reframe what it means to be a human in every knowledge system'. She makes the case for the power of Mi'kmaw perspectives amid 'the vast potential of diverse knowledge systems to enrich our lives'. This includes a deepened understanding of ecology that emerges from continued experience within particular places, and which refuses to be consumed with the notion of power over land and people. It foregrounds the knowledge preserved through centuries of experience in small boats at the water's edge. It values oral storytelling and dialogue, challenging the supremacy of the written word with all its ties to authority and power.

III

The Loafers of Scilly Cove

In the Newfoundland archives, there are an unusual number of slim studies of wooden boats and offcuts from old magazine articles on boat folklore. In one, 'The Inshore Boats of Newfoundland', Duane Collins insisted that 'various designs of small wooden boats may be the most recognizable part of our material culture', while in another, Crystal Braye wrote of the punts of the Avalon Peninsula as 'iconic symbols of Atlantic Canada' that are 'ingrained in Newfoundland and Labrador's cultural landscape'. In the early 2000s, Braye was a folklorist, travelling the province collecting oral histories. Her informants told of days spent in the woods seeking the perfect stem post, and of the care required to lead a team of dogs in hauling boat timber from high spruce and fir woods down to shoreline villages. She describes how 'boats, adapted for local environments, also reveal the unique histories experienced by different regions of the province'. She shows, too, how the scale of innovation by independent builders has made Newfoundland's boatbuilding quite different from that of regions more tightly bound by tradition. Many of the studies in the archive emphasise the continued significance of the small boat, citing song lyrics such as 'we still keep our time by the turn of the tide', or quoting local fishermen who insist that, should necessity force them to do only one, they'd repaint their boat before they'd repaint their home. They also tend to quote Winston Churchill, who is said to have referred to Newfoundlanders as 'the best small boat men in the world'.

Just as the landscape and culture of each Newfoundland bay is different, so is its history of wooden boats. This broadly divides into two regional traditions, shaped by Newfoundland's identity as an ocean crossroads. In the and east, and on north-facing coasts, where communities looked to England and Ireland, there exists a punt culture. These boats have deep rounded bottoms that displace large volumes of water as the laden vessels cut the waves. In contrast, in the south, where communities look to Nova Scotia, Maine, and the Grand Banks there is a dory culture. Flat-bottomed dories are closer to planing hulls, which lightly skim the waves. But within each tradition the regional varieties are countless and of great social significance. As Braye puts it, the small region known as the Bay of Islands, had a host of different localised markers:

> Builders in Lark Harbour–York Harbour use three planks per side, whereas builders in Benoit's Cove only use two. Dories built in Cox's Cove, on the north side of the Humber Arm, can be distinguished by their higher stems and may be painted grey instead of orange, which was once common throughout the Bay of Islands.

Such distinctions often related to the availability of materials, or to the specific types of catch made locally, but sometimes they were simply aesthetic markers of local distinctiveness and communal identity, practised, as one of today's leading boatbuilders, Jerome Canning, puts it, 'just to be different' and to generate community cohesion.

As the weather improved, I made my way to the Bay de Verde Peninsula in the hope of exploring the punt culture and the distinctive ways of life it made possible. This peninsula splits Conception Bay in the east from Trinity Bay in the west. Its oldest settlements, such as Harbour Grace, which dates back to a French initiative in 1517, were the first outports Europeans founded on the island. Local memory suggests that fishermen from the Channel Islands and Bristol were coming to these sites decades before the island was 'discovered'. My journey would start near Carbonear and travel up the peninsula's east side before rounding the tip and paddling down the west coast through the boatbuilding villages of Trinity Bay.

Skies were blue once more when I set off from Bristol's Hope, with Carbonear Island ahead. Known to early settlers as 'the Gibraltar of Newfoundland', this island was already a central site of early European activity when, in 1679, a wealthy local merchant Thomas Oxford demanded a fortress be constructed there. Certain visions of Newfoundland's past have long sustained the notion that settlements before the eighteenth century were illegal, forbidden by British legislation that insisted the island remain in the same state as when it was 'discovered'. The first settlers, in this interpretation, were fugitives and deserters from West Country vessels, as well as fishers who simply stayed illegally over the winter to secure the best sites and a head start on the spring fishing season.

Recent historians have argued that this narrative of illegality is misleading. The Newfoundland fishery was so important that 350 vessels were crossing from Europe to the bays each year by 1578, by which point British and French fisheries had come to eclipse Iberian interests in the area. Estimates of the annual catch at that date range from 75,000 to 200,000 tonnes; either figure would render this one of the largest of all European industries. Attempts at founding settlements, though many failed, were a corollary of this significance. There was no real line between extensive informal activities and supposedly official endeavours. Descriptions of even the most legitimate settlements give the impression of moral and social disintegration. Clergy, it was often noted, were rare in the outports, while pirates lurked in every shadow. For centuries, stories have been shared of figures like the Harbour Grace pirate Peter Easton, who saved the 'Irish princess' Sheila NaGeira from the Dutch before, in the 1610s, terrorising the eastern seaboard of North America himself. Such was the reputed lawlessness of the island's communities that he was said to be able to recruit 5,000 local fishermen to his crews.

There have been many different interpretations of the culture and economy of these communities. Some have argued that from the seventeenth century to the early twentieth the punt culture was based almost exclusively on subsistence and exchange; 'people', one of the ethnographer James Faris's informants told him, 'had never seen money from their births to their graves'. Others, such as the historian Peter E. Pope, author of *Fish into Wine: The Newfoundland Plantation in the Seventeenth Century* (2004), contend that these outports possessed a cash economy of 'precocious consumerism' which reveals the precise ways in which 'capitalism scattered Europeans across the Atlantic'.

The fortifications on Carbonear Island date from an era when these communities were made still more precarious by competition between English and French interests. This broke into open warfare during European conflicts such as the Nine Years War. In 1696, a small French militia swept across the Bay de Verde Peninsula, causing British settlers to flee their homes. Many took refuge on Carbonear Island while their abandoned homes burned. A second French attack took place in 1705, when every British settlement in Trinity and

Conception Bays was sacked, with the exception of the island. The aftermath revealed some nuances of the Newfoundland situation. Many English and Irish indentured labourers were taken prisoner in the 1705 raids and put to work as servants for the French. By 1709, according to Newfoundland planters, the French had brought these servants so much to their side that '40 or 50 English and Irish . . . have declared themselves subjects of the King of France and have several times taken up arms against the English'. Newfoundland identities were already becoming more complex than simple echoes of European loyalties.

Today, Carbonear Island is a major site for the archaeology of early British North America. But it's also a bird reserve where bald eagles nest. I was quickly becoming used to the ways in which the most significant historical sites in Newfoundland are also nature reserves or seabird colonies. Overhead, as I paddled, there were ospreys, as frequent in many parts of Newfoundland as buzzards in Britain. But even they weren't quite so charismatic as the little belted kingfishers that hunted from the sea rocks. These large-billed piebald birds, with their quirky blue-black crests and glowing chestnut bibs, shape the experience of this shore, where limited underwater vegetation means they can see their prey with ease. When I landed in a little bay called Perry's Cove, a couple who were watching their dog splash in the water told me they thought of the kingfishers' rattling call as 'a teacup shaking in a saucer'.

As I edged beneath silver and orange cliffs topped by stunted fir trees, I passed large numbers of lolling grey sunfish, while vivid white squid-jigging boats of many sizes passed along the bay. As the hours went by and I moved nearer the end of the peninsula, the sea gathered more roll and churn until, a few hundred metres beyond the headland at Western Point, a huge fin whale slid silently past my boat and left me feeling tinier than I ever had before and unsure whether I could trust my senses.

Eventually, as I reached my turning point, the striped cliffs grew in scale, as did the swell that broke on them. The sound of moving water grew louder than I'd heard it since the storm. I was entering Baccalieu Tickle, one of the richest fishing grounds in Canada, whose name derives from Iberian terms for cod. Breaking waves soon rushed me ashore on Baccalieu Island, and I clambered up to the top of the five square kilometre sea rock. Had I been here two months earlier, I would've shared the little craggy mound with a number of Leach's storm petrels that I still find impossible to comprehend: 3.4 million. And they wouldn't have been alone. The island, at the height of summer, is said to host the greatest diversity of seabirds in all of eastern North America.

Beneath the guano lies an immense depth of history. Early Portuguese maps, from decades before Columbus, refer to a land labelled 'Terra do Bacalhau', which may have indicated the whole of Newfoundland. Tiny Baccalieu Island itself has been marked on maps since 1556. Centuries of European sailors used the island's seabirds to navigate by. As one French traveller, Eugène Ney, put it in 1828:

> They are called Baccalao birds and are useful pilots that Nature seems to have provided for mariners, whom they warn of the closeness of the coast, especially when hidden by fog.

Countless songs and stories relate the rock's pivotal role in sea journeys. The most famous song, 'The Cliffs of Baccalieu', has been recorded by dozens of Newfoundland musicians, many of whom are rooted in Gaelic-speaking Irish and Hebridean traditions. It recalls a boat bound for Newfoundland from the fisheries of Labrador when a nor'easter laden with snow grips the sea: 'the wind swept down upon us making day as black as night/Just before we made the land of Baccalieu'. With waves beating down, and the deck rails tilting beneath the sea, the island looms suddenly upon them. Trapped between the rocks and the gale in blinding sleet that 'would cut you through and through', the seafarers win their battle with the ocean where many others had failed. The combination of big ships passing through with small boats fishing the tickle makes this a place of great cultural significance.

In recent years, Baccalieu Island has been a focal point for innovative studies that entwine biological sciences and historical study to understand how settler society has changed the behaviour of seabirds. Biologists have penned articles such as the multi-authored 'Linking 19th Century European Settlement to the Disruption of a Seabird's Natural Population Dynamics', while Peter Pope's research after *Fish into Wine* turned to seabirds. He drew on diverse sources of Basque and British textual evidence, as well as archaeology, to argue that when settlers arrived in Newfoundland, its north coasts were one vast seabird colony. He showed how transatlantic ships deliberately and consistently sought out spots close to cliffs where seabirds could be caught. Sailors ate the birds and their eggs by the million, and the marine eggs of Newfoundland, like the sugar of the Caribbean, and the furs of the Arctic, were a building block of modernity. It was these texts that finally made sense for me of that most distinctive feature of Newfoundland culture, which sees nature reserves, historic sites, seabird colonies, and fortifications piled one atop another.

I didn't dare spend the night on Baccalieu, since the weather was too unsettled to guarantee a safe return from the island the next day. And the morning seas did indeed run white, recalling the 'Ode to Newfoundland' in which a Barbadian-born governor of the island once declared his love for the northerly 'wind-swept land' that always looked best 'when blinding storm-gusts fret thy shore/and wild waves lash thy strand'. I made my way south along the western shore of the peninsula on foot and by road for a final day of sea travel in the sheltered waters of Trinity Bay and a visit to the cove in which boats that fished the tickle were built.

Founded in the seventeenth century, Scilly Cove was shaped by merchants from Poole who brought many Dorset people to the wooded slopes above its little bay. In 1675, an English naval officer and captain of the annual convoy to Newfoundland, Sir John Berry, made a census of the island's settlements. In Scilly Cove, he listed three 'planters' (the name for Newfoundland's well-to-do middling sorts, who, despite their comforts, were far less wealthy than the merchants). Their households included forty indentured servants as well as eight boats and three fishing stages. When Berry returned the following year, however, the cove's fortunes had increased dramatically: the same three planters had eighty-one labourers and sixteen boats.

In these early years of settlement, boatbuilding was just part of every community's annual round of tasks. The whole operation of the art was made distinctive here by the nature of the materials themselves. White spruce, balsam fir, and juniper (the Newfoundland name for larch) grow in volumes on Newfoundland shores. But these woods are all far softer than the oak commonly used for keels and masts in Europe. The result was that boatbuilding, care, and repair took an unusually large proportion of a community's time, and boat traditions developed in ways that took the short lives of vessels for granted. It was far less a specialised craft than in many other places.

Gradually, Scilly Cove gained repute as a place with good forests and excellent carpenters. Families further along the peninsula, where the fishing was excellent but the forests poor, might exchange their labour or its fruits for the finest watercraft. Often these informal arrangements were just a case of skilled boatbuilding families passing on the boat they'd used for a season or two when they built new vessels. But, in this way, Scilly Cove boats came to populate the whole of the peninsula, frequenting every inch of coast I'd travelled. One variety, used to fish off the end of the peninsula, was even known as the 'Baccalieu skiff'.

KTAQMKUK/NEWFOUNDLAND

Today, Scilly Cove, renamed Winterton, is one of the few places in Newfoundland to retain its boatbuilding heritage. In the 1970s, a folklore student, David Taylor, visited the outport to study boatbuilding traditions. I listened, through the hiss of cassettes, to the interviews he conducted, as well as to those later recorded by Crystal Braye. I admired the gentle, easy way they chatted boats with the quiet, introverted boatbuilders. When Taylor arrived, the local museum was set up as a generalist collection, like most of the new folk museums of the 1970s. He persuaded them to specialise in the boats that made the town distinctive. This would, he insisted, inspire local pride in ways nothing else could. Today, the old United Church school is one of the world's leading boatbuilding museums. It houses, in a shed behind the school, the workshop of the master boatbuilder Jerome Canning, and succeeds in keeping a whole tradition afloat.

I arrived at about 10 a.m. to find Jerome in his workshop. During the time I spent there, a steady flow of locals arrived in pick-ups or on motorbikes to talk boats or local affairs. With thousands of visitors to the workshop every year, it seems that bustle must be a daily affair. The schoolhouse displayed photos of children building model boats to float in the harbour, or helping construct full-size boats. A small but steady income came from selling community-built vessels.

On this day, Jerome was working on a beautiful little rodney for a Newfoundlander living in the United States. The rodney is the smallest and most modest Newfoundland punt, easily worked by a single rower. Its name is thought to come from an old English dialect term meaning 'an idler, or loafer; a casual worker; a disreputable character'. In one of David Taylor's interviews, the Winterton boatbuilder Eleazor Reid explained that rodneys were indeed made to be used by 'casual workers':

Say now, when a man get up [in years, and] he'd be too old to be working clear of home or going away fishing, he had a single-handed Rodney, fifteen or sixteen feet. He'd go out here alongshore, go alongshore fishing, you know.

A pair of short oars (often only seven feet), and sometimes a longer steering oar, would be each boat's standard equipment. Although many photos show one elderly rower in a rodney, others show three children each wielding one of the three oars. The so-called 'wine-glass'-shaped cross section of the hull means that, despite the boat's transom, a rodney is essentially double-ended at the waterline and supremely easy to row. Where bigger boats might be reserved for lengthy fishing trips, these little craft were the ultimate multi-purpose vessels.

Photographs of early twentieth-century Newfoundland show dozens of rodneys moored along the flakes. One of the boat museum's interviewees, Edwin Bishop, suggested their sheer numbers meant that it wasn't just the elderly who used them. The young treated them like other children might use tricycles. He described how, because fishermen used them as tenders for skiffs moored out 'on the collar', there were always dozens that children could take to scull about the bay and visit new places. Preferring sailing to rowing, Bishop and his friends scrounged flour bags to make sails. He talked about even the small boats as social spaces where conversations would have qualities that briefer ones round town never could. He described a neighbour challenging him about boatbuilding on a Sunday, and recounted his response: he was expressing his faith by building a boat just as much as others did when they voiced it in church, and God would want him to use his skills this way.

Another interviewee, Fred Hiscock, described a further use for the rodney. He talked about the forty-two-foot Baccalieu skiffs that sailed out for two weeks at a time. Despite being undecked, and often rowed with long spruce oars, these skiffs would carry two rodneys for handlining in the tickle. Of the five crew, two would row each smaller boat while the fifth would stay on the anchored skiff, cleaning and salting the catch. Hiscock himself liked to row to Baccalieu Island and had two favoured spots, which were known locally as 'Falmouth' and 'London'. At Falmouth there were a few shacks. But London was just a ladder up the cliffs.

Hiscock and his generation were famed for their intuition and ready improvisation in the 'found-timber methodology' of building these boats. In the seasons that marked a turn from fishing to boat-building, he 'went in the woods' to seek out 'what I thought would suit the water . . . I never had no moulds.' As a younger boatbuilder put it, if there was a boat inside the tree,

> The old fellas, they knew when they looked at it. They could know, I suppose, by the tops of the trees. We was in [the woods] one time, I suppose there was four feet of snow or more. We was boiling a kettle and, ah, I don't know if my father said, or my uncle, one of them, he said, 'There's a fine knee under that juniper tree.' You know, just looking at it.

But if the boatbuilders of old were legend, so were childhood summer days. One local I met in Canning's workshop broke into an ear-to-ear grin as he recalled taking his childhood rodney out when the capelin returned each June. He'd row back with a boat twice the weight it started, having witnessed humpback whales chasing the tiny shoaling fish through the bays. After a day of hearing such love for boats pour forth, and of using the resources of the museum, I found myself chatting to a family who had rodneys moored nearby, equipped with carefully maintained traditional engines, which used the extremely simple 'make-and-break' method of the early twentieth century. We headed out together into Trinity Bay and, with a pair of handlines, caught dinner.

One topic that arose repeatedly was the way state bureaucracy in the era of resettlement had threatened to end boatbuilding traditions completely. In the 1960s and 1970s, building boats had been strongly disincentivised by an array of well-meaning but incredibly clumsy initiatives. One had been a programme designed to assist fishers in buying new boats, which placed astonishingly rigid restrictions on the shapes of vessels and on who made them. This both moved boatbuilding out of the community and threatened to render little local harbours obsolete. The scheme specified boats too heavy to be pulled ashore in winter, something the exposed mooring of Winterton required. New conditions for state benefits forbade recipients from engaging in boatbuilding either for sale or for their own use (perversely, someone drawing any kind of benefit could buy themselves a boat). As David Taylor wrote of one of his boatbuilding informants, 'as much as he might want to build a boat, he admitted that it would be wiser for him to "sit on his arse" than risk losing his unemployment checks'. It only takes one generation of such dramatic disincentive for a tradition to unravel.

In the wake of the changes since the 1990s, from renewed interest in wooden boat traditions and the resurgence of Mi'kmaw identity, to the cod moratorium and its strict conditions on the use of boats, the place of traditional vessels in Newfoundland remains unsettled and unclear. Few would deny that bark canoes and wooden boats are the most distinctive and definitive objects of the island's cultures, but few could agree on what this should mean for the island's future. There's an opportunity in the further changes that will inevitably come over the next decades for the rarely attempted experiment of privileging the small-scale and localised, with their associated values of care and stewardship, over the industrial and extractive. A Newfoundland with its heritage of small boats reinvigorated, and tied to island identities, would be a wonder to behold.

7

Maine and Massachusetts
Forest Seas

I

Canonical Coasts

EVERY AUGUST WEEKEND, thousands of little boats are launched onto sheltered inter-island seas on the Maine and Massachusetts coasts. This is a mass embrace of ocean freedom that's accentuated by the contrast with urban life and the physical constraints of nearby cities such as Boston and New York. And these are canonical coasts. Writers elsewhere in this book deserve far more attention than they receive. Those on these northeastern coasts of the United States are the household names of watery literature: Melville, Thoreau, Longfellow. The world's most celebrated marine biologist, Rachel Carson, lived on Cape Cod. The most significant coastal historian in the world, John Gillis, spent his summers on Great Gott Island, Maine. The most revered of all small-boat artists, Winslow Homer, lived on an island-like peninsula here and used little wooden carvel-crafted rowing boats to depict human struggle with nature's overwhelming force. Every tiny island or bay has its poets, painters, craftspeople, and thinkers who have layered the coasts and oceans with meaning.

I was also drawn here by the fact that the number of different small-boat styles on these coasts is unrivalled, as is the number of people who learn boatbuilding methods. This was the first place, in 1605, that a canoe was ever described in text, though the historiography of the people whose lands these are, the Wabanaki Confederacy (the 'People of the Dawnlands'), contains records in rock art, wampum belts, sand paintings, and oral histories that take canoe-borne knowledge back millennia. In later eras, access to small boats here has been uniquely easy and even democratic. Hundreds of styles have been invented or developed on the edge of Maine's vast forests: whitehalls, peapods, dories, punts, barques, gundalows, nutshell prams, shellback dinghies, skiffs, catboats, brigs, jiggers, sloops, yawls, pinks, snows, ketches, shallops, galleys, lobster boats, and many more. Boat styles from far away, including wooden Finnish boats and Cornish pilot gigs, have found second homes among these countless bays and islands too. Tradition here means invention and improvisation not commitment to past forms. One boatbuilder I met put this in a way that seemed to sum up local attitudes: 'I'm not a traditional boatbuilder, but I build traditional boats.' At boatbuilding workshops, schools, and camps, new traditional boats are developed every year: nowhere is wooden boatbuilding more future-oriented, and nowhere has it been possible to take more measures to ensure its survival.

Commercial boatbuilding in the towns fed family use and repair of little boats in rural coves. This was a relationship unmatched elsewhere. Huge fleets of schooners once went out for cod from burgeoning ports such as Gloucester or Portland. The multitudes of tiny rowing boats the schooners carried with them had afterlives long beyond their ocean uses. These dories were built cheap but strong. Sometimes they were stacked eight-high on deck. Places such as Lowell's Boat Shop on the Merrimack River mastered the art of building them exceptionally speedily: in the 1890s, Lowell's alone built almost a thousand a year. Lowered from the ship's deck into wild offshore waters, dories carried pairs of fishermen who rowed out to lay longlines or seine nets. Many of Winslow Homer's most powerful paintings are of these cranky little boats cresting awesome seas. Rowing these craft feels like riding a bike with loose handlebars: every little push, whether of your oars or from a wave, nudges you about. Once you're used to their quirks, though, they're stable and seaworthy as can be.

Because dories, like their rowers, would take a battering each summer, they were frequently replaced. Hundreds of cast-offs were scattered along the shores each autumn. Young people grew up with uniquely easy access to ocean, rivers, and lakes. Freedom of the sea has long been a boon for thousands of New England teens. Many row and sail alone years before they learn to drive a car. This results in many locals having stories of lone childhood voyages through treacherous seas which are both hair-raising and awe-inducing.

When commercial interests moved into the Maine forests, a frenzied timber trade, often likened to a gold rush, boomed. This too was built on boats that had brief commercial lives before being distributed to local teens for a few cents each. The loggers used quick and easy builds to make vessels that could be lashed together to bring rafts of trunks downstream. These 'batteaux' were long flat-bottomed craft, improvised and seemingly crude. But even the roughest examples were praised by observers:

> They are light and shapely vessels, calculated for rough and rocky streams, and to be carried over long portages on men's shoulders, from twenty to thirty feet long, and only four and a half wide . . . in order that they may slip over rocks as gently as possible . . . The batteau is a sort of mongrel between the canoe and . . . a fur-trader's boat.

This observation came from Henry David Thoreau, author of books such as *Walden* and *Civil Disobedience*. Thoreau spent months of his life travelling this region by boat, and though he rarely wrote about the boats themselves, the author of *Walking* represents a boat-bound vision of the world as much as he does a pedestrian one.

Local folk culture, too, embodies the vision of life built on rugged wooden row boats. There are hundreds of songs about Maine boats and their builders caring for one another in a simple but generous symbiosis. In Gordon Bok's 'Saben the Woodfitter', an ageing seafarer is caught in rough weather in a boat as old as he is. As he sleeps his nights in the leaky hull he is haunted by dreams of his vessel's life: 'he dreamed he saw her building . . . and he dreamed he saw her dying in the sea'. He strikes a bargain with his vessel that he will take her apart, plank from plank, prevent her spending more days on the rough ocean, if she can just hold herself together long enough to reach the shore.

> And they say she took him home then, put him on the shore.
> She gave him her timbers to build his house,
> her plank for his wall and her keel for his rooftree,
> and she wrapped him up in her old brown sail
> and laid him down,
> sang him to sleep
> while the winter wind came off the western ocean:
>
> East wind's rain and north wind's clearing,
> Cold old southwest wind's a fair wind home.
>
> One bell, two bells, don't go grieving,
> All our bad times past and blown alee.

In the words of the local poet Derrek Schrader, such a fisherman has the responsibility for 'beating the sun to morning' each day. To make a living, he must be standing, feet planted squarely on his dory's flat wooden floor, and rocking with the swell before 'the sun curls over the tips of waves'. It's equal hardship and joy to be so far into the ocean that he's the first in the United States to see the dawn.

I'd arrived on the seas of these dawnlands as October became November: a month later than the season I'd left Newfoundland. The whole sea seemed to smell of forest. Golden leaves speckled the beaches. Islands appeared first as rafts of spiky spruce tops. Only as tides carried me closer did land break the horizon. Grey seals basked, like woodland creatures, in forest shade, while chipmunks scuttled through breakers. Even the great blue herons, legs submerged in saltwater, looked unsettled when raucous forest jays skimmed the waves. The wooded shore had an almost spring-like liveliness, though the people at these overlaps of tree and sea were busy bringing boats ashore for winter or shuttering summer houses to return to cities.

II

The Island of the Desert Mountains

In 1604, Samuel de Champlain, the French soldier and navigator who would establish New France as a permanent colony in the Americas, arrived at a formidable island with a vast indented coastline:

> It is very high, with notches here and there so that it appears, when one is at sea, like seven or eight mountains rising close together. The tops of most of them are without trees, because they are nothing but rock . . . I called it the Island of the Desert Mountains.

He described the location of Mount Desert Island, as it became known, at the edge of an enticing ocean world where 'the quantity of islands, rocks, shallows, banks and breakers is such everywhere that it is strange to see'. He recalled myths of a great indigenous city, said to be in this region, with pillars of crystal and silver and pearls as common as pebbles.

Over the following two decades, French and English interest in Mount Desert Island waxed. The first thoughts of those who passed these regions, 'ouergrowen with all sorts of excellent good woodes', was always the building of 'boats, barks, or shippes'. In London, in 1622, John Haviland printed, on behalf of the New England Joint Stock Company, *A Briefe Relation of the Discovery and Plantation of New England*. As well as detailing the woody riches of the shore, this described the fauna at great length. The moose, a creature barely known to the English at the time, received particular attention. The *Briefe Relation* detailed every aspect of the moose's appearance and every use to which indigenous peoples put it. It told how a great many could be seen on Mount Desert Island, and how Wabanaki people pursued them into the sea and then used boats to round them up or kill them. On this island, the authors surmised, it might be possible for settlers to capture moose and bring them into domestic service like horses or oxen.

The *Briefe Relation* then gave an equally acquisitive description of the riches of the region:

> Fish of seuerall sorts, rich Furres, as Beauers, Otters, Martins, blacke Fox, Sables, &c. There are likewise plenty of Vines, of three kindes, and those pleasant to the taste, yet some better then other. There is Hempe, Flax, Silkgrasse, seuerall veines of Ironstone, commodities to make Pitch, Rosen, Tarre; Deale boords of all sorts, Sparres, Masts, for Ships of all burdens; in a word, there comes no commodity out of *France*, *Germany*, or the *Sound*, but may be had there, with reasonable labour and industry . . . There is no want of any thing, but of industrious people, to reape the commodities that are there

to be had . . . We purpose from henceforth to build our shipping there, where wee find all commodities fit for that service, together with the most opportune places, that can bee desired.

As I paddled from the mainland to reach this 'opportune place', the sheltered sound was a frenzy of ducks, grebes, loons, and seals in windless, waveless skies and seas. I continued east, past Canoe Point, and layer upon layer of two centuries' tourist infrastructure. At the town of Bar Harbor are centres of Wabanaki life, including the site of a famous 'Indian village' to which the Penobscot, one of the peoples of the Wabanaki confederacy, travelled in the nineteenth and twentieth centuries, to sell birch baskets and other wares to visitors.

But by the time I turned south, the sea's moods were different. Deep-blue surf and swell rolled wildly in. There were rarely buildings, just a band of yellow-grey rock and concrete where the toll road through the national park hugged the shore. The day was filled with salt-rime, sunburst, and gannet dive, till my heart was truly singing with the salty pleasure of it all but my boat was filled completely with water. Sloshing through the big seas felt like wading through swirling syrup. As evening set in and the sky purpled dramatically, I landed, and emptied my boat of sea. I was beside a bulky, whitewashed seamark on a tiny skerry called East Bunker Ledge.

The pewter ocean and its dark, wooded shores were ravishingly beautiful. Flocks of geese filled the sky and loons cackled on the water. But any sense of wildness was offset by the names of these waters. I was in the centre of Eastern Way, with Western Way and Gilley Thorofare nearby. East Bunker Ledge is a crossroads rather than a place that's off the beaten track. I feared that by low tide there'd be seals wishing to haul themselves ashore. And so I launched once more. I became quickly accustomed to challenges in finding places to sleep. Attitudes to property are different here than on most coasts. They're far more like those of cities. The people of Maine have unusual degrees of restriction on their access to coastal land. Private property extends by state law to the low-tide line, so beaches sometimes bristle with 'Keep Out' signs in ways I've never seen elsewhere. I arrived a week after rallies held on the shore to protest against local people's banishment from their beaches.

But the pay-off for launching again was immense. As I looked back into the orange sky, the skerries and rock ledges I'd passed seemed to float in the air, magically lifted metres above the sea so I could see the sky beneath them. Any seals watching my boat might see a vessel floating through salty ether on the edges of reality. These being islands that inspired swathes of verse, I was unsurprised there was a description of precisely the phenomenon I'd just seen. When the poet Robert Lowell died, his fellow poet Elizabeth Bishop memorialised him in verse. The two had each written of singing to seals in the regions I was in, and Bishop's poem was set among the islands and filled with the rigging of schooners, the flora of coastal spring, and the songs of goldfinches and sparrows. His absence, she wrote, seemed to leave their favourite island drifting in air – 'afloat in mystic blue' – despite being in reality 'anchored in its rock'.

I paddled on till the sun set among a group of islets, the Cranberry Islands, that nestle in the large bay of Mount Desert Island's southeast corner. I landed on the rocky edge of the northernmost islet, where a steep cobblestone beach rose to a wooden ladder that led to spruce woods and a cabin that was empty and secured for winter. I decided to wrap myself up and rest at the water's edge. More flocks of geese passed slowly over the hills of the national park. Waves and cackling loons were the only sounds as I settled into an illicit night's sleep; in the morning, I cleared the plastic from the tideline to bin in the nearest town as recompense for my trespass. Country music already blared across the water from the stereos of little working boats.

I paddled to Mount Desert Island's southwestern settlements in search of boatbuilding heritage. I'd already learned I was five years too late to meet the last generation of island builders of traditional wooden rowing boats. But everyone I spoke to directed me to the part of Southwest Harbor known as Manset, where many boatbuilders had spent their days. There were still lots of people who'd known them and who met the mention of their names with smiling praise. I wandered into Ocean House boatyard, where several builders of modern boats were constructing or repairing yachts, and asked around after anyone who owned or used traditional craft. But all the stories they told me were of the generation who'd recently passed. One man I spoke to there had been taught to build dories by one of the iconic figures of that generation, Ralph Stanley, but had not built one for decades.

Stanley's was the name that cropped up everywhere. He was tradition bearer as much as craftsman; his ancestors had settled on the Cranberry Islands in 1755 and he knew the songs and stories of the islands like no one else. His carpentry was devoted not just to making boats but also violins. This folksy link exists in many places, but was worn with pride in Maine, where fiddles and model boats are often mounted side by side.

Recollections of Stanley's boatbuilding often claim that the first vessel he built was an engine-powered lobster boat. But that's to ignore the true origins of his passion: while still a schoolboy in the 1940s, and working with a few borrowed tools, he'd built a fifteen-foot rowing dory that was his pride and joy. This tendency to forget the rowing boats was something I came across frequently: it was possible to find written records of the sailboats a builder had made – the sloops and ketches – but it was only in conversations with local people that lists of the smaller, rowed boats poured forth. Stanley and his school friend would row their little dory round Greening Island or out to Great Cranberry on after-school evenings. This is how he built the sea knowledge that made him a legendary local figure.

Stanley learned how to build this boat by wandering into all the local shops (in Maine, places a British person would describe as boatbuilding 'workshops' are just 'shops'). There, he simply observed the quiet, introverted boatbuilders who had neither the words nor inclination to describe the details of what they did. His driving need, he said, was to build a vessel to gain for himself the freedom of the sea. But as soon as a community sees a person build a good craft, everyone wants one like it: the orders pour in, the boats spread along the coast, and a reputation wells up from little waves into a great groundswell.

The reputation Stanley built was for boats that were fast but supremely comfortable and practical. People who saw him sail said he always seemed to be at leisure on the sea: so attuned to wood and water that everything looked comfortable and easy. Many of the themes I'd seen elsewhere cropped up in descriptions of his work: he saw boats as alive, with their own spirits; he could imagine in a blown-down tree the precise behaviour of a finished boat on the water; and he had an artistry and ease with traditional tools, such as the adze, which in other hands would seem crude and clunky.

When he got tuberculosis in the late 1950s, Stanley turned full time to working with wood and gave up seeking an income from sailing or fishing. Whenever a tree blew down, Stanley would be first on the scene. If he couldn't see a boat in it, a fiddle would appear instead, with elegant boat-like curves on a miniature scale. Stanley passed the boatbuilding mantle to his son, Richard, who now builds fibreglass-topped motorboats just a few miles from Southwest Harbor. But in his later years, Stanley's quest was to spread his knowledge further. He aimed to 'keep the wood alive' by teaching at WoodenBoat School on the mainland a few miles west. All talk it seemed, like all local boatbuilding careers, circled back to this centre at the village of Brooklin. So it was time to launch through the island maze once more.

III

A Saltwater Campus

I'd hit fiercely choppy waters as I passed from a night on the little Pond Island towards the safety of Eggemoggin Reach. But, once there, I was in a soft and gentle seascape that felt as much like an inland lake as the sea. The forests that reached to the shoreline, overhanging gentle pebble beaches, only increased that impression. In the mid-twentieth century, the village of Brooklin was far larger than it is today, thanks in part to factories for canning sardines and beans. But the later years of the century saw many industries abandon these bays for places better connected by road. Traditional boatbuilding, on the other hand, grew dramatically, so that the village now has a feel much less industrial than in the middle of the last century. Brooklin boatyard, *WoodenBoat* magazine, and WoodenBoat School are the most famous of several institutions and endeavours that mean the boats here outnumber the population of 800.

Although the growth of this activity bears all the hallmarks of the Atlantic-wide 1970s revivals, there are also ways in which its origins attest to the distinctiveness of Maine culture. In 1965, a young college dropout with the air of a 'scraggle-headed, long-haired teepee dweller' stumbled into a boatyard on Long Island Sound which happened to be committed to wooden boatbuilding in ways few then were. Jon Wilson arrived with a generalised enthusiasm for watercraft, but work as a yard hand here sparked a lifelong passion for wood and a desire to comprehend the seemingly supernatural skills of past boatbuilders.

He began his own workshop in Maine, but realised that, since he wasn't the fastest worker and could only ever build so many boats, the impact he could have this way would be localised and limited. He believed more sweeping action was needed since wooden boatbuilding was close to extinction everywhere it once thrived. The question before him, then, wasn't just how to make his workshop successful; it was how to revive the whole beautiful art, or even just slow the process of its disappearance. His grand ambition was to find a way to enthuse 'a few thousand' people. Despite a total lack of experience in printing, he settled on the idea of a magazine as a way to build his imagined community. 'You have to appreciate,' he insisted, 'how naively I asked this question. I had no idea what I was thinking about. I just thought "Why not?"'

In any other state, someone with no idea how to start a boatbuilding magazine might have failed for lack of mentoring. But Wilson found that John Gardner, 'the father of the modern wooden boat revival', was just a short sail away. In Wilson's words, Gardner combined the Maine virtues: 'a towering scholar' who could 'hew heavy timbers with a broad axe'. Gardner was ready to help, but had a very traditional idea of how a boatbuilding magazine should operate: a simple and functional black-and-white journal that gave novice boatbuilders the information they required to learn the craft. Wilson's ambitions were to reach those who didn't yet know they were novice boatbuilders at all. He set out to conjure curiosity and delight with lavish colour images and friendly, poetic prose. As one commentator put it, 'Everything in *WoodenBoat* looks as though it was photographed at 3 o'clock on a summer afternoon on golden pond.'

What makes this endeavour so characteristic of Maine is that, despite this professional, glossy aesthetic, the base for the new magazine was a cabin in the woods without electricity or running water, just a telephone a kilometre down the road which was screwed to the trunk of an old white pine. Wilson feared the prospect of anything costly, after watching another coastal magazine collapse because of the expense of office space in New York. To his surprise and satisfaction, his first edition, in 1974, sold 9,000 copies. But what followed was yet more unexpected: every year for the next decade the circulation grew by 10,000. The growth was such that John Summers, writing in *Material History Review* in 1992, argued that 'the story of the persistence of wood as a boat-building material is to a very large extent the story of the persistence of *WoodenBoat*'.

Later, after several tribulations, including a burglary and fire at the premises, a twist of good fortune allowed Wilson and *WoodenBoat* to buy the saltwater campus I'd just arrived at. Wilson itched for a practical, hands-on, branch of the magazine's unexpectedly successful efforts: 'I wanted [the magazine's mission] to be expressed in three dimensions.' Soon he was collaborating with others such as Joel White, who would become another of the region's most prodigious innovators, to design new wooden boats with simplified construction processes and versatile handling. The first they created, the nutshell pram, was just seven and a half feet long and designed for almost any purpose: rowing, sculling, sailing, or towing. Plans or kits of pre-cut wood could be bought direct. Joel White described his first royalty cheque for these plans as the proudest moment of his life: it meant being one of the architects of a new movement, not just a remnant of a dying trade.

Before I arrived in Brooklin, I'd seen photos of the area arrayed with dozens of diverse sail- and rowing boats equipped for regattas. But now, after the end of another heady sailing season, there was just a pair of chipmunks dashing round the rocks. I wandered up to the storage sheds, where Jon Wilson's successor as director, Rich Hilsinger, was busy securing boats for the winter. After a brief chat about the array of boats built that summer, he showed me up to the shop which, in a way that's characteristic of the boat school's ethos, is always left unlocked.

I was taken aback by the scale and beauty of the place. In Britain, these would be the grounds of a great country house, like the setting for a particularly marine Jane Austen novel. The offices themselves were built as the home of a family of four in 1916, but contain thirty-five impressive rooms. They sit up the hill from a large complex of handsome and sturdy workshops, two large buildings to accommodate visiting students, a retail space where boat plans, hoodies, hats, and books can be bought, several boatsheds, and launches onto both a small lake and the ocean. The walls of the workshops are plastered with notes, sketches, doodles, and messages from countless mentors and students over forty years. There are now a hundred classes each summer for 800 boatbuilders of all skill levels.

I've yet to meet anyone who has been here who doesn't speak of these grounds as salty heaven on earth. The WoodenBoat staff and I talked through the roster of tutors past and present, discussing the ways in which most of them are not just boatbuilders but also impassioned activists for the small communities they live in and against the threats, social and environmental, that face them. Brad Dimock and Cricket Zarn, for instance, are legendary boat people, instrumental in introducing and adapting the Atlantic dory to the Colorado River, where these little boats have become a celebrated success story in galvanising community resistance to the damming and destruction of waterways. Their boats, initially all named after rivers destroyed by dams, appear in campaigns around the world, especially with photos of Cricket standing with an oar in each hand, masterfully weaving her adapted dory through shockingly intense white water. The presence of so many activists on the school's roster impressed on me that, even in their leisure revival, wooden boats are still working boats. They drive, without a wisp of nostalgia, major social and environmental agendas.

I stayed in Brooklin for the night and talked to people as I strolled around. On the far side of the village from the boat school, I bumped into a group of teenagers launching a Cornish pilot gig. Then, as I walked through the village centre, I noted how many residents were still in sea clothes. I was struck by the way the community and the boat school seem aligned. There was nothing here of the conflict between a local community and its biggest source of incomers which happens in many places: no outsiders looking down on a rural place, and no residents mocking visitors' naivety about the realities of coastal life. I made a firm commitment, there and then, to make it back to Brooklin when the summer schools were in full flow.

IV

Meanings of Home

From Brooklin, my two-day journey northwest to Belfast would eventually pass across the mouth of the Penobscot River. Along the way, shorelands opened out into fields as well as forest, scattered with homes, businesses, and roads that clustered where river and sea merged. To the Penobscot Nation, these tidal headwaters are sacred. Fresh water gathered from vast swathes of forest flows into salt tides and brings burgeoning life from both directions. Bark canoes made from the region's plentiful paper birches permitted an intensely mobile way of life within the river's vast watershed (which accounts for two thirds of what is now the state of Maine). Thousands of miles of smaller waterways are linked together by the great river highway itself. Many of the clans into which the Penobscot are organised are named for the river's creatures: eel, dragonfly, sturgeon, eagle. These animals provided tools, such as beaver-tooth chisels, with which canoes were built. Eight thousand Penobscot once lived around the river and coast, using long poles to punt upstream, and paddling out to islands for clams, oysters, and fishing. Their canoes, smaller than those of the Beothuk, are exceptionally versatile for flat water, sea, and rapids. Penobscot life was mobile and seasonal, with boats and coasts the mediums for summer living, and forests the winter heartlands. Each autumn, canoes were sunk in still, shallow water, then recovered in the spring. This kept their bark pliable over many years.

Birchbark canoes were present in large numbers when Europeans first landed. But we have almost no evidence concerning much of the early European activity. Even the captains of Basque and Bristol ships, which visited these shores long before supposed 'first contact', were illiterate, and they were tasked with secrecy concerning the fishing grounds and forests that they found. Further obfuscation was created by the politics of European states and their 'doctrine of discovery'. This had been used by the Catholic church since the fifteenth century to grant nations rights of dominion over all lands 'not yet claimed by a Christian sovereign'. In this way, first contact was claimed repeatedly, even when the indigenous people encountered were clearly quite accustomed to trading with Europeans. Christianity was used as a measure of humanity, much as being settled rather than mobile was in later centuries. In this way, 'discovery' became a fiction which encouraged seafarers to concoct stories of heathen savages who lived crude lives in vacant lands. The politics of 'discovery' prevented any recognition of indigenous sophistication and sovereignty. Words such as 'vacant' in this discourse conveyed a specifically European vision in which all uncultivated land was 'waste' except in so far as its potential for 'civilised' agriculture could be conjured in the mind's eye. As late as 1605, English ships were still claiming to be visiting vacant shores where 'no Christian had been before', despite well-attested events such as English ships stealing 'three hundred dried moose skins' from advanced indigenous cultures on the same stretch of coast twenty-five years earlier.

Many of the European texts from this era are also unhelpfully imprecise in their geographical descriptions. In 1605, a 'light horseman' rowing boat, captained by the Englishman George Waymouth, entered the mouth of a great river, kidnapped indigenous people and stole several canoes. These events were published as part of an account of Waymouth's journey, and for centuries historians have argued about whether the river the book described was the St George or the Penobscot. For Waymouth's river to be the Penobscot, his crew would have had to row eighty miles in twenty-five hours. Believing this to be impossible, most historians assumed his river to be the St George, despite considerable inconsistencies between topography and text. In 2002, a group of local historians and rowers decided to settle this issue. They painstakingly built a replica of Waymouth's light horseman and successfully proved that the distance was no barrier to identification with the Penobscot. What could seem, in a different context, to be a matter of historical trivia matters deeply where the historical interactions of a colonial power and an indigenous people are at stake.

Other evidence concerning early encounters tells a very different story from that contained in the documentary record. It seems that Basque loanwords in indigenous languages predate Columbus. Penobscot memory held stories of sightings of 'large canoes' filled with unfamiliar people – white skinned, hairy, and noisy – many decades, or even centuries, before the larger influxes began. Early encounters played major roles in Penobscot oral histories. When the big ships were eventually sighted, they were compared to great swans. This was a many-layered metaphor. The colour white, in Penobscot lore, denoted origins in the east. The ships' sun-bleached sails billowed like the wings of swans swimming in threat displays. Their bows were crusted white with salt to match the pale people on them. They arrived and left at the times the swans migrated.

By the late nineteenth century, a few Penobscot elders were recording their people's history in texts such as Joseph Nicolar's *The Life and Traditions of the Red Man* (1893). This work provides

Penobscot retrospectives on the era when European rowing boats began to mix with the canoes of the bay. It recounts the things reported back by the 'spiritual men' chosen to follow these new people and observe their habits. Nicolar tells, too, of early prophecies that warned of the visitors' dangerous combination of power that could undermine the natural order, along with a lack of the morality that might prevent them doing so. Because news travelled fast and far in indigenous societies, shared at large summer camps and through trade, a people's first sighting of Europeans was rarely a surprise. The indigenous experience of first contact was therefore profoundly different from what Europeans imagined it to be.

By 1605, French and English seafarers were endeavouring to begin a fur trade from the coasts of Maine. Because birchbark canoes were the only way to access the interior, they relied heavily on indigenous paddlers and guides. Penobscot memory recalls this moment as the start of new divisions between the bands of the coast. But this was not the most profound impact of the arrival of big ships in a world of small boats. By 1620 (the year of the Pilgrim Fathers), the diseases Europeans brought with them had wiped out an estimated 75 per cent of the indigenous population. Many past camps and settlements lay empty, and European commentaries on squalor and savagery multiplied. Since the medical knowledge of elders had failed to see off the new diseases, significant damage was also done to the social prestige of leaders and to tribes' self-confidence.

From this moment onwards, interactions between Penobscot and Europeans revealed profoundly different world views, especially regarding the relationship of humans to land and sea. Divergent understandings of concepts relating to home, property, and family led to wildly different expectations of what the outcomes of their negotiations meant. For a long time, historians wrote as though the picture of Penobscot life given by official records was accurate. By the early nineteenth century, the Penobscot had been dispossessed of almost all their lands, and the official record suggested their lives were contained within sedentary settlements on the islands of the Penobscot River. Only recently have scholars such as Micah Pawling worked collaboratively with Penobscot historians to reveal a different picture, in which old canoe networks persisted and usage of the coast was far greater than other historians once assumed. Pawling writes that divergent visions of what constituted 'home' stand at the heart of misconceptions:

> Maine officials attempted to draw lines around homeland and build roofs over it, but they failed to contain it. State policies and goals failed, in large part, because they struggled to hit a moving target.

When, in 1857, Henry David Thoreau travelled by canoe with a Penobscot guide, Joseph Polis, their contrasting visions of home were evident from the interactions Thoreau recorded. As they approached the seat of Penobscot tribal government, Old Town Island, Thoreau asked Polis whether he was glad 'to get home again'. Polis responded, 'It makes no difference to me where I am'; to which the uncomprehending Thoreau noted: 'Such is the Indian's pretence always.'

The Penobscot vision that home was a portable idea, present anywhere canoes could go, can in fact be seen in hosts of nineteenth-century sources, where Penobscot mobility brushed up against the idea that home was an item of private property. In 1825, a reporter for the *Eastern Argus* noted that

> in the spring and fall the tribe, which consists perhaps of three or four hundred, all assemble at Old Town . . . In the cold winter months they go into the forest and stay, where they can procure wood for their fires without much labor, and in the summer season they scatter . . . on the rivers and on the sea shore.

There are many reports of groups visiting sites that remained fine sea-fishing spots, or places where salmon had once been caught before dams and weirs blocked the rivers. In these places by the shore, they'd cut wood and build wigwams. The owners of this private property frequently petitioned the state for compensation for their damaged wood-lots. Sometimes they would try to force indigenous peoples away, but were answered by the Penobscots' assertions that property owner's had no right to block customary land use.

By the twentieth century, the point where the river splits around the Penobscot Nation's reservation at Old Town Island had become the canoe-building capital of the eastern United States. In 1912, the Old Town Canoe Company was producing 4,000 canoes a year. Penobscot people made up a significant proportion of its sixty-strong workforce. This organisation was at the forefront of experiments with new methods and materials, such as lightweight woods and canvas. Early in its history, the company was committed to working with wood and resisted new materials such as aluminium and fibreglass; in the 1940s, the managing director even had on his desk a sign that read: 'If God wanted fiberglass boats, he would have made fiberglass trees'. When, in the 1970s, Old Town finally embraced those materials, the company licensed a nearby outfit, Island Fall Canoes, to continue to build its classic wooden designs.

It was in part because of this strong commitment to tradition in the building of canoes that there were individuals in the region, such as Steve Cayard, who kept many old traditions alive. When several different Wabanaki peoples sought to revive birchbark canoe building at the turn of the century, it took the pooling of many different communities' knowledge to achieve this goal. In 2002, Cayard was invited to run workshops on Old Town Island and help restore techniques of building with bark that the communities themselves had lost. Through the Penobscot workforce at Old Town Canoes, and the methods practised by individuals such as Cayard, the productive interaction of settler and indigenous boatbuilding has made this region a beacon of hope for the survival of birchbark knowledge and skill.

Before leaving Maine, I went to meet members of a group called Come Boating, who race Cornish pilot gigs on both sides of the Atlantic. And I took a tiny wooden pram out from Lowell's Boat Shop onto the Merrimack River. My short oars barely creaked as they span through the slow, dark stream and the water lapped at the edges of jetties. This was the only time in my life I've been able to hear the hand tools of a busy traditional workshop while on the water: saws creaked and hammers clanged, ringing out on a gentle breeze as though it was 1890.

V

A Steep Mountain of Water

I hired a car for the journey south and borrowed a sea kayak for the rougher waters I'd soon face. It was with trepidation that I realised I'd be leaving the chatty calm of the boat schools and boat shops for a world once populated by a boat called the 'surf dory'. By 1890, the dory family had branched into a large clan. The Grand Banks dories are the true workhorses, with carrying capacity prioritised over ease of rowing. Swampscott dories, 'the aristocrats of the dory clan', are at least as able on rough seas, but are gentler to handle. The surf dory is the natural lifeboat and one of the most capable vessels on earth in the heavy, broken surf of Cape Cod.

These seas were the sharpest contrast to those of Maine. The extravagantly long and sandy beaches often have a sudden, heavy dump onto shore that makes safe landing near-impossible. Offshore swell is chaotic and speeds in with uncomfortably short wavelengths: there's never a moment to relax in a flat trough or rounded peak.

Where tides ran, they ran exceptionally strong, making advanced planning of each leg crucial. The swell was exactly like a Winslow Homer painting, and the ducking and diving of my kayak resembled his sea-swept dories. To make matters worse, a dramatic drop in temperature was predicted to bring the first snow. I decided to try and cover the bulk of the most threatening seas in a single day, paddling from Provincetown in the north along beach after sea-eaten beach to land on the east side of the town of Wellfleet, from where I could spend a less frantic second day exploring the historic boat-building coast.

Before setting off, I spent my evening reading books about the region and I was struck by just how different being a hundred yards offshore would make my view of the coast. Henry James, in *The Bostonians* (1886), wrote descriptions that were a world away from the place I was witnessing:

> the Cape was the Italy, so to speak, of Massachusetts; it had been described . . . as the drowsy Cape, the languid Cape, the Cape not of storms, but of eternal peace . . . Bostonians had been drawn thither, for the hot weeks, by its sedative influence . . . In a career in which there was so much nervous excitement as in theirs they had no wish to be wound up when they went out of town . . . They wanted to live idly, to unbend and lie in hammocks, and also to keep out of the crowd, the rush of the watering-place.

Thoreau was the only nineteenth-century writer I found whose prose echoed my experience. Rarely a seafarer, he visited Cape Cod four times between 1849 and 1857 in order to learn a little of this ocean 'of which a man who lives a few miles inland may never see any trace, more than of another world'. He described Massachusetts as a pugilist braced to fight the ocean, locked in endless conflict as land and sea grappled to heave each other aside. In this vision, Provincetown was 'a sandy fist' and Cape Cod itself was 'the bared and bended arm of Massachusetts . . . boxing with northeast storms'.

This description was shaped by his first visit in 1849. Travelling after a storm, he witnessed the aftermath of a shipwreck in which a brig carrying emigrants from Galway had foundered on the rocks. The drowned were being packed emotionlessly into coffins. This led him to his first sympathy with coastal people who, after the incident, 'would watch there many days and nights for the sea to give up its dead'.

I set out from the shelter of Provincetown, knowing that in passing round the hook of the cape's northern headland I'd face almost every sea condition. With each kilometre of the spiral out from the bay – travelling south, then west, then north, then east, then south again – the scale of the seas grew. With them, the qualities of the air transformed. In Provincetown, the skies had been bright and clean, with just a few cumulus clouds zipping overhead. By the time I was paddling the exposed east coast, everything was dazzling seaspray and salt haze. Each wave sparkled aggressively as its foamy peaks caught the sunlight. I thought I'd reached the height of the sea's roughness long before I truly had, and I stayed far offshore, where breakers strafed through hundreds of yards of shallow seas. It wasn't long till arms, eyes, and brain ached from the pulse of heaving ocean.

Black forms hurried past or bobbed by. Many were surf scoters: stunning black seaducks whose comfort on these waves felt disconcerting as I laboured past them. Others were seals, whose speed in rough seas is always disorienting. My strongest association when I remember this cape journey isn't the bright gleam of violent swell, but the strange behaviour of these seals. Whether in these rough waters or in later sheltered seas, I found myself, more than ever before, seeming to be living in their communities. Even a quick pause to catch my breath was often enough to find eyes and noses all around. In rough seas, they'd just race past repeatedly and circle by, like wet greyhounds, but wherever there was anything stiller, there'd be snorting, spluttering, heavy breathing, and all the signs of happy lazing. Never was there any of the tail-slapping with which seals often warn boats off. Sometimes a huge bull seal would lounge beside the boat: infinitely more powerful than me, with a neck thick as a moose's and a strong, unblinking stare. But, even then, I had the feeling I was somehow seen as useful, and I loved the sense of being part of these sea flocks.

If landings on surf-strewn stretches were always brutal, they were at least predictable. There was no danger here of unseen rocky reefs, since the whole world was simply sand, water, seal, and sunlight. Every landing felt like a rugby match: bruising tackles but, ultimately, safety. Wide stretches of beach were empty, with just occasional deckchairs, family strolls, and people fishing (seemingly with great success). There were none of the crowds that would have lined the sands three months earlier.

In Wellfleet, I crossed the cape and paddled from the sheltered harbour to the historic sites of the Great Island peninsula, where a seventeenth-century tavern and other early settler structures had been sited. There were many small boats, and the shores were alive with local people picking clams. Then suddenly, in shallow water near a stretch of sand lined with straggly pitch pine, a blue shadow in the water grew at alarming speed. Before I could process what was going on, an eight-foot mako shark had passed me and slowed to a drift, its great fin cutting the surface. These huge sharks, as heavy as a grand piano, use their speed and weight to hunt: they barrel into prey at fifty kilometres an hour, then circle back to their stunned victim, rows of razor-sharp teeth bared. As well as seals, they hunt animals as fast and powerful as swordfish and other sharks. I should have felt relieved to see this awesome great blue shape at all (since if it mistook me for prey I wouldn't have spotted it till the water was already scattered with boat and paddler), but I didn't have quite that clarity of thought during one of my most heart-stopping moments on the sea. It was a reminder that these waters, populated by great whites, hammerheads, and many other species, are very different from the seas I'm used to. The reason seals clung to boats like comfort blankets suddenly became clear.

After landing, I went to visit Walter Baron, whose workshop in the woods is filled with many kinds of little boat. Baron's story echoes those of many others round New England. There was no history of boatbuilding in the family, but he grew up with the freedom to take to the water in the dories that scattered coast, lake, and river. With a love of boats, but a career in house carpentry, he subscribed to magazines such as *WoodenBoat* and occasionally repaired the odd small vessel. Then he began building simple plywood prams and soon branched out into dories and skiffs. In the years since, he has built dory-skiffs for the town of Wellfleet, skiffs to be raffled off by the Wellfleet Historical Society, Greenland kayaks, and countless other styles for private buyers. It's entirely in keeping with the boatbuilding cultures of New England, however, that he has followed this love for elegant wooden boats wherever it led. In recent years, he has specialised in the fast-rowing vessels of Savo in Finland. When a couple from up the coast, Leigh Dorsey and Dameon Colbry, wanted a wooden boat to row the Race to Alaska, it was Baron they approached to build it. They already owned one of the Finnish boats he builds (*Norppa*, meaning 'Ringed Seal'), but commissioned him to construct a sturdier ocean version, *Mursu* ('Walrus'). He explained to me what it took to make a small two-person boat that could handle huge swells, with the threat of capsizing, and seas filled with dangers, such as thousands of huge driftwood logs. The adaptations, such as using white oak gunwales instead of pine and adding a couple of extra ribs, showed the impact that even small shifts in the handling of wood could have.

From Wellfleet onwards, Cape Cod's outward edge isn't a great wall of unbroken sand, as before, but is breached by the sea to reveal marshlands and salt flats behind. Amid the ocean's chaos, each paddle into marshes felt like entering some unreal and Edenic space. They were near silent but for birdlife. My longest break from the swell was in the marsh maze of Nauset Bay. This was where Samuel de Champlain landed on Cape Cod in 1605, finding the thatched homes, bark canoes, and plots of corn, beans, and squash of the Wampanoag, the indigenous peoples of the cape. He named it Port de Mallebarre (the 'Port of Dangerous Shoals') but centuries of sea have transformed the geographies he witnessed. By the nineteenth century, the waterways of this large marsh were criss-crossed by small wooden barges, rowed or poled, which supplied the bedding and feed for livestock for many miles around. There are still Cape Cod residents who recall the salty milk produced by animals fed on marsh grass. The last living example of these flat-bottomed boats sits beside the water at the western extremity of the bay.

The marsh's great chronicler, Wyman Richardson, arrived when the era of the hay barges was giving way to tourism and leisure. In articles for *The Atlantic* (collected as *The House on Nauset Marsh* in 1955, he described both the life of the marsh and 'the joy of the sea'. His prose is full of leisurely observation of other species, from gyrfalcons to sea bass. But one such piece revealed all the perils for young people of the easy availability of dories on these shores. He discussed the difficulty of launching a boat from the dunes beyond the marsh, emphasising the need to choose the right moment, when the surf was at its smallest:

> Take her out then, if you must; take her out surely and quickly, and never, never think of turning back. Likely you will have to climb over a steep mountain of water, and you may smash down so hard in the next trough that the bow goes clean under, but if you have figured correctly, and if you keep heading out, you will make it.

I thought of the times I've launched a kayak in surf and been flipped in a somersault back over my head to flop back onto the beach, and I wondered at the idea of Richardson, as a young boy, launching an open dory in seas that scale.

Richardson then discussed the far greater challenge of timing a landing. 'It is still another thousand times more difficult,' he wrote; 'I know, because I have been there.' He told of the time he and two friends took a dory along this coast, not quite aware of the treacherous seas they were embarking on, but too 'young and stubborn' to give up at the point they should have. He recounted unforgettable moments when they were too close to a submerged sandbar and huge waves reared up as if to take the little boat in their jaws. Luckily, the waves broke just beyond them rather than baring white teeth with the boat still at the swell's lip. The boys, nerve spent, turned towards shore opposite what was then a lifeboat station. It was only at this moment that they became aware of the eternal difficulty of attempting to land in rough seas: the impossibility of judging, from behind, where the waves begin to break. They held their position, awaiting some clue as to how they could safely time their push into the surge. But none came. Eventually, the far larger lifeboat dory was rowed out to their rescue. When they were loaded into the lifeboat, their own little dory was simply cut loose and abandoned to the sea. After a full fifteen minutes waiting for the perfect moment, the captain cried out, 'Now!'

> The boat came to life as the crew bent to their oars. Then ominously a wave . . . rose higher and higher astern. The lifeboat came up on the wave's crest, and, gathering speed, slowly started to point her bow downward. All at once she began to yaw to port. The Captain, with his steering oar over the starboard quarter, put all his weight on it, but could not straighten us out. Quick as a flash, the stroke oarsman jerked his oar out of the lock and slid it over

the same quarter. This proved to be just enough to bring us around, and we shot in, riding the wave, at what seemed to me the speed of light ... Had we yawed around just a little further, nothing on earth could have stopped us. In a jiffy we would have turned broadside to the sea, and been rolled over and over like a bobbin on a spinning machine.

Richardson insisted dories were designed so that, with their great flat bottoms, they always came through surf and landed right side up. The advice for anyone out on a rough sea is thus to lie down in the bottom of the boat, ignore their peril as best they can, and simply let the trusty vessel do its thing, unhindered by human error. Sure enough, the boys' little dory soon turned up on the beach, upright and bone dry inside.

But it's the marshy world of the hay barges and flat-bottomed duck boats, not the surf-strewn shores of the dories, that Richardson described most beautifully. He spends long days on the waterways, absorbed in important tasks, such as seeking out a bird whose call he can't place (it turns out to be frog). He watches eels by electric torchlight from a night trip in a flat-bottomed punt. He lies in a boat with a friend while a 'duck hawk' (a peregrine) sends a flock of hundreds of sandpipers twisting back and forth as though they had a single mind. He recounts the arrival of 'the Big Owl' (a great horned owl) and the new songs, from crooned duets to blood-curdling screams, that the owl and his partner add to the marsh. He tells how this pair transform the behaviour of the whole place, the night herons leaving and the crows changing their roosts.

It's entirely typical of Richardson that as soon he hears the call of the great horned owl, he begins to squeak like a mouse in the vain hope of breaching the divide between species. One of the greatest sea poets, Vincent Ferrini, was also writing in the Massachusetts of the 1940s. In his huge seven-volume sequence, *Know Fish*, he insisted that 'there are as many realities as there are creatures/& substances'. But Richardson's life and work feel devoted to proving the reverse: his humans and hawks, foxes and flounders, occupy the same realms of being and are only a whistling lesson or two away from mutual understanding.

South from Nauset Marsh, there is often sandy shelter from the swell. These final stretches of the cape were staggeringly beautiful, with more wildlife than I'd expected to see at so famous a sea resort. Crabs scuttled below, fish of many sizes shoaled like reflected constellations, and waders lined the shores. A red-tailed hawk looked me in the eye from a patch of cordgrass. Great egrets stood statuesque and ghost white, no sign of concern at the passing boat, perhaps because the tide dragged me by like driftwood and I didn't raise a paddle as I passed. I hadn't expected to feel so transported in time.

To my surprise, the further I travelled, the more small boats crossed my path, and suddenly I was seeing things that seemed to be scenes from Henry James or Virginia Woolf. There were families, dressed in blue and white linens, taking skiffs out to small sandbars in the surf. These were the kind of slivers that, in most regions, people would be told were too dangerous to set foot on. But here, families erected deckchairs and had picnics, swell breaking to their east and tides racing to their west, as though this were the most normal thing to do. I paddled late into the night as a huge harvest moon rose over the sandbanks, making the coast look like an orange-tinted daytime. Temperatures remained intensely warm through the clear-skied days, but dropped dramatically once the sun set. The wind was constantly shifting, and when I settled to sleep on a small island made only of sand and cordgrass, the night felt calm, bright, and delicious. Then the breeze swung easterly and the soundworld was suddenly filled with the surf that still raged just beyond my dune.

Next day, I paddled into the town of Harwich. The toll the journey had taken on me was greater than I'd expected. I had ripped clothes, and damaged sunglasses beyond repair. Easterly winds were building and temperatures dropping every day. It was clear the weather would block my most ambitious goals. So I took a lift west and caught the ferry to Nantucket.

Nantucket is the island from which the whale hunt in *Moby-Dick* sets off, though Melville hadn't visited before he wrote the book. What drew me there was an incredible tradition of improvisatory boatbuilding and a heritage of portraying boatbuilders sympathetically. Everywhere in Maine and Massachusetts I'd seen the work of women who'd painted and photographed the lives of little boats. The photos taken in the 1890s by Martha Hale Harvey depict dories with a skill and sensitivity no other lens has ever captured. Most of her photos exist only as glass plates in the Cape Anne Museum, and the physical commitment she required to take her photos of dories landing and launching in rural places must have been as great as the trials of any offshore fisherman. On Nantucket, however, it was the painter Elizabeth Coffin who battled the elements to depict life at the shoreline.

In an era when Nantucket was known for commercial ships that pursued whales to the ends of the earth, Coffin portrayed the smallboat world of the island's shore. She painted seaweed-gatherers, clam-pickers, young boys landing dories on the shore, and, in one of her most famous paintings, the interior of a boatbuilder's workshop. In this work, from 1893, a grizzled old sea captain turned boatbuilder, Barzillai Burdett, sits carving a decoy for duck hunting and telling sea tales to the nineteen-year-old Chester Pease, who would himself take up boatbuilding later in life. The pair sit in front of a carpenter's workbench, while the bow of a carvel-constructed rowing boat protrudes into the foreground at the scene's edge.

I'd been told before I headed to Nantucket that such people and such stories were long gone, and that there were no builders of traditional boats on the island today, but the island's maritime heritage drew me there anyway, and after my experience on Cape Cod I suspected I might find more than mainlanders imagined. I spent my first night in Nantucket town. When I went for breakfast in a coffee shop next morning, I found residents willing to help me decide whether to devote my time to paddling east or west. Taking their guidance, I paddled the long western strands to Tuckernuck and Esther islands where much of Nantucket's driftwood gathers and where Martha's Vineyard was a purple-grey mound on the horizon. There were many boats out on the sheltered western waters, and the occasional wooden vessel on the shore. The scrubland birds of Nantucket's interior glided out to sea, while ducks skulked wherever reed interrupted the long sandy stretches.

I paddled into the largest harbour on Nantucket's west, Madaket, where shoreline houses sloped down to the reed-fringed sea and little wooden jetties cut into supremely sheltered water. Small boats, including tiny tenders and many kayaks, scattered the ocean end of the long, river-like harbour, but the sheltered end was a world of yachts, outfitters, and builders of modern boats. The first person I saw as I headed for a landing place was the owner of Madaket Marine, who'd been one of those I met by chance over coffee. She showed me round the large workshop where the modern yachts are built and asked the others on the shop floor whether any knew of wooden boatbuilding on the island. A name was mentioned – the Ottisons – and soon I was being driven across the island to visit this boatbuilding family. We arrived on the edge of another beautiful coastal marsh, where a creek meandered past large collections of driftwood and reclaimed timber to the exact mud flats where Elizabeth Coffin had painted boys picking clams.

This plot at the water's edge is a love song both to wood and to the sea it's salvaged from. The three Ottisons who live here, Albert, Karl, and Susan, are sons and daughter-in-law of the couple who established the house and first built a catboat and a dory here. That was in an era when farming, fishing, and clam-picking were a way of life on an island of 3,000 people. Today, the world the Ottisons have built on their eight acres by the salt flats aims to preserve some aspects of that culture ('the only thing grown' on Nantucket now, Karl says, 'is houses'). The willows on the plot were planted by Karl forty-two years ago, from cuttings taken when a storm blew down harbourside trees that had witnessed the comings and goings of centuries of seacraft. The plot's trees are treated with a kind of sacred significance: Karl and Susan were even married beneath a creekside apple tree.

On this land, the family have collected vast amounts of timber, driftwood, brushwood and other organic resources. Using their homemade sawmill, they've built from these a house, workshops, and sheds, and made boats, bowls, baskets, brooms, and countless other things. They take great pride in recycling this haul from the sea: building beauty from what others might see as waste, and finding function in what others might imagine to be useless. In constructing boats, the family even made their own nails, doing all they could to work from their own resources and become, as Susan puts it, the tradition-led 'recycling unit for the island'. Masts and keels of great ships that sank a century or more ago have become the perfect structural underpinning for their eminently boatish home. The feats of seafaring and construction this small family engaged in to bring these huge timbers from Tuckernuck Island by little boat, and form a home around them, beggar belief. On the walls are half models of boats of various sizes, and salvaged pieces of nineteenth- and twentieth-century wooden vessels can be found everywhere: acting as furnishing, built into walls, or mounted on them.

Large commercial interests have attempted to buy this prime piece of coastal real estate in order to replace its nature-filled foliage with tourist infrastructure. But, in 2005, the Ottisons secured their land's future: it will, when they eventually leave it, be managed, intact, by the Nantucket Land Bank, for the people of the island. It's a little piece of boatbuilding heritage that exemplifies the significance of stubborn individuals who both build traditional boats and ensure that the coasts we share with other species maintain at least a little of their historic vitality and cultural significance.

8

Barbados
Sea Flower, Sea Moss, Moses Boats

I

Bajan Moses

I'D BEEN PADDLING since dawn, past large expensive hotels and vast marina complexes and was reaching mid-morning on the third day of my circumnavigation of Barbados. The heavy, gentle swell – blue as the cover of a travel brochure – regularly blocked my view of shore. Frigate birds swung overhead and the shells of turtles, the size of dinner plates, occasionally broke the surface. The sounds of human activity swirled on the breeze. The swell took each clang, grind, or shout and span it till its point of origin was lost. Families were claiming spots on hotel beaches, cars were on the move, and yachts were being readied for launch.

As I edged a mile beyond a grand marina, my soundworld changed. It was suddenly more serenely beautiful than anything I'd heard at sea before. A dozen or more harmonised voices sang a hymn that rang out – clear and vibrant – across the ocean. Song seemed to merge with swell and breaker – amplified on peaks and smothered in troughs – to become something elemental.

BARBADOS

I nudged my boat towards the land. Soon I was immersed in the praise song and could see the open door of the whitewashed wooden Pentecostal church the voices came from. I could also see something I hadn't witnessed in my previous three days on Bajan (Barbadian) waters: an array of wooden boats of many styles and sizes lined up beneath the palms. There were lumps of rock and iron on the beaches: ballast for traditional working boats. Houses, also built from planks of wood, lined the small beachside road, and there were already locals seated in open-sided bars between road and water. The village I'd reached, Six Men's, is different from any other place on the Bajan coast. In its boatbuilders and its poets, it expresses island culture in ways that carry threads of the island's past into the future.

Over the following days, I watched the life of the village unfold. Grey kingbirds perched on overhead wires. Green monkeys clasped mangoes as they bounded through the treetops and sat to eat on the roofs of houses. The smells of roasting breadfruit and pot-fish boils drifted across the beach. Dominoes were slammed onto barrel tops, in the game that's a Bajan national pastime, and the clunks and laughter echoed everywhere.

But as often as possible, I took to the sea. I was never alone. Heads might emerge from waves at any time as young people swam out with nets and fishing spears. Tiny wooden craft, called 'Moses boats', were rowed, paddled, and motored from the beach. Sometimes they had a single occupant, at other times whole families were aboard. Danny, who makes the village fish pots (large wood and mesh traps for catching the many inshore species known here as 'pot fish'), took out a boat that was instantly recognisable by the scale of the fish pots perched in it and the presence of his wife and daughter. When I rowed out far into the swell towards St Vincent, other Moses boats were always there. I photographed them perched atop mountainous waves. They hung on the rolling water, anchors dropped and leaning prodigiously, while their occupants casually made their catch.

The narrow seafront street in Six Men's was often packed with people. At its southern end, women sat on steps preparing flying fish. Further along, there were bars, charcoal grills, and social spaces, all open-sided wooden structures. At the north end of the street was the social club, where the dominos are flung; overhead, the names of villagers lost at sea were inscribed on a beam as a reminder of old friends and of the Bajan saying that 'de sea en got nuh back door'.

The morning after I arrived, I wandered down to the seafront just as a large wooden boat came in. An unassuming area of the roadside suddenly bustled as skipper and crew prepared their catch. The people who gathered round introduced me to the fish by names such as 'red bellies', 'sweet lips', and 'old men'. I asked about the wooden rowing boats, and many remembered watching fleets of fishers in the past 'rowing those Moses' out to fishing grounds before engines and refrigeration arrived. They talked about rowing boat and motor-boat races that used to take place from Six Men's to Spike's Town (Speightstown) and how they, as children, would clamour to get on board the fastest boats in the hope of riding the winning vessel. And I heard stories of local heroes, such as the formidable Ruby Rollock, known as 'the Sheriff', who for many decades organised the sale of fish on the seafront. Conversation turned to the marinas that meant it was no longer possible to walk along the beach to Speightstown as people of Ruby Rollock's generation did. The general view seemed to be that these huge disruptive developments were against the course of nature. They were possibly even the cause of the recent rapid erosion of Six Men's beach, which meant that the places games were played and pigs kept two decades ago were now under water.

By the time the fish was sold, I had my introductions to Six Men's current boatbuilders, known simply as Guts, Pedro, and Babbs. That afternoon, I visited Guts's yard, and met his grandson, who was currently being trained to take on the boatbuilding mantle. An array of wooden and carbon-fibre hulls lined the space. Here it was possible to see how the boats were laid down: keel placed on a level, then stem, stern post and transom added, one by one, before this spidery frame had a beamy hull formed round it.

When Pedro popped by, he talked of the wooden boat he was restoring that would take him out on the week-long ocean journeys every seafarer here seemed to live for. He talked me through the wood he used and where it came from. Whitewood from St Vincent, greenheart from Guyana, pine from Belize, and resilient mahogany that, till a few years ago, would have come from the slopes of Barbados itself.

Both boatbuilders make their boats for local Bajan buyers. Among fishers here, there seems to have long been a hierarchy of aspiration. It's possible, without a boat but with a wetsuit and a fishing spear, to supplement another living. With a little Moses boat, a fisher can make a very modest living from days on the waves. But it seemed the aspiration, for everyone, was to own the bigger 'ice boat' which can give a seafarer freedom of the sea for days on end. I was struck by the love with which people spoke of the ocean, and the pride taken in the ability to work it independently. To build your own boat, take it to sea for a catch that could feed a family and be sold locally, with some fish left over to give away, was to live the Bajan fisher's dream. Pedro gave the impression that each day the boat was on land awaiting materials was just an intermission from the real life that happens on the water.

As in all boatbuilding centres, poets and singers are significant figures in Six Men's. Indeed, the fisherman in the Moses boat is a common feature of song and verse. Tales of rowing home with empty nets evoke sympathy with a folk figure who's characterised by the contrast between his great value to the community and 'his rough clothes and appearance' (not to mention his bawdy songs). Today, two brothers, born in a house that now lies beneath the Six Men's sea, write poetry that explores how the village's past 'has knitted/ boat and man/and sea/as one'. Frank and Antarrah Gilkes's poetry is full of small vessels setting out from 'this smiling mile' of gentle shore where the boys once played 'sand ball war' and beach cricket. It contains 'bellowing towers' of December sea that thrashed the anchored Moses boats ashore. It celebrates 'sun burnt, crusty hand/ fishermen' and 'raw fishy crates/of daily flying fish'. The stories they tell stretch back to the islands' indigenous people, 'Arawakan Taino/ Kalinago Carib/who canoed/between the islands/of this chained history'. They use the ancient name for the island, Ichirouganaim, thought to mean 'Red Stone with White Teeth'. And they write of a dream for a Caribbean that will reject environmental destruction by embracing its own distinctive culture and politics:

> We must now
> rise up
> to paddle
> the canoe
> that transported
> our Kalinago
> predecessors
> across this island chain,
> to once more
> regain
> lost affinities . . .

The alternative is to see 'the unique magick/smell/and sounds/of this seascape . . . gone/gone/gone/gone'.

Despite being 'dissected and concreted', what remains at Six Men's is still incomparably important: a place where sea knowledge and community thrive against the odds. The writing of poetry and building of wooden boats helps bulwark a distinctive way of life – a culture of global significance – against immense globalising pressures.

Moses boats are the smallest wooden craft I'd seen at work anywhere, and they've been used to fish these seas for centuries. They leave few remains for archaeologists. In its short lifetime, each boat was worked to breaking point; then, at the end of its seagoing days, it was absorbed into a house as a doorframe, rafter, or firewood. They leave almost no textual documentation. Most historic mentions tend only to emphasise the dearth of information, such as a letter to a newspaper in 1887 which asked for assistance in identifying what the term 'Moses boat' – which the letter writer had found in an eighteenth-century document – denoted. The query went unanswered. Caribbean dictionaries and encyclopedias often attempt to describe the boat, but in their discrepancies and divergences they do as much to obscure as to clarify the vessel's stories.

Some claim the boat was named for a man named Moses who invented the style. To others, the boat's beamy middle meant 'its shape resembled . . . the cradle in which Pharaoh's daughter found the infant Moses'. For others still, such as the *A–Z of Barbados Heritage* (2003), scale is more significant than shape: 'The boat was probably named because of its tiny size, which can bring to the imagination [a] boat-like reed basket.' Like many small boats, these vessels also crop up on the decks of big ships. In the early nineteenth century, for instance, sailors aboard Caribbean schooners described each ship having a single Moses on davits at the vessel's stern, 'for bringing barrels of rum and molasses from a beach'.

But a handful of nineteenth-century travellers from Europe or North America recorded their experience in Moses boats on longer voyages. In the 1870s, for instance, the American ornithologist and antiquarian Frederick Ober travelled to seek the indigenous peoples of the Caribbean. To reach the smallest islands, he was rowed in a Moses boat, and he wrote four sentences that are among the longest written responses these vessels have ever received. He began well enough: 'The Moses-boat is a peculiarly strong boat built for transporting sugar and other heavy freight through the heavy surf.' Immediately, however, he turned to comparing the boat to the bowl in which three fools in the Mother Goose nursery rhymes set out to sea:

> In shape it is something like the famous craft in which those 'three wise men of Gotham' departed on their sea-voyage. It is very buoyant, and owes its great strength to numerous knees and thick planking. Regarding its name, whether it was named for Moses the great 'lawgiver,' or for the man who built the first of the kind, will forever remain a mystery.

Often propelled by a rower or two, each with a pair of small oars, the boat was sometimes used by a single standing sculler rotating one long paddle through the sea. Today's Bajan culture is gloriously innovative and improvisatory in its use of these vessels: small boats are propelled in every way it's possible to imagine them moving. Many of these Moses boats have a distinctive shift in sheer towards the bow (like an upturned nose), which makes them instantly recognisable, though many today have fibreglass shells to add longevity to their wooden frames.

The seas between Caribbean islands were once filled with small wooden boats like the Moses boat. The indigenous Lokono (also known as Arawaks) and Karifuna (Carib) people had canoes of many shapes. Some were dugout tree trunks that, according to Columbus, reached ninety feet long and carried forty people with provisions. Later sailing canoes, gommiers, yoles, canots, and pirogues all owed something to that heritage. They were built for long stretches of shallow turquoise sea, and glistening golden sand, where big ships might anchor a mile or more offshore and large fleets of little rowed boats would mediate between ship and island. The sailing ships, scrupulously documented in archives, passed in their thousands, and the traffic of tiny boats such as Trinidadian droghers and Nevisian lighters, ferrying goods ashore, was thus crucial but uncelebrated for centuries. They linked not just ship and shore, but coastal settlements too, as the key carriers of news and songs as well as goods. In this way, they defined the making of the modern Caribbean.

Much familiar maritime culture emerged from the mixing of mariners in the ports and beaches these little boats put into. The sea shanties British sailors took to all corners of the world, for instance, bear remarkable resemblances to the songs sung by enslaved African peoples: as the leading historian of Caribbean seafaring Julius Scott put it, 'the very practice of shantying may have its roots in the interaction of sailors and black dockworkers on the shorelines of the West Indian islands'. Since many boat styles that performed these interactions decayed into non-existence by the early twenty-first century, the Moses boat of Barbados is a rare survivor from this era.

As the most easterly island in the Antilles, this was the first call of the transatlantic schooners and the focal point of early European efforts to convert the 'masterless' Caribbean into the rigidly ordered capitalist production of plantations. This quest for control was brutal, but always incomplete: slave owners never achieved total dominion over the enslaved. One of the greatest threats to their control was the seafaring prowess of many of the West Africans they forced across the ocean. Numerous legal codes revealed slaveholders' determination to control the sea, but the very frequency of their repetition betrayed their failure. Slaveholders frequently worried that it was 'a very dangerous thing to let a negro know navigation', but the need for a functioning workforce in an island world riven with seaways meant indentured servants and even slaves were frequently given control of rowed and sailed boats. The anthropologist Marco Meniketti has speculated on the meanings that this time at sea may have held:

It is a compelling thought to contemplate the brief periods of autonomy and freedom experienced by enslaved mariners of African heritage working for the Caribbean plantations as they filled their sails on the open sea. The period in which they sailed between islands on plantation business must have been bittersweet joy. Away from overseers and land-based colonial law, they connected distant plantations with island capitals and carried on commerce at neighbouring islands on behalf of their white owners, returning, perhaps, only because they had families they did not care to leave behind.

All seafarers were considered potentially unruly by plantation owners, so legislation also aimed to prevent bustling ports and rural beaches hosting informal economies of exchange between African slaves and European, particularly Irish, sailors. A Waterford merchant, James Kelly, observed in 1838 that 'Sailors and Negroes are ever on the most amicable terms'. He noted their 'mutual confidence and familiarity', as well as 'a feeling of independence in their intercourse', which contrasted with their 'degradation' at the hands of plantation owners. Many of these sailors had been forcibly pressed into naval service or tricked into merchant vessels against their will. Indentured servants, whether Indian, Irish, or Scottish, had also been violently co-opted by officials seeking cheap labour.

It's a dramatic illustration of the singular focus of the sugar society the British built in Barbados that, despite it being amid some of the richest seas in the world, the salt fish that became the staple diet of the enslaved was imported from Newfoundland: the northern fisheries provided the calories on which the workforce that produced Europe's sugar boom was sustained, and few Atlantic coasts were unsullied by the horrors that empire and Enlightenment wreaked upon the world.

But small boats still spelled freedom. In a novel called *The Fourth Century* (1964), one of the islands' great philosophers, Édouard

Glissant, voiced the view from the little boat. Its protagonist, Mathieu Béluse, sets out to find a Caribbean perspective on history. He turns to a local storyteller, Papa Longoué, an 'old man of the forest . . . [who] knows the oral tradition and its relationship to the powers of the land and the forces of nature'. Longoué tells Béluse the story of two of their ancestors, who were brought, four centuries ago, from Africa. The Béluse ancestor remained enslaved for his whole life, but his Longoué friend escaped and fled to live in one of the communities of the escaped who were known as maroons. The Antilles islands, to the historic Longoué, were not defined as colonies with borders and authorities, but as interconnected spaces in seas of freedom. He asks, 'Why always flee to the interior?' When he stood tiptoe on island hills, other islands could be spotted:

> People say it's the same land as this; the earth goes under the sea and comes back up over there, then it goes back under again and comes back farther away, on and on like that . . . Why forget the sea? They just had to steal a skiff and if they didn't dare do that (not wanting to alert people again or not wanting to be chased all over the place because of a stolen skiff) they could make one in the woods . . . They had to get there! Have confidence in the sea!

Glissant's work was part of the cultural renaissance that swept the islands in the late twentieth century. This saw the region's boats as an inheritance to be embraced. In Barbados, the resurgence might be dated as early as the late 1960s, when new generations of poets and musicians emerged from the coastal villages. But it is sometimes traced instead to 1983, when Barbados hosted the Caribbean Festival of the Arts. The Bajan historian Ralph Jemmott writes that 'Barbadians who had only known sporadic droplets of cultural expression found themselves swept up in a flash-flood of artistic creativity . . . a catalyst for the creative flowering that was to follow'.

This involved the first recognition of the Moses boat, celebrating the many historic links between small boats and freedom. Moses boats named after the cultural renaissance often emphasise the link, whether by accident or design, between the liberator of the Hebrews from Egyptian slavery and this vessel of unsung resistance to colonial control: these range from the wordplay of 'Isreal' to the simplicity of 'Freedom' and 'Exodus'.

II

Holiest Grails

Before I could leave Six Men's and take my little boat beyond the shelter of the island's west, I had a pilgrimage to make on foot. One of the world's greatest poets of small boats spent much of his youth in a wooden boat workshop nearby. Kamau Brathwaite's work shows the centrality of the small boat to Bajan culture. His poetry is vivid and dreamlike. Its logic, like tides, often seems to circulate in all directions. But one material substance ties his imagination to Barbados's gentle slopes: his writing is filled with the wood from which boats are built. Brathwaite imagined the craft of poetry as parallel to the art of carpentry, and loved the workshop of his great uncle, Bob'ob, just a few minutes' gentle stroll from Six Men's beach in the village of Mile and a Quarter. Both poet and boatbuilder, Brathwaite insisted, made wood (whether planks or paper) the medium for the new Bajan nation.

Brathwaite saw West Africa and the West Indies as twin 'timber cultures' that 'used wood well'. He celebrated the humble but profound artistry with which the functional beauty of boat or drum was drawn from modest tree trunks. After visiting Ghana, he wrote of the genius of carpenters who coaxed images of their ancestors from sacred trees in the form of masks, and he wrote of seeing the fingerprints of his great-uncle Bob'ob's work in the figurines of Ghanaian carpentry. He celebrated the way in which ancestral African peoples held the manual skills of woodworking in high esteem and showed great respect for natural materials.

In Brathwaite's collection *Islands* (1969), the image of Bob'ob is entangled with that of the Yoruba blacksmith deity, Ogun. Brathwaite depicts the African gods arriving in the Americas. They are hobbled and changed by the voyage of the middle passage: Bajan Ogun is a carpenter instead of a blacksmith. In this altered world, Uncle Bob'ob's workshop is a boat: 'That Mile&Quarter ship'. The Bajan boatbuilder expresses his ancestry with plane and saw, straddling forest and ocean, past and future, Africa and the Americas:

With knife and gimlet care he worked away at this on Sundays,

explored its knotted hurts, cutting his way
along its yellow whorls until his hands could feel

how it had swelled and shivered, breathing air,
its weathered green burning rings of time,

its contoured grain still tuned to roots and water.
And as he cut he heard the creak of forests:

green lizard faces gulped, grey memories with moth
eyes watched him from their shadows, soft

liquid tendrils leaked among the flowers
and a black rigid thunder he had never heard within his hammer

came stomping up the trunks. And as he worked within his shattered
Sunday shop, the wood took shape . . .

If the act of working wood near the Six Men's shore was formative for Brathwaite's world view, so too was leaping in the sea from the places where Moses boats launched and landed. He was such a sea child that the local newspaper once (to his great pride) referred to him 'cleaving through the water like a slim destroyer'.

In *Barabajan Poems* (1994), a book dedicated to Bob'ob, Brathwaite tried to encapsulate a Bajan outlook on life, building his experience of Barbados, Britain, Ghana, Jamaica, and New York into an outward-looking island vision. Another naturalistic theme runs alongside wood grain in these poems: crystal water pours over and through porous stone. Barbados is the only coral, rather than volcanic, island in the long chain of the Antilles. Almost riverless, its water comes from pools deep in the coral rock that had once been an ocean bed. In *Barabajan Poems*, beautiful explorations of a marine creative process make sea moss and Moses boats the holy grail of an island faith that blends stone and water, past and future:

> So I am growing up here and dreaming of how to write something that wd catch the gleam the word of water clink & pebble where th(e) wave folds on/to the sand, the fans of sunlight in the water, its various colours & histories, coralline grains settling/ xploding// fish crab sails empty shells whorls worlds of sea-floor sea-flour sea-flower sea-moss moses boats deeper more morose colours holiest grails, how ewathing flows underwater . . . the waves comin in/ comin in/ tidelect tidelect tid- electic con/nect/ing . . .

Barabajan Poems is far more powerful than any ordinary history book in evoking the making of Bajan culture through its era of transition from colonial rule to independence. Its format and style are deliberate challenges to the idea of academic prose or official documentation, which Brathwaite saw as forms of strangulation for non-European subjects. It shows how we need to turn to the boatbuilder and poet, not the archive, if we are to understand a wave-washed place on its own profound and indispensable terms. In a public lecture in 1987, Brathwaite voiced this gap between history and reality when he asked, 'Is the Archives quietly tucked away up there in Black Rock above ye olde Lazaretto rocks aware of . . . the Bob'obs . . . of Barbados?'

This might sound like a local vision, but, with it, Brathwaite sought to unite Atlantic littorals: when he sought 'new meaning of the MARGIN(S)', he evoked Bajans and West Africans alongside 'Inuit warriors and queens'. He evoked makers and craftspeople, materials worked by hand, and stories that were entertainment and philosophy, memory and prophecy, all rolled into one flowing vision of fierce and gentle, interconnecting sea.

III

You Never Say 'Like' about the Sea

I'll never know how I tore myself away from Six Men's. Where the west coast had been blissfully benign, the headlands of the north were a baptism of foam. First the coasts became forested and ever more rural. Then, as Atlantic exposure increased, the rock became bare and pitted. This was some of the most sea-ravaged land I've ever witnessed, and the swell at the northernmost cliffs churned with geometric complexities that threatened to leave me spinning on the spot. Shadows of reef sharks lurked below. Just when paddling felt hardest, a boom in the distance dragged my attention offshore. Over and over again, a huge humpback whale breached and slammed into the sea. That the force of its landing was enough to be heard across the waves, even when white-topped swell blocked the view, felt miraculous.

There was no respite turning south: every stroke demanded an intensity of focus that I've rarely had to sustain for so long. Little more than half an hour in, I tried to wipe my salt-encrusted sunglasses and lost them to the ocean. I stayed offshore, away from the reflected complexities of easterly swell, and saw little of the coast for my first twelve kilometres. Even offshore, the heavy smell of sargassum hung over every paddle-stroke. Sometimes the rotting algae was flung into the air by my paddle and I wondered what kind of strange shaggy bear I must've looked like.

I was shocked, in the very worst conditions, to pass local divers in wetsuits with their mesh bags trailing behind. These fishers must have been tossed around so wildly by the sea that I was amazed they had much choice where the dizzying ocean swept them. By the time I tumbled onto the beach at the town of Bathsheba, my every limb ached, my skin was dry and cracked, and my vision was blurred by staring at sunlit sea all day. Despite the mounds of shoreline sargassum, and the rapidly setting sun, the beach was still busy with children paddling in rockpools and surfers enjoying the waves I'd shuddered at.

On land, little herds of goats populated the dry grass, while the forests were filled with small birds and lizards. Teenagers fished from sea stacks, some of their fishing rocks reached only by narrow planks balanced at a height. Everything existed in a haze of seaspray that left rainbows in the corners of my vision.

Kamau Brathwaite often threw this stretch of coast into his verse, with lines such as:

> wave teeth fanged into clay
> white splash flashed into spray
> Bathsheba . . .
> bloom of the arcing summers . . .

In another Brathwaite poem, it was onto the Bathsheba beach that the Igbo gods waded from Africa, and out of the surf-strewn sea to build Bajan culture. Brathwaite described himself as a boy from the calm seas of 'the sunset side of the island', but always aware that just a few miles east, at Bathsheba, the coast

> stood ragged and fear and red in the sky/line like thun
> der made visible
>
> and the sea over there was a giant of i:ron
> a rasta of water with rumbelling muscles and turrible turrible hair.

He recalled being taught English literature in his Bajan school, its rhythm and sound designed, he felt, 'to capture the experience of falling snow', where he required a soundworld that captured 'the Barbadian experience of hurricanes'.

Over a few Banks beers in Bathsheba bars, I was told of the iconic figures of the coast from here to Conset Bay, a couple of miles south. One, Coreen Bradshaw, known as 'Feeney', had passed away less than a month before. The people in the bar credited her as being the first independent full-time fishing woman in recent decades of Barbados history, and she sailed from Conset Bay. 'You'd never call her a fisherwoman,' one man stated, impying that your life might be in danger if you called her anything but a fisherman. They talked of her wandering round town in her sea clothes as if to indicate to everyone that she was only on dry land on sufferance. They made her sound like someone with an uncanny knowledge of the ways of the ocean. But Feeney's life, for all her skill and the respect it gained her, was never easy: she lost her boat and was forced to spend her later fishing years as crew on others' vessels.

Many women followed in Feeney's wake, so much so that the Barbados Fisheries Division now celebrates the 'Barbadian Matriarchy of Fishing'. Like Feeney, Andrea Chapman and Keisha Carrington head out to sea alone or in small crews, in Moses boats or other vessels of their size, and make their living from the water. Chapman talks of the excitement, as a child, of watching the bustle of fishers at the shoreline, noting who was coming in and who setting out in little boats. You never say 'like' about the sea, she insists, but always 'love', and you can always rely on the ocean. She bemoans today's education system that teaches people nothing of the sea – none of the skills required to love the water with intimacy – and insists on the need to get young people in boats in order that they understand this source of independence and cultural pride. Instead, she says, children are taught that small-scale fishing is a dead or dying trade. Carrington, too, talks of the sea in terms of the desire and passion that draw her to the waves and off the land. She speaks of the power to provide for people, and of the satisfaction of knowing she can battle the elements as well as anyone else. It's rare to hear Bajan fishers talk in ways that don't embody this paradox of cultural prestige and economic paucity.

IV

The Flying Fish

I'd timed my circumnavigation to end in the town of Oistins, on the south of the island, and to coincide with the annual festival when Bajans gather to honour their boats. Old men sat in small craft hauled ashore. Blue-and-yellow Bajan flags bearing the black trident expressive of a marine identity rippled in a stiff breeze. Competitions in boning flying fish and skinning mahi mahi drew crowds of hundreds to stages set up in the boatyard. Local legend Tyrone 'Dolphin' Shorey won the latter, as he has for every one of the last eighteen years. Races followed, including one in which intensely competitive racers carried trays on their heads in imitation of generations of flying-fish vendors. The wind flung many trays into the crowd and made this into high-octane sport. Only the event that involves competing to climb a greasy pole, like a ship's mast set up in the boatyard, seemed to raise emotions higher.

Around the cheering onlookers loomed hulks of wooden and fibreglass boats in various states of repair. The seafront street was lined with stalls selling fishcakes, beers, and mangoes slathered in salt and chilli. Gospel music from a bandstand enveloped most of the village, except where, past the palm trees at the east end of the bay, the roll of the gentle blue ocean drowned out almost everything.

As the sun set, I swam into the glistening bay to watch the festival unfold. Dozens of others were in the warm water and many little boats on which islanders had arrived lay at rest. Nets were being cast from the jetty into the sea, seeming to come up full every time. The long sweep of the fish market, stalls, and boatyard were visible to my left. On my right were the gentle slopes where some of the first free villages on the island had been founded after a plantation owner, William Reece, granted half an acre each to forty freed slaves in 1838. The links of the current cultural renaissance to two centuries of history were evident all around.

This little bay was the heart of the flying-fish fisheries on which much island identity has been built. From the earliest descriptions of the island, the presence of these charismatic fish arcing over the waves has been noted with wonder. As one visitor put it in 1789,

> I have seen them spring out of the water by thousands together before the ship's bows; and in dark nights they frequently dropped on board. They are about the size of a large herring, and of a very delicious flavour. In Barbadoes they call them Spike's Pigeons, as they are caught in the greatest numbers off the coast near Spike's Town.

In the same era, another observer, George Pinckard, described how these fish acted as a supplement to salt cod. They were 'pickled, and salted, and used as a very common food' by enslaved peoples on the island's plantations. Other commentaries note big ships being met on the water by hosts of Moses boats loaded with fruit and fried flying fish to bring sailors their first fresh food after weeks at sea.

The Barbadian-Canadian writer Austin Clarke wrote several novels with titles such as *The Origin of Waves*. He also penned memoirs of his childhood in 1930s Barbados, such as *Growing up Stupid under the Union Jack*. But some of his most vivid writing on cultures of the sea and his Bajan childhood are contained in *Pigtails 'n Breadfruit: Rituals of Slave Food* (1999). Here he recalled the days when fisherwomen from Oistins and neighbouring Rockley walked through all the villages selling flying fish 'all-a-penny':

> Always in the evenings, after four o'clock, there were the voices of women walking through the villages and neighbourhoods with heavy trays or baskets on their heads, padded for comfort and laden with freshly caught fish . . . 'Fish? Fish here! Come and get muh! Fish! Fish here! All-a-penny!' These women advertised their produce with shrieks, walking miles and calling out until the last fish was sold.
>
> 'All-a-penny' means, literally, all you can carry for the price of a penny. It meant also that the catch was bountiful. During these all-a-penny evenings, my mother would buy three dozen for the price of one shilling. Before I went to bed that night, the fish would be cleaned, scaled, gutted, cleaned a second time, soaked in lime juice and salt, seasoned and fried (or steamed). And my mother and I would eat them all!

By 1948, seeing the flying-fish fleet come in under sail was marketed as one of Barbados's great cultural attractions, though tourists were warned to beware the roads between the fleet's key landing place at Tent Bay, near Bathsheba, and the market at Oistins: every fisher, pausing for no impediment, would rush the few miles overland to be the first to get their fish to market. In the 1950s, flying fish began to appear on stamps and coins, and a competition to develop a distinctively Bajan drink produced a cocktail called the Flying Fish. Then, in the 1960s, the fish replaced the image of a harbour policeman as the principal icon to promote the island. By 1966, the Barbados Tourist Board's official guide was entitled *Barbados: Land of the Flying Fish*.

This growing identification of Barbados with its fleet of independent wooden boats worked strongly in Oistins' favour. By the 1960s, almost all bank holidays were occasions for celebratory gatherings and boat races here. The fishing festival itself was established in 1967, and in the 1980s increasing efforts were put into presenting Oistins as a place for Bajans to spend their weekends. In 1983, the fish market was substantively overhauled to become Bay Gardens, where the boatyard and fish markets sit among stalls and restaurants as well as spaces for dancing and roller-skating. Friday-night fish fries gradually became a cultural institution, helping dramatically to revitalise the town from its mid-century condition. On a stage in the heart of Bay Gardens, musicians perform. Sometimes, surprise appearances from the island's great calypso stars, such as the Mighty Gabby, turn a fish fry into a singalong of calypsos like 'Bajan Fishermen' that recount the triumphs and tribulations of the Bajan shoreline. These calypso stars are, along with the poets, the standard bearers of the island renaissance.

Bajan calypsos frequently tell of the emotions raised in fishers and observers by the unpredictable yields of the ocean. Almost every calypso performer is directly connected to this heritage. The Mighty Gabby talks of having spent all his youth in or on the water, constantly immersed in salt. His grandfather was a fisherman with a sailed Moses boat called *The Monkey*. This had no compass or electrical equipment. Indeed, it didn't even have a rudder, so to tack he threw huge blocks of iron from one side of the boat to the other as he travelled long ocean distances.

One of Gabby's most famous songs, 'Jack', protests at the excesses of the modern tourist industry, which separates Bajans from the shores that are their inheritance. Gabby wrote this song after being asked in a hotel to sing 'some local music', at which point Jack, a corporate lawyer from the Tourist Board, sneered at the idea the local fishing villages had anything that could be called 'culture'. In the song, Jack uses the police to force Bajans off the beaches he has illegally decided are for wealthy hotel guests only. 'Dat cyan happen here in this country,' Gabby sings. 'I want Jack to know that the beach belong to me.' 'Tourism vital,' he continues, 'I cyan deny,/But cyan mean more than I and I.' It's hard to imagine the shores of Barbados without Bajan people launching Moses boats from beaches and cooking breadfruit on the sand. Six Men's – precarious but infinitely precious – must be one of the most important small-boat centres on the planet.

Epilogue

To Understand What's Beautiful

OVER THE COURSE of the year's travels, I asked many people what qualities they felt made a good boatbuilder. Some responded by discussing practicalities, using phrases such as 'jack of all trades'. They emphasised the improvisation required to cope with new challenges on each unique boatbuilding project. They stressed engineering talent and insisted a good boatbuilder couldn't be a perfectionist: the most crucial skill of all was knowing how to respond well to mistakes you'd already made. Even if boats might be among the most beautiful things that can be built, these responses emphasised that there's no such thing as perfection.

Other answers praised the emotional characteristics of the best builders: patience, determination, and stubbornness. It wasn't a job, they insisted, for anyone who gave up easily. Nor, given the time-consuming nature of the tasks, was it a role for anyone who hadn't fallen deeply in love with the process as much as the outcome. Many revelled in losing their sense of time and space within a task as ordinary and as mundane as it was rewarding. Sometimes, boatbuilders who put things this way were the ones giving me simple but time-consuming tasks, like sanding away old paint from the Galway *gleoiteog*, *Loveen*: I felt this response as a lesson they were trying to teach me.

There were few answers, however, that prioritised practicality and technique over beauty and feeling. Sometimes this was about touch, whether the satisfaction of working with wood itself, or of the connection to the elements the finished boat allowed, when 'you can sit down' in your creation 'and trail your fingers through the water' with total trust that the work you'd cared so much for would care, in turn, for you.

But sight was the sense most frequently mentioned, and 'the eye' of the boatbuilder was talked of as an almost mystical quality. To some, this 'eye' was shorthand for a complex set of skills that were essentially mechanical: to know from the sight of a specific untreated tree trunk exactly what boat might issue from the wood and how it would respond to the brute forces of swell, storm, and time. But this was always expressed in aesthetic terms. Seeing the beauty in the wood was linked to a prophetic sense of the graceful lines it might produce: like Michelangelo visualising a living David in the quirks of a block of marble. Jon Wilson, the former director of WoodenBoat School, expressed this in unusually explicit terms:

> To me, a great boatbuilder is one who understands, first of all, what's beautiful. A person who has an eye for the sweep of the sheer, the turn of the bilge, the tuck below that. Someone who understands how trees grow, realizing that the material, when it gets cut, shaped, fitted, and fastened in place is going to have to live there for the rest of its life.

One boatbuilder even used the word 'supernatural' in describing how beauty was in fact the measure of practicality. 'If it looks fair it is fair' is a saying every English-language boatbuilder knows. When a builder refers to making a boat 'eye-sweet', the implications are that functional perfection follows naturally from visual grace.

There was one final category, however, in the responses boatbuilders gave. This suggested that the qualities of a good boatbuilder included a sense of responsibility to past communities: that the boatbuilder was essentially a kind of historian. Jerome Canning, in Newfoundland, puts it like this:

> While you're building one, the whole sense of what the boat is and where it comes from, actually, what you inherit is a lot of tradition. And this is how I look at it, it's very ancestral, so actually participating in that, you get a feel for that ancestral sort of history.

This connection takes many forms. For some, it's a matter of repeating the actions of ancestors to learn how they engaged with materials from spruce root to pine plank. A boat might only be seen as traditional if the tools and skills used to craft it have been handed down through generations. For others, the key characteristic of past boatbuilders was their ability to improvise with the best tools available, hence the distinction drawn in New England that 'I'm not a traditional boatbuilder, but I build traditional boats'. But even these boatbuilders made frequent reference to the question of how their predecessors, a century or two ago, might have handled the tasks they faced.

This commitment to historical knowledge took many forms, from knowing the genealogy of everyone in the area, to reconstructing knowledge of tides and fishing grounds, or rebuilding detailed vocabularies of local dialects and their words for wild or wooden things. A stubborn unwillingness to accept the inevitability of loss, whether of skills, communities, or memory, was a constant theme. So was the principle that caring for the past was an investment in the future. Indeed, one of those I spoke to on the Isle of Lewis insisted that 'we need to get rid of the idea that traditional comes before modern'. That same day, she told me, too, that we should never call the traditions surrounding boats or crofting 'intangible cultural heritage': 'It's not heritage, it's life.' Others expressed an unlikely optimism that many of the problems of the present might just be fleeting trends – that nurturing this venerable world for one more decade might be just enough to lead to long-term recovery of skills, values, communities, and environments.

To me, that's the greatest strength of these boats and the small, local worlds sustained by them. They nurture tiny, guttering flames of hope. In the knowledge that the world and the ways it has been navigated have been wildly different from how they seem today, they prove beyond doubt that the world will be different again. Perhaps it's only in this way – by knowing how different the past and present *could* have been – that we can conjure and nurture visions of a better future. The years leading up to my North Atlantic journeys were undoubtedly the darkest and most difficult of my life. But I can't imagine a better recipe for optimism than spending time on water and in workshops with people whose passionate investments in the past are focused, always, on futures that attend more fully to the details of land, sea, sky, and community than I'd ever known was possible.

On the day I finished writing the last chapter of this book, I downloaded plans for a Fiddlehead Canoe. Twelve feet long and clinker built, with a draught as shallow as a dory's, its form – if I get it right – will be nearly as elegantly tapered as the boats of the Faroe Islands. I swapped some of my history books, with boatbuilders I'd met, for basic boatbuilding tools: a saw, a steam box, and a block plane, as well as bronze screws and copper rivets. And I phoned and Zoomed boatbuilders in Barbados, the Faroes, and Maine as I planned the task of building a wooden boat from scratch in the back room of a house in central Birmingham. The smell of fresh pine shavings is now like a portal back to Sápmi. I don't know, yet, if this vessel will ever see salt water, but to build it is to believe. It spells three things: solidarity with marginal, ocean-edge attitudes; hope for a future of watery freedom; and trust that giving time to something beautiful can change the world.

Select Bibliography

Aamold, S., Haugdal, E. & Jørgensen, U.A. (eds), *Sámi Art & Aesthetics: Contemporary Perspectives* (Aarhus UP, 2017)

Adam, R. & MacLeoid, F., *Cas-Cheum An Leodhas* (Acair, 2006)

Adney, E.T. & Chapelle, H.I., *The Bark Canoes & Skin Boats of North America* (Smithsonian, 1964)

An Lanntair, *Between Islands* (Acair, 2020)

Anichtchenko, E.V., 'Open Passage: Ethno-Archaeology of Skin Boats & Indigenous Maritime Mobility of North American Arctic' (University of Southampton PhD, 2016)

Aubinet, S, *Why Sámi Sing: Knowing through Melodies in Norther Norway* (Routledge, 2023)

Bahar, M., *Storm of the Sea: Indians & Empires in the Atlantic's Age of Sail* (Oxford UP, 2019)

Barrowman, R.(ed.), *Dun Eistean, Ness, Isle of Lewis: the Excavation of a Late Medieval Clan Stronghold* (Acair, 2015)

Bateman, M. & Purser, J., *Window to the West: Culture & Environment in the Scottish Gàidhealtachd* (Clò Ostaig, 2020)

Battiste, M., *Visioning a Mikmaw Humanities: Indigenizing the Adacdemy* (Cape Breton UP, 2016)

Bavington, D., Murton, J. & Dokis, C.A. (eds), *Subsistence Under Capitalism: Historical & Contemporary Perspectives* (McGill-Queens, 2016)

Bayliss-Smith, T. & Mulk, I., 'Sailing boats in Padjelanta: Sámi rock engravings from the mountains in Laponia, northern Sweden', *Acta Borealia* (1999)

Beckles, H., Black Rebellion in Barbados: The Struggle Against Slavery, 1627-1838 (Antilles, 1984)

Bogadóttir, R., & Olsen, E.S., 'Making Degrowth Locally Meaningful: the Case of the Faroese Grindadráp', *Journal of Political Ecology* (2017)

Bogadóttir, R., 'The Social Metabolism of Quiet Sustainability', *Sustainability* (2019)

Booker, M.M., *Nantucket Spirit: the Art & Life of Elizabeth Rebecca Coffin* (Mill Hill, 2001)

Brathwaite, K., *Rights of Passage* (Oxford UP, 1967)

– *Masks* (Oxford UP, 1968)
– *Islands* (Oxford UP, 1969)
– *Gods of the Middle Passage* (Bloodaxe, 1982)
– *Barabajan Poems* (Savacou North, 1994)
– *Born to Slow Horses* (Wesleyan UP, 2006)

Brattland, C., 'Mapping Rights in Coastal Sami Seascapes', *Arctic Review on Law & Politics* (2010)

Brú, H., West, J., trans, *The Old Man & his Sons* (Paul S. Eriksson, 1970)

Buitléar, C.D., *Húicéir na Gaillimhe* (Cian de Buitléar, 2005)

– *An Churach Adhmaid* (Cian de Buitléar, 2005)
– *An Churach Canbháis* (Cian de Buitléar, 2005)

Bulbek, C. & Bowdler, S., 'The Faroes Grindadráp or Pilot Whale Hunt: The Importance of its 'Traditional' Status in Debates with Conservationists', *Australian Archaeology* (2008)

SELECT BIBLIOGRAPHY

Bursey, L., *Vessel: Stories from the Edge of the World* (University of Waterloo MA, 2023)

Campbell, A., 'Atlantic Exchanges: the Poetics of Dispersal & Disposal in Scottish & Caribbean Seas', *Journal of Postcolonial Writing (2019)*

Cannon, M., *Carrying the Songs* (Carcanet, 2007)

– *The Parchment Boat* (Gallery, 1997)

Champlain, S.D. & Grant, W.L., *Voyages of Samuel de Champlain* (Scribner's, 1907)

Chapelle, H.I., The National Watercraft Collection (Smithsonian, 1960)

Chase, B.C., *Codbones* (Wrinkled Sea, 2023)

Chivers, M., *Shetland's Boats: Origin, Evolution & Use* (Shetland Bookshop, 2022)

Claesson, S., 'Sustainable Development of Maritime Cultural Heritage in the Gulf of Maine' (Boston University PhD, 2008)

Cole, P., *Coyote & Raven Go Canoeing: Coming Home to the Village* (McGill-Queen's, 2006)

Commun Eachdraid Nis, *History with Heart & Soul: The Place Names of North Lewis* (CEN, 2021)

Compton, N., *Iain Oughtred: A Life in Wooden Boats* (WoodenBoat, 2009)

Conaghan, P., *The Zulu Fishermen: Forgotten Pioneers of Donegal's First Fishing Industry* (Bygones, 2003)

Cope, M., *The Photography of Archie Chisholm: Life & Landscape in the Outer Hebrides (2018)*

Crichton Smith, I., *Towards the Human* (Saltire, 1986)

Cronin, N., 'Ground Truths: Deep Mapping Communities in the West of Ireland' in Mayer, Lynch, Wall & Weltzein (eds), *Thinking Continental: Writing the Planet One Place at a Time (1997)*

Crummey, M., *River Thieves* (Doubleday, 2001)

Cunliffe, B., *Facing the Ocean: The Atlantic & Its Peoples* (Oxford UP, 2001)

Cunningham, C., *Building the Greenland Kayak* (Ragged Mountain, 2002)

Cusack, T., *Art & Identity at the Water's Edge* (Routledge, 2012)
— *Framing the Ocean, 1700-the present* (Ashgate, 2014)
Dahl, J., *Saqqaq: An Inuit Hunting Community in the Modern World* (Toronto UP, 2000)
Dalton, M., *The Vernacular Strain in Newfoundland Poetry* (Breakwater, 2022)
Dana, K.O., '"When a Lapp is out on the High Fells": Literary Voice & Cultural Identity for the Sámi', *Scandinavian Studies* (2003)
Dean, M., *Inheriting a Canoe Paddle: The Canoe in Discourses of English-Canadian Nationalism* (Toronto UP, 2013)
Dimock, B., Rust, C., Brooks, D. & McKay, G., *How the Old Fella Done It: Building the Shelburne Dory with Milford Buchanan* (Fretwater, 2013)
Drabinski, J.E., *Glissant & the Middle Passage* (Minnesota UP, 2019)
Duncan, A., *Hebridean Island: Memories of Scarp* (Tuckwell. 1995)
Dzik, J.A., 'Settlement Closure or Persistence: A Comparison of Kangeq and Kapisillit, Greenland', *Journal of Settlements and Spatial Planning* (2016)
Ecott, T., *The Land of Maybe* (Short, 2020)
Edmonds, J., *Small Craft* (Sea Crow, 2022)
Edwards, K.J., '"On the Windy Edge of Nothing": A Historical Human Ecology of the Faroe Islands', *Human Ecology* (2005)
Elder, J., Fève, N., & Robinson, T., *Connemara & Elsewhere* (Royal Irish Academy, 2014)
Ell-Kanayuk, M. & Aporta, C., '"The Sea is Our Mainstay": Shipping and the Inuit
Homeland' in Bartenstein & Chircop (eds), *Shipping in Inuit Nunangat* (Brill, 2023)
Erickson, B., *Canoe Nation: Nature, Race, & the Making of a Canadian Icon* (UBC, 2013)
Ferguson, C., *Lewis in the Passing* (Birlinn, 2007)
Finneran, N., 'Slaves to Sailors: the archaeology of traditional Caribbean shore whaling c.1850–2000. A case study from Barbados & Bequia (St Vincent Grenadines)', *Nautical Archaeology* (2016)
Frederiksen, K., *100% Inuk* (Iperaq, 2012)

SELECT BIBLIOGRAPHY

Gaini, F., *Among the Islanders of the North: An Anthropology of the Faroe Islands* (Fróðskapur, 2011)

Gardner, J., *The Dory Book* (International Marine, 1978)

Building Classic Small Craft (McGraw Hill, 1977)

Garland, J., *Lone Voyager: the Extraordinary Adventures of Howard Blackburn* (Touchstone, 2000)

Gearheard, S.F., Kielsen, H., Hunytington, H., Leavitt, J.M., Mahoney, A.R., Opie, M., Oshima, T. & Sanguya, J. (eds), *The Meaning of Ice: People and Sea in Three Arctic Communities* (IPI, 2017)

Gilkes, F. & Gilkes, A., *Sea Water & Sand: A Collection of Poems* (2022)

Gillis, C.M., *Writing on Stone: Scenes from a Maine Island Life* ( )

Gillis, J., *The Human Shore: Seacoasts in History* (Chicago UP, 2012)

– *Islands of the Mind* (Palgrave Macmillan, 2004)
– *The Shores Around Us* (CreateSpace, 2015)

Gladwin, D. & Cusick, C. (eds), *Unfolding Irish Landscapes: Tim Robinson, Culture and Landscape* (Manchester UP, 2016)

Glissant, E., Wing, B. trans, *The Poetics of Relation* (Michigan UP, 1997)

– *The Fourth Century* (Bison Books, 2001)

Gmelch, G., & Gmelch, S.B., *The Parish Behind God's Back: The Changing Culture of Rural Barbados* (Waveland, 1997)

Golden, H., *Kayaks of Greenland* (White House Grocery, 2006)

Gøthche, Morten, *The Faroese Boat: Boatbuilders, Craftsmanship & the Use of Clinker-Built Boats in the Faroe Islands, 1830-1975* (Viking Ship Museum. 2014)

Grant, K., '"The Streaming Ocean of the Roadways": Hebridean Gaels & the Sea in the early 19th century', *Proceedings of the Society of Antiquaries of Scotland* (2018)

Guichon, D., *Birch Split Bark: Deconstructing the Canadian Canoe Through Poetry* (University of Calgary PhD, 2006)

Harries, John, 'A Beothuk Skeleton (not) in a Glass Case: Rumours of Bones & the Remembrance of an Exterminated People in Newfoundland' in J-M Dreyfus & É Anstett (eds), *Human remains in society* (Manchester UP, 2015)

Haviland, J., *A Briefe Relation of the Discovery & Plantation of Newfoundland* (Bladen, 1622)

Haviland, W., *Canoe Indians of Down East Maine* (The History Press, 2012)

Heinesen, W., Jones, W.G., trans, *The Tower at the Edge of the World* (Dedalus, 2018)

Heinesen, W., Jones, W.G., trans, *The Lost Musicians* (Dedalus, 2018)

Hermanstrand, H., Kolberg, A., Nilssen, T.R. & Sem, L., *The Indigenous Identity of the South Saami Historical & Political Perspectives on a Minority within a Minority* (Springer, 2019)

Hessler., S. (ed.), *Tidalectics: Imagining an Oceanic Worldview through Art & Science* (MIT, 2018)

Hunte, W. & Oxenford, H.A., 'The Economics of Boat Size in the Barbados Pelagic Fishery', *Proc. Gulf Carib. Fish. Inst* (1986)

Jamieson, R.A., *Nort Atlantik Drift* (Luath, 2007)

Jemmott, R.A., *The Barbadian Cultural Renaissance* (CreateSpace, 2016)

Jentoft, S., 'From I to We in Small-Scale Fisheries Communities', *Maritime Studies* (2020)

Joe, Chief Mi'sel & O'Neill, S., *My Indian* (Breakwater, 2021)

Joensen, F., *Boats & People: Faroese Fishing Vessels* (Estra, 1978)

Joensen, J.P., *Pilot whaling in the Faroe Islands* (Faroe UP, 2009)

Johnston, G. (ed.), *Rocky Shores: An Anthology of Faroese Poetry* (Wilfion, 1981)

Karetak, J., Tester, F. & Tagalik, S. (eds), *Inuit Qaujimajatuqangit: What Inuit Have Always Known to Be True* (Fernwood, 2017)

Katic, M. & McDonald, M., 'Experiencing maritime pilgrimage to St Mac Dara Island in Ireland: Pilgrims, hookers, & a local saint', *Anthropological Notebooks* (2020)

Keller, C., 'Furs, Fish, & Ivory: Medieval Norsemen at the Arctic Fringe', *Journal of the North Atlantic* (2010)

SELECT BIBLIOGRAPHY

Kent, N., *The Sámi Peoples of the North: A Social & Cultural History* (Hurst & Co, 2018)

Kent, R., *Salamina: Greenland Journals* (Harcourt, Brace & Co, 1935)

Kolodny, A., '"This Long Looked For Event": Retrieving Early Contact History from Penobscot Oral Traditions', *Native American & Indigenous Studies* (2015)

Körber, L.A. & Volquardsen, E., *The Postcolonial North Atlantic Iceland, Greenland & the Faroe Islands* (Nordeuropa-Institut Berlin, 2014)

Laugrand, F.B. & Oosten, J.G., '"We're Back with Our Ancestors": Inuit Bowhead Whaling in the Canadian Eastern Arctic', *Anthropos* (2013)

Leonard, S.P., '"Spoken language is a prison": phenomenology of speech & ways of speaking in North-West Greenland', *Polar Record* (2016)

Lee, D.S., *The Maine Lobster Boat: History of an Iconic Fishing Vessel* (Down East, 2022)

Leslie, J., 'Socio-Economic Monitoring in Oistins, Barbados', *CERMES* (2010)

Lien, S. & Nielssen, H., 'Absence and Presence: The Work of Photographs in the Sámi Museum, RiddoDuottarMuseat-Sámiid Vuorká-Dávvirat (RDM-SVD) in Karasjok, Norway', *Photography & Culture* (2012)

Lipman, A., *The Saltwater Frontier: Indians & the Contest for the American Coast* (Yale UP, 2015)

Lloyd, D., *Irish Times: the Temporalities of Modernity* (Field Day, 2006)

Luukkanen, H. & Fitzhugh, W., *The Bark Canoes & Skin Boats of Northern Eurasia*

Loo, T., *Moved by the State: Forced Relocation & Making a Good Life in Postwar Canada* (UBC, 2019)

(Smithsonian, 2014)

Marshall, I., *The Beothuk* (Breakwater, 1989)

– *Beothuk Bark Canoes: An Analysis & Comparative Study* (Ottawa UP, 1985)

MacCaig, N., *Collected Poems* (Chatto & Windus, 1985)

Martin, T., *Craft Learning as Perceptual Transformation: or Getting the Feel in the Wooden Boat Workshop* (Palgrave Macmillan, 2021)

Mac Cárthaigh, C., *Traditional Boats of Ireland: History, Folklore & Construction* (Collins, 2008)

Mac Giollarnáth, S., Mac Con Iomaire, L. & Robinson, T. trans, *Conamara Chronicles: Tales from Iorras Aithneach* (Indiana UP, 2022)

MacIntosh, D.C., How to Build a Wooden Boat (WoodenBoat, 1987)

Macleòid, F. (ed), *Nis Aosmhor: The Photographs of Dan Morrison* (Acair, 1997)

– *Muilnean Beaga Leòdhais* (Acair, 2009)

MacLeod, G., *Muir is Tir* (Acair, 2005)

Maclean, M. & Carrell, C., *As an Fhearann: Clearance, Conflict, & Crofting* (Mainstream, 1986)

Mac Polin, D., *The Donegal Currachs* (Cottage, 2007)

Martin, M., *A Description of the Western Isles of Scotland* (Andrew Bell, 1703)

MacGeoch, C., *Sulaisgeir: Photographs by James MacGeoch* (Acair, 2016)

MacDonald, D., 'Lewis Shielings', *Review of Scottish Culture* (1994)

MacDonald, C., *Aig an Airigh* (CEN, 2012)

MacDonald, D., *Lewis: a History of the Island* (Steve Savage, 1978)

McConney, P., Atapattu, A. & Leslie, D., 'Organizing Fisherfolk in Barbados', *Proc. Gulf Carib. Fish. Inst* (1999)

McPhee, J., *The Survival of the Bark Canoe* (Biblio, 1975)

Meldgaard, M., *Ancient Harp Seal Hunters of Disko Bay* (Oapen, 2004)

Meniketti, M., 'And Now They Are Gone: documenting the last sailing lighter of Nevis, West Indies', *International Journal of Nautical Archaeology* (2012)

Mikes, J., *Contextualizing & Reconstructing a Model Birch Bark Canoe* (Buffalo State College MA, 2022)

Milner, C., *Ralph Stanley: Tales of a Maine Boatbuilder* (Down East, 2004)

Moores, T., KayakCraft: Fine Woodstrip Kayak Construction (WoodenBoat, 1999)

Morgan, M., 'Highway to Vision: This Sea Our Nexus', *World Literature* (1994)

Morris, J.N., *Alone at Sea: Gloucester in the Age of the Dorymen, 1623-1939* (Godine, 2010)

Morris, M., *Scotland & the Caribbean* (Routledge, 2015)

SELECT BIBLIOGRAPHY

Mosbech, A., Johansen, K.L., Davidson, T.A., Appelt, M., Grønnow, B., Cuyler, C., Lyngs, P. & Flora, J., 'On the Crucial Importance of a Small Bird: The Ecosystem Services of the Little Auk (*Alle alle*) Population in Northwest Greenland in a Long-Term Perspective', *Ambio* (2018)

Mowat, F., *The Rock Within the Sea: A Heritage Lost* (Little Brown, 1968)

– *Bay of Spirits* (McClelland & Stewart, 2006)

Murray, H.C., *Of Boats on the Collar: How it was in one Newfoundland Fishing Community* (Atlantic, 2007)

Nicolar, J., *The Life & Traditions of the Red Man* (Self published, 1893)

Nolan, H., *Land of the Rock: Talamh an Carraig* (Breakwater, 2022)

Nuttall, M., 'Water, ice, & climate change in northwest Greenland', *Wiley Interdisciplinary Reviews* (2022)

O'Farrell, K., *Hegarty's Boatyard* (Ilen River, 2019)

Olson, C., Butternick G.F. (ed.), *The Collected Poems of Charles Olson* (California UP, 1987)

Ó Sabhain, P., *The Centrality of the Galway Hooker to Dwelling in the Island & Coastal Communities of South West Conamara* (NUI Galway PhD, 2019)

Paul, D., *We Were Not the Savages: A Mi'kmaq Perspective on the Collision Between European & Native American Civilizations* (Fernwood, 2003)

Pawling, M., 'Wabanaki Homeland & Mobility: Concepts of Home in Nineteenth-Century Maine', *Ethnohistory* (2016)

Petersen, H.C., *Skinboats of Greenland* (Viking Ship Museum, 1986)

Pluymers, K., *No Wood, No Kingdom: Political Ecology in the English Atlantic* (Pennsylvania UP, 2021)

Peere, I., *Death & Worldview in a Ballad Culture: the Evidence of Newfoundland* (Memorial University PhD, 1992)

Petersen, R., 'On Ethnic Identity in Greenland', *Inuit Studies* (2001)

Philbrick, N., *Away Off Shore: Nantucket Island & its People, 1601-1890* (Penguin, 1994)

Pollard, C., *New World Modernisms* (Virginia UP, 2004)

Pope, P., *Fish into Wine: The Newfoundland Plantation in the Seventeenth Century* (North Carolina UP, 2004)

Pyle, D.C., *Clean Sweet Wind: Sailing with the Last Boatmakers of the Caribbean* (Ragged Mountain, 1998)

Qitsualik-Tinsley, R. & Qitsualik-Tinsley, S., *Skraelings* (Inhabit Media, 2014)

Raffan, J., Bark, Skin, & Cedar: Exploring the Canoe in Canadian Experience (Harper Collins, 2000)

Ragazzi, R. & Nerici, G., 'Discourses, practices & performances in Sámi museology at Tromsø University Museum', *Nordic Museology* (2019)

Rasmussen, K., *The People of the Polar North* (Kegan Paul, 1908)

– *Eskimo Folk Tales* (Glydendalske, 1921)
– *Observations on the Intellectual Culture of the Caribou Eskimos* (Glydendalske, 1930)
– *Eskimo Poems from Canada & Greenland* (Pittsburgh UP, 1973)

Rawlence, B., *The Treeline: the Last Forest & the Future of Life on Earth* (Penguin, 2022)

Reckin, A., 'Tidalectic Lectures: Kamau Brathwaite's Prose/Poetry as Sound-Space', *Anthurium* (2003)

Riquet, J., *The Aesthetics of Island Space* (Oxford UP, 2019)

Robinson, B., & Heller, A.S., 'Maritime Culture Patterns & Animal Symbolism in Eastern Maine', *Journal of the North Atlantic* (2017)

Robinson, T., *Stones of Aran: Pilgrimage* (Lilliput, 1986)

– *Connemara: A Little Gaelic Kingdom* (Penguin, 2011)
– *Connemara: Listen to the Wind* (Penguin, 2006)
– *Setting Foot on the Shores of Connemara* (Penguin, 1996)
– *Tales & Imaginings* (Lilliput, 2002)

Robson, M., *Someone Else's Story* (Acair, 2018)

Savory, E., 'Wordsongs & Wordwounds / Homecoming: Kamau Brathwaite's *Barabajan Poems*', *World Literature Today* (1994)

Schneider, P., *The Enduring Shore: a History of Cape Cod, Martha's Vineyard & Nantucket* (Henry Holt, 2000)

Scott, J., *The Common Wind: Afro-American Currents in the Age of the Haitian Revolution* (Verso, 2018)

Scott, R., *Galway Hookers: Working Sailboats of Galway Bay* (Ward River, 1985)

Seifert, M., *Rewriting Newfoundland Mythology: the Works of Tom Dawe* (Galda, 2002)

Severin, T., *The Brendan Voyage* (Hutchinson, 1986)

Shetterly, S.H., *Notes on the Landscape of Home* (Down Wast, 2022)

Silvan, E., 'Constructing a Sami Cultural Heritage: Essentialism & Emancipation', *Ethnologia Scandanavica* (2014)

Singleton, B.E., 'Love-iathan, the meat-whale & hidden people: ordering Faroese pilot whaling', *Journal of Political Ecology (2017)*

Skogvang, B, 'Development of Cultural & Environmental Awareness Through Sámi Outdoor Life at Sámi/Indigenous Festivals', *Frontiers in Sport & Active Living* (2021)

Slayton, E.R., *Seascape Corridors: Modelling Routes to Connect Communities Across the Caribbean Sea* (Sidestone, 2018)

Sonne, B., *Worldviews of the Greenlanders: An Inuit Arctic Perspective* (Alaska UP, 2017)

Standen, D., 'Canoes and *Canots* in New France: Small Boats, Material History & Popular Imagination', *Material Culture Review* (2008)

Steffler, J., *The Grey Islands* (McClelland & Stewart, 1985)

Stephen, I., *Boatlines* (Postscript, 2023)

Svanberg, I., Kuusela, T. & Cios, S., '"Sometimes it is Tamed to Bring Home Fish for the Kitchen": Otter Fishing in Northern Europe & Beyond' in *Swedish Dialects & Folk Traditions* (2015)

Taylor, D., *Boat Building in Winterton* (National Museums of Canada, 1982)

Taylor, L., *Occasions of Faith: an Anthropology of Irish Catholics* (Lilliput, 1995)

Teien, K, 'Moltekrig på Hedmarksvidda', *Tidsskrift For Utmarksforkning* (2019)

Thisted, K., 'On Narrative Expectations: Greenlandic Oral Traditions about the Cultural Encounter between Inuit and Norsemen', *Scandinavian Studies* (2001)

Thomson, D., *The People of the Sea* (Turnstile, 1954)

Thoreau, H.D., *Maine Woods* (Ticknor & Fields, 1864)

Turi, J., DuBois, T. trans., *An Account of the Sámi* (Nordic Studies Press, 2011)

Valkonen, S, Aikio, A, Alakorva, S, & Maga, S (eds), *The Sámi World* (Routledge, 2022)

Walden, S., *Places Lost: In Search of Newfoundland's Resettled Communities* (Lynx, 2003)

Watt, R., '"Aa My Mindin": Moving through loss in the poetic literary tradition of Shetland' (University of Stirling PhD, 2018)

— *Moder Dy* (Birlinn, 2019)

Weaver, J., *The Red Atlantic: American Indigenes & the Making of the Modern World* (North Carolina UP, 2014)

Webb, J.A., *Observing the Outports: Describing Newfoundland Culture, 1950-1980* (Toronto UP, 2015)

White, C., *One Man's Journey: The Mi'kmaw Revival in Ktaqmkuk* (Memorial UP, 2023)

Wicken, W., *The Colonization of Mi'kmaw Memory & History, 1794-1928* (Toronto UP, 2012)

Wickler, S, 'Visualizing Sami Waterscapes in Northern Norway from an Archaeological Perspective', in Westerdahl (ed), *A Circumpolar Reappraisal* (Archaeopress, 2010)

Wylie, J., *The Ring of Dancers: Images of Faroese Culture* (Pennsylvania UP, 1981)

— *The Faroe Islands: Interpretations of History* (Kentucky UP, 1987)

— 'Dwelling & Displacement: Tim Robinson & the Questions of Landscape', *Cultural Geographies* (2012)

Index

A–Z of Barbados Heritage 233
Adams, Emma and John 165
Adney, Edwin Tappan, *The Bark Canoes and Skin Boats of North America* 121
Adolf Frederick of Sweden 123
Àirigh nan Linntean (the 'Shieling of the Pools') 38–45
Alaska 140, 219
Aleutian Islands 123
Americas, the 62–3, 122–8
An Capal (Galway hooker) 26, 28, 31
Andersson, Alex 91
andovsmaður (crew member) 111–12
Arnaquq-Baril, Alethea, *Angry Inuk* 116
Aron (Inuit artist) 133–4

Babbs (Bajan boatbuilder) 230
Baccalieu Island 188–9, 190, 193
bád mór ('big boat') 28, 35
báid iomartha ('rowed boats') 29–31, 32, 37
Baie Verte Peninsula, Newfoundland 163
Bailey, Peter 26, 27, 28, 30–1
Bajan Moses *see* Moses boat
Baker, Angela 171
Ballads/songs, traditional *see* songs/ballads
Barbados 15, 228–48

bark, tree 63, 84, 123
   birchbark 63, 121–3, 146, 172, 176–9, 209–10, 212, 214–15
Baron, Walter 219
Barrow, Alaska 140
Bathsheba, Barbados 242–3
batteaux 197
Battiste, Marie, *Visioning a Mi'kmaw Humanities* 183
Bay de Verde Peninsula 186
Bay of Islands, Newfoundland 184
beamy boat 56, 68, 231, 233
Bearasay, Lewis 46
Béluse, Mathieu 237
Beothuk people 12, 172, 173–4, 178–82
Bergen, Norway 100
Bergman, Ingela 87–8
berry foraging 85, 86–7
Berry, Sir John 190
Betts Cove, Newfoundland 172
birds
   Atlantic 124–5
   Barbados 228, 229
   Faroe Islands 96–7
   Greenland 150–1, 156
   Maine 199, 202
   Massachusetts 217, 222, 225

Newfoundland 187
Sápmi 89
Bishop, Edwin 192
Bishop, Elizabeth 202
Biskupsstóð, Jákup á 104
Blankskáli, Kalsoy Island 103
boatbuilders/boatbuilding
    Algonquin 121
    Barbados 230–1
    boat forms 9–10, 54–5, 68–9, 176–7, 181–2
    boat styles 8, 58, 196, 234–5
    Canyard and 214–15
    'carvel' construction 62
    'caulking' 62
    'clinker' construction 62–3
    commercial 11, 196
    Faroe Islands 94–5, 102–3, 104, 105–6
    iron rings 103
    language of boats 67–8, 93
    'lapstrake' construction 62–3
    launches 15
    'loom' 68
    Maclean on 60–1
    Maine 203
    Newfoundland 184, 190, 193–4
    qualities of 249–52
    'rowlocks' ('oarlocks') 68
    Sámi 73–6, 81–91
    sewing 73–4, 81
    structures of 62–9, 140–1
    'thole pins' 66, 68, 95
    tools 209
    'transom' 66–7
Bob'ob (Bajan carpenter) 238, 239, 240
Bogadóttir, Ragnheiður 112, 113
Bok, Gordon, 'Saben the Woodfitter' 198
Borve, Lewis 40
Boyd's Cove, Newfoundland 180, 180–1
Bradshaw, Coreen 'Feeney' 243
Brathwaite, Kamau, *Barabajan Poems* 238–41, 242–3
Bratland, Camilla, *Coastal Sámi Atlas* 80

Braye, Crystal 183–4, 191
Bríkar (agricultural terraces) 98
Bristol, Canada 185
Brooklin, Maine 205
Burdett, Barzillai 224
bygdarsøgur ('village histories') 107

Callanish, Lewis 45
Canada 167, 172, 175
Canning, Jerome 185, 191, 251
canoes 63, 122–3, 172–3, 176–9, 181–2, 196, 209–14
Cape Cod 21, 58, 195, 215–20
carbon fibre boats 65
Carbonear Island 185, 186–7
Caribbean basin 125–6
Caribbean Festival of the Arts (1983) 237–8
caribou 152–3
Carloway, Lewis 45
Carrington, Keisha 243–4
Carson, Rachel 195
carvings, Dorset 145–6
Cayard, Steve 214–15
Champlain, Samuel de 199, 220
Channel Islands, Canada 185
Chapelle, Howard, *The Bark Canoes and Skin Boats of North America* 121–2
Chapman, Andrea 243–4
chipmunks 199, 207
Christianity 76, 87, 210
Churchill, Winston 184
Chydenius, Anders 123–4
Clarke, Austin 246
cleits (beehive buildings) 42–4, 45–6, 50
clinker boats 62–3
cloudberries 85, 86–7
Coastal Sámi people 73, 78, 80, 82, 87
cod 90, 108–9
Coffin, Elizabeth 224, 225
Colbry, Dameon 219
Collins, Duane, 'The Inshore Boats of Newfoundland' 183
commercial shipping 10–11

INDEX

Conamara/Connemara 25–37, 62, 68, 121
Conception Bay, Newfoundland 185, 187
Conne River, Newfoundland 4
Conset Bay, Barbados 243
Cornish pilot gig 208, 215
Covid-19 pandemic 27
Cranberry Islands 202, 204
Cree people 126
Crummey, Michael, *River Thieves* 173–4
Cuishader, Scotland 39
currach (Irish wicker round boat) 15, 25, 29–30, 35, 63, 122
cyclones, Arctic 161–2

Danish Icelandic Company 100
Danny (fish pot maker) 229
Davidge, Bud, 'Outport People' 169–70
Dawe, Tom 170
Denmark 100–1, 133
Dimock, Brad 208
diseases 212
Disko Bay, Greenland 154
dogs, sled 19, 140, 159, 160–1
Dòmhnull Cam Macaulay 46–8
donkey boats (*báid iomartha*) 25–37
dories 184–5, 196–7, 203, 208, 215, 219, 221–2, 224
Dorset culture (Paleo-Eskimo) 144–6, 147
Dorsey, Leigh 219
double-ended boats 66–7
Drew, Tammy 175
Duncan, Angus 59, 60
duodji (Sámi handicraft) 86, 88–9, 90

East Bunker Ledge, Maine 201–2
Easton, Peter 186
Eged, Hans 148
Eggemoggin Reach, Maine 205
Ehrenmalm, Arvid 76–7
Eiði, Faroe Islands 102
Eilean Fir Chrothair/'Island of the Men of Croir' 45–6
Eilean Mhealasta, Lewis 50–1, 52

enslaved peoples 125, 235, 245
Eric the Red 147
European seafarers 210–12
Exploits River, Newfoundland 173, 178–9
Eysturoy, Faroe Islands 99

Fálástak (down feathers) 85
Fálástakladdak 85
Faris, James 186
Faroe boats 63
Faroe Islands *see* Føroyar/Faroe Islands
Faroese boats 67
Ferrini, Vincent, *Know Fish* 222–3
Fiddlehead Canoe 252
Filiscleitir, Lewis 40
Finland 123
First Nations peoples 172, 173, 174, 177, 180, 209
fish, rowing out for 106–17
Fitzhugh, William, *The Bark Canoes and Skin Boats of Northern Eurasia* 122–3
Flannan Isles 57
flying fish 244–8
Forest Sámi people 73
Fornais/Furnace 29
Føroyar/Faroe Islands 15, 66, 92–117
foxes, Arctic 142, 150
France 187
Frederiksen, Katti, 'Ijaajjajjaa' 131, 132

Gaisgeir, Lewis 51
Gallan Head, Lewis 45, 50, 52
Galway Bay 15
Ganstotl, Lewis 49, 50
Gardner, John 206
Gaup, Ánte Mihkkal 88
geographic structure, of villages 101–2
Ghana 238–9
Gilkes, Frank and Antarrah 232
Gillis, John 195
Gjógv, Faroe Islands 102
gleoiteog (small Galway hooker) 28, 30, 35, 249

Glissant, Édouard 126, 236–7
God's Pocket, Newfoundland 163, 172
Gøthche, Morten 107
'Great Awakening', Canada 175
Great Bernera, Lewis 45, 46, 54, 57–8
Greenland *see* Kalaallit Nunaat/Greenland
Greenpeace 116
grindadráp (pilot whale hunt) 116–17
Guts (Bajan boatbuilder) 230–1

Hammerfest, Norway 70
Hans (Mearrasiida) 82–3
Hansen, Hans O. 80
Harbour Grace, Newfoundland 185, 186
Harris, Scotland 59, 60
Harvey, Martha Hale 224
Haviland, John, *Briefe Relation* 200–1
Heinesen, William, *The Lost Musicians* 93
herbs, pungent 149
Hiller, Harry 169
Hilsinger, Rich 207
Hiscock, Fred 192–3
hjallur (wooden buildings) 110
Højgaard, Samson 109
Homer, Winslow 195, 197
hookers (Galway fishing boats) 25–37, 62
Horwood, Harold 170

'ice boat' 231
icebergs 150, 151–2, 154–60
Iceland 64, 100
Igbo gods 242–3
Ilulissat, Greenland 154, 161
indentured labourers 187, 236
Indian Burying Place, Newfoundland 172, 174
inflatable boats 21, 94, 96
Ingold, Tim 87
Inis Mór/Inishmore 28
Innu people 12, 180
Inuit people 12, 16, 116, 130–62, 179, 180
inussuit ('waymarker cairns') 152
Ireland 8, 10, 25–37, 62, 68, 78, 121

Jack (Bajan Tourist Board) 248
James, Henry, *The Bostonians* 216
James VI 46
Jamieson, Robert Alan 118
Jeddore, John Nick 173
Jemmott, Ralph 237
Joe, Billy 178
Joe, Mi'sel 174, 175, 177, 178
Joensen, Sigurð 108
John Du Craig 47–8

Kaikkonen, Konsta 80
Kalaallit Nunaat/Greenland 15, 19, 63–4, 100, 121, 130–62
Kalm, Pehr 123–4
Kalsoy Island 102, 103–6
Kangeq islet 133, 149
Kapisillit, Greenland 141–3, 149
Kapisillit River 149
Karifuna (Carib) people 234
kayaks 7, 15, 16, 123
    sea 21, 38, 70–1, 215
    See also qajaq (traditional Greenland kayak)
Kellingin ('Witch' Faroe stack) 99, 103
Kelly, James 236
killiaq (slate) 143
Kollafjørður, Faroe Islands 113
Koryak people 123
Ktaqmkuk/Newfoundland 10, 12, 13, 62, 146, 163–94
Kuommarsaari island 90

Langabhat, Loch 41–2, 44
languages, island 3, 11, 22
    Faroese 93, 100–1
    Gaelic 12, 18
    Greenlandic 131, 135, 159
    Maliseet 121
    Sámi 78, 80, 85–8
    Shaetlan 118–20
leath bháid ('half boat') 28
Leítir Mealláin/Lettermullen 27

INDEX

Leitir Móir/Lettermore 29, 30
Leòdhas/Lewis 21, 38–61, 251
Linnaeus, Carl 76
'living thing', boat as 8, 65–6, 89
Loch an t-Sròm/Strome 49, 50, 51–2
Lokono (Arawaks) people 234
Loo, Tina, *Moved by the State:* . . . 170–1
Lowell, Robert 202
Lowell's Boat Shop, Massachusetts 196–7, 215
luomemeahcci (cloudberry landscape) 86
luondu ('inner nature') 86, 87
Luukkanen, Harri, *The Bark Canoes and Skin Boats of Northern Eurasia* 122–3

Mac Giollarnáth, Seán 32, 33–4
MacCaig, Norman 9
MacDara, St 33–6
MacDonald, Shane 175
Mace Pier, Connemara 32
Mackenzie,, W. M. 44
Maclean, Allan 60–1
Macleod, Finlay 50
MacLeod, George (Seoras Chaluim Sheorais) 57
MacLeod, Neil 46, 47
Macrae, Alexander 51–2
Madaket, Massachusetts 225
Maine, USA 65–6, 146, 195–227
maqittagaq ('portable qajaq') 154
Marshall, Ingeborg 181
Martin, Martin, *Description of the Western Islands of Scotland* 49, 52–3
Massachusetts, USA 195–227
Mathisen, Hans Ragnar 13
meahcci (landscape word) 86–7, 108
Mealaisbhal, Lewis 57
Meaning of Ice, The 158
Mearrasiida (Coastal Sámi Sea Competence Centre) 80, 81–3, 84, 86
Meniketti, Marco 235–6
Merrimack River 196, 215
Miawpukek First Nation 173, 178

miðamaður (semi-mystical seafarer) 108
Mighty Gabby (Bajan singer) 247–8
Mikladalur, Kalsoy Island 4, 105
Mi'kmaw people 12, 173–6, 178–80, 182–3
Mitchell, Arthur 43–4
Mitchell, Mattie 173
monkeys 229
Monkman, Kent 'Miss Chief Eagle Testickle ', *mistikôsiwak (Wooden Boat People)* 126–8
Morrison, Dan 38–9
Morrison, David, 'Fair- Haired Scholar' 46
Moses boat 228–38
Mount Desert Island 199–205
Mountain Sámi people 72–3
Mowat, Farley 13, 170
Mykines Island 102–3

NaGeira, Sheila 186
Nantucket, Massachusetts 224–7
Nauset Bay, Massachusetts 220–3
Nazi Germany 78
Ness, Lewis 38–41, 52, 54, 56
Nevisian lighters 235
Newfoundland *see* Ktaqmkuk/Newfoundland
Ney, Eugène 188
Nicholson, John, 'the Seer' 40–1
Nicolar, Joseph, *The Life and Traditions of the Red Man* 211–12
Nielsen, Qaerngaaq 159–60
North America 121–2, 127–8, 177, 186, 187
North Atlantic Drift 17–23, 64
North Rona, Scotland 38
Norway 21, 55, 78–80, 100
Notre Dame Bay, Newfoundland 163, 165, 173, 180
Nova Scotia 174, 177, 184
Nunataq (summit/ridge protrusion) 152
Nunatarsuaaq, Greenland 152, 153
Nuuk Fjord 136, 137–9, 141, 147, 148–50
Nuuk, Greenland 15, 132, 134–5, 142

Ó Sabhain, Pádraig 27, 29
Ober, Frederick 233–4
Oileán Mhic Dara/St MacDara's Island 32, 33
Oileán Muiríleach/Strawbeach Island 33
Oistins, Barbados 244–7
okpik, dg nanouk, 'Inupiaq Women' 130–1
Old Town Island, Maine 213, 214
Omma, Ola 91
Oshima, Toku 160
otters 90–1
Ottison family 225–7
Outer Hebrides 4, 9, 18, 49
Ove (Mearrasiida) 82, 83, 86

Páll, Nólsoyar 103
Panipak, Jacopie 157–8
Pawling, Micah 213
Pease, Chester 224
Pedro (Bajan boatbuilder) 230, 231
Penobscot Nation 209, 211–14
Penobscot River 209
Peter Joe (Algonquin boatbuilder) 121
Petersen, H. C., *Skinboats of Greenland* 16, 17
Pilley's Tickle, Newfoundland 179, 181
pilot gig, Cornish 68
Pinckard, George 245
pitcher plant 165
Placentia, Newfoundland 169
poetry 108, 118–20, 130–2
Bajan 202, 232, 237, 238, 239, 240
Polis, Joseph 213
Pope, *Peter E.,* author of *Fish into Wine:* ... 186, 189
porpoises 71
Porsanger Fjord 71, 83
'priest holes' 55
Provincetown, Massachusetts 216–17
púcán (Galway hooker) 28, 30
punts 183, 184, 191–3

Qaannat Kattuffiat (Greenland Kayak Association) 134–5
qajaq (traditional Greenland kayak) 15, 63–4, 130–62
terminology 134
Qajartuarpo ('to kayak simply for the joy of it') 130–5
Qalipu First Nation 173
Qoornoq, Greenland 138

'Raaga Tree' (Watt) 119–20
Rasmussen, Carl, *Spring Day Returning from the Hunt* 136–7, 138
Reece, William 245
Reid, Eleazor 191–2
reindeer 84
Renaissance, European 84
Richardson, Wyman, *The House on Nauset Marsh* 220–3
Rink, Hinrich and Signe 133
Risin ('Giant' Faroe stack) 99, 103
Robinson, Mairéad 26–7
Robinson, Tim 14, 18, 25, 26–7, 121
Rockley, Barbados 246
rodney (Newfoundland boat) 163, 191–3
Ròg, Little Loch 51
Ròg, Loch 45, 48–9
roles, fishing crew 111–12, 193
Rollock, Ruby, 'the Sheriff' 230
Rose, Robert N. 69
Rua, Páidín 32–3
Russia 79, 81, 122
Ryd, Yngve 91

'Saat i da Blöd' (Watt) 118
St John's, Newfoundland 179
St Olaf's Day 15
St Petersburg 84
St Vincent, Barbados 229–32
Saksun Church, Faroe Islands 98
salmon 41, 49, 84, 141, 214
salted fish 83–4
Sámi boats 63

INDEX

Sámi people 12–13, 70–91
Sandnes farm, Greenland 147–8
Sápmi 70–91
Saqqaq people 143–4, 146
Scammell, Arthur 168
Scarp, Lewis 54, 58–61
Scheffer, Johannes 75–6
schooners 196
Schrader, Derek 198–9
Scilly Cove, Newfoundland 190–1
Scotland 38–61, 64, 78
Scott, Julius, *The Common Wind* 126, 235
'sculling' 67
Sea Sámi people 73, 78, 80, 82, 87
Seaforth estate, Lewis 51–2
seals 97, 199, 217–18, 219
seaweeds 28, 32–3, 49
Sermermiut, Greenland 161
sgoth (Scottish wooden boat) 39, 54, 56–7, 60
sharks 218–19, 241
Shawnadithit ('last Beothuk') 174, 182
Shetland Islands 9, 56, 118–20
'Shieling of the Pools' (Àirigh nan Linntean) 38–45
Shorey, Tyrone 'Dolphin' 244
Six Men's, Barbados 15, 229
skerries 93
skiffs, Baccalieu 190, 192–3
skin boats 63, 64, 122
    See also umiaq
Skolt Sámi people 81
Slættanes, Faroe Islands 96
sloops, sailing 101
Smallwood, Joey 172–3
Snook's Arm, Newfoundland 163–7
soapstone lamps 144–5
songs/ballads
    Barbados 231, 237, 247–8
    'The Cliffs of Baccalieu' 188–9
    English hymns 41
    Faroe Islands 103
    Greenland 146, 153–4

Newfoundland 14, 168, 169–70
'oar songs' 46
'Saben the Woodfitter' 198
yoik chant 88
Spike's Town (Speightstown), Barbados 230
spisse (Sámi boat) 82, 89
Stac Dhòmhnuill Chaim/'Dòmhnull Cam's Fort' 47
Stanley, Ralph 203–5
Stanley, Richard 204
Stephen, Ian 57
Stewart, Lord Robert 56
Stoodley, Vey 171
Streymoy, Faroe Islands 99, 102
Stride, Derek, *Gwitna'q* 176, 178
Sturluson, Snorri, *Heimskringla* 74–5
Suda, Sasha 127–8
Sula Sgeir, Scotland 38
Summers, John 207
Svabo, Jens Christian 105, 111
Sweden 77, 123
'sweeping' 67
swordfish 146, 218

Tagaq, Tanya, *Tungijuq (What We Eat)* 116
Tangafjørður fjord 109
táttur ('literary ballad') 103
taxation 56, 79, 100, 112, 153
Taylor, David 191–2, 194
Tent Bay, Bathsheba 246–7
Thoreau, Henry David 198, 213, 216–17
Thule peoples 147, 148
tidal movements 50, 94, 154
tides 10
timber 9–10, 54–5, 68–9, 190, 231
Tjørnuvík, Faroes Islands 102
Tórshavn, Faroe Islands 94, 107
tríbekkur ('three-thwart boat') 94
Trinidadian droghers 235
Trinity Bay, Newfoundland 185, 186, 189, 193
Trøllanes, Kalsoy Island 105

Tromsø, Norway 79–80
Tryphon of Pechenga, St 81
Tuke, James 25–6
Tuniit people 146–7
Turi, Johan, *Account of the Sámi* 77, 85–6
turtles 228
Twillingate, Newfoundland 181

Umanaq island 144
umiak/umiaq (Inuit open boat) 16, 130–62
Umivik, Greenland 152
Út á Lónna, Faroe Islands 97
útróður ('rowing out') 107–8

Viking Norse 75–6, 99–100, 147–8, 149

Wabanaki Confederacy 196
Wabanaki people 200–1, 214
Walden, Scott, *Places Lost* 171, 174

walrus ivory 147–8
Wampanoag people 220
Watt, Roseanne 118–20
Waymouth, George 211
Wellfleet, Massachusetts 216, 218–19
whales/whaling 84, 114–17, 124, 134, 138–9, 156, 187
White, Calvin 173
White, Joel 207
Williamson, Kenneth 95
Wilson, Jon 205–6, 207, 250
Winterton rodney 62
Woodburn, James 145
WoodenBoat magazine 205, 206–7
WoodenBoat School, Brooklin 205, 208

yoal (Shetland rowing boat) 55
yoik (chant-like song) 88

Zarn, Cricket 208